America's Early Whalemen

America's Early Whalemen

Indian Shore Whalers on Long Island, 1650–1750

John A. Strong

THE UNIVERSITY OF ARIZONA PRESS

TUCSON

The University of Arizona Press
www.uapress.arizona.edu

ISBN-13: 978-0-8165-3718-1 (cloth)
ISBN-13: 978-0-8165-4151-5 (paper)

Cover design by Sara Thaxton
Cover art: *Whalers* by David Bunn Martine, Shinnecock Reservation

Publication of this book is made possible in part by the proceeds of a permanent endowment created with the assistance of a Challenge Grant from the National Endowment for the Humanities, a federal agency.

Library of Congress Cataloging-in-Publication Data
Names: Strong, John A., 1935– author.
Title: America's early whalemen : Indian shore whalers on Long Island, 1650–1750 / John A. Strong.
Other titles: Native peoples of the Americas.
Description: Tucson : The University of Arizona Press, 2018 | Series: Native peoples of the Americas |
    Includes bibliographical references and index.
Identifiers: LCCN 2018009207 | ISBN 9780816537181 (cloth : alk. paper)
Subjects: LCSH: Indian whalers—New York (State)—Long Island—History—17th century. | Indian
    whalers—New York (State)—Long Island—History—18th century. | Algonquian Indians—New
    York (State)—Long Island—History—17th century. | Algonquian Indians—New York (State)—Long
    Island—History—18th century. | Whaling—Long Island Sound (N.Y. and Conn.)
Classification: LCC E99.A35 S75 2018 | DDC 639.2/8089973074721—dc23 LC record available at
    https://lccn.loc.gov/2018009207

Contents

List of Illustrations — vii

Foreword — ix

Preface — xi

Acknowledgments — xiii

1. The Whale in Aboriginal Long Island Culture — 3

2. Drift Whales: A Contentious Asset — 21

3. Sachems, Entrepreneurs, and Conflicting Sovereignties — 41

4. Origins of "Ye Whaling Design" on Long Island — 57

5. New Needs, Old Traditions: The Cultural Impact
of "Ye Whale Design" — 79

6. Debt Peonage and Indentured Servitude — 99

7. Papasaquin's World: Politics, Economics, and Family
in Seventeenth-Century Long Island — 127

8. Leaving the Shore: The End of an Era — 151

Appendix 1. Examples of Whaling Contracts — 164

Appendix 2. Whaling Contracts by Season — 171

Appendix 3. St. George Manor — 175

Appendix 4. Estimates of Shore Whale Catches, 1697–1734 — 177

Appendix 5. Names of Indian Whalers and English Investors
on the Whaling Contracts, 1670–1685 — 179

Notes — 203

Bibliography — 211

Index — 225

Illustrations

Figures

1. North Atlantic right whale and calf *Eubalaena glacialis* — 2
2. North Atlantic right whale mouth with baleen plates — 3
3. Baleen plate — 3
4. *Curious Method of Catching Whales*, Theodore de Bry — 9
5. *Harpooning Whales*, Theodore de Bry — 10
6. Antler harpoon points — 14
7. Painted whalebone pestle — 15
8. Late Woodland engraved mica tablet — 17
9. Beached whale at Smith Point, Long Island, October 10, 2014 — 22
10. Whale oil lamps — 22
11. Baleen plates used for corset stays, boxes, and buggy whips — 23
12. Replica trying furnace with iron trying kettles — 30
13. Whale oil skimmer held by Mataukus Tarrant, Shinnecock Nation — 31
14. Whaleboat — 58
15. Drawing of whaling crew attacking a whale on 1722 map of Gardiners Island — 59
16. Whaleboat and crew — 60
17. Whaleboat crew attacking a whale — 62
18. Harpoon held by Mataukus Tarrant, Shinnecock Nation — 63
19. Whaling lance held by Mataukus Tarrant, Shinnecock Nation — 64
20. Whales in New York Harbor — 66
21. Indian crews flensing whale — 73
22. Indians mincing blubber — 74
23. Indians bailing oil into cooling vat — 74
24. Shore trying station — 75
25. Iron pot from Montaukett burial site at Pantigo, East Hampton — 85
26. Green glass bottle inscribed with the name Wobetom — 96
27. Papasaquin handing Wyandanch's gun to Ninigret — 131

Maps

1. North Atlantic right whale seasonal migratory corridor — 6
2. Long Island in the seventeenth century — 24
3. Whaling stations on eastern Long Island, 1686–1687 — 44

4. Map of Mastic Peninsula, showing the Floyd and Tangier Smith
    Estates and the approximate locations of the Unkechaug villages   107
5. Ryder map of western Brookhaven Town (1670)   124

Tables

1. Debts recorded for the first and last seasons   115
2. Value of shares for the 1706–1707 season   118
3. Whalers who endorsed the 1703 Confirmation and
    their employers   149
4. 1710–11 whaling season   152

Foreword

Native Peoples of the Americas is a multivolume series that covers North, Middle, and South America. Each volume takes unique methodological approaches—archaeological, ethnographic, ecological, and/or ethnohistorical—to culture areas and regions and to themes that link areas across time and space. This volume looks at Long Island Sound and the whaling industry that developed there. John Strong, a prolific author of many books and articles about Long Island peoples, has turned his historical lens on the whaling industry that came to consume the lives of the Unkechaug, Montaukett, and Shinnecock peoples during the seventeenth and early eighteenth centuries. As Strong states in his introductory remarks, his "primary goal here is to open a window on the cultural transition experienced by the Native peoples of Long Island. . . . Most of the 340 whalers who appear in these documents were able-bodied men in their twenties and thirties, born shortly after the first English settlers arrived. They were the first generation to reach maturity in a changing world increasingly dominated by an alien culture."

Strong worked with descendant Native peoples from Long Island groups in addition to mining the historical documents concerning the enterprise of whaling. Whereas both Natives and settlers primarily (but not exclusively) harvested beached whales, as demand for whale oil grew in the colonies, specially designed boats and techniques were constructed to go after North Atlantic right whales, kill them, and tow them to shore for processing. This industry grew and soon consumed the lives of Long Islanders, alienating them from their land and diminishing the power of their sachems. By the late eighteenth century, whalers had to resort to long-distance travel because local whale populations had declined due to overharvesting. Long Island Natives were hired for deep water whaling that took them on long voyages all over the world in search of whales. As Natives lost land, more and more of them took to the sea and became indebted to the whaling companies through "contracts" and the purchase of highly prized European commodities like iron and copper pots, coats, and powder and shot.

The well-organized volume follows the timeline of whaling off the New England coast. Strong's contribution is severalfold: the book begins with a history of the Native peoples of Long Island, the relationships between Long Island Natives with each other and the mainland (especially the Pequot and Niantic), and the archaeological evidence for the use of whales. Strong also provides insight into the rich ceremonialism that surrounded these animals. He then gives a detailed account of Native whaling, the taking of drift whales, the construction of whaling boats, and the composition of whaling crews. Further, he looks at relationships between Natives and settlers and how and why Native men joined English whale crews. And Strong also contributes his well-known and familiar historical accuracy in following the lives of some of the Native whalers, like Papasaquin, a Montaukett sachem. This biography provides an emic account of the ways in which whaling shaped individual lives and communities from the mid-seventeenth through the mid-eighteenth centuries.

America's Early Whalemen: Indian Shore Whalers on Long Island, 1650–1750 will be a timely and insightful addition to the series Native Peoples of the Americas. This book is rich in historical detail, and it firmly places the Montauketts, Shinnecocks, and Unkechaugs in an expanding world system as important and highly sought-after players.

Laurie Weinstein, PhD
Series Editor, Native Peoples of the Americas
Danbury, Connecticut, June 2017

Preface

I began working with the primary sources for this book soon after I joined the faculty of Southampton College in 1965. I was surprised to discover the wealth of seventeenth-century material in the town archives on eastern Long Island that related to local Native American communities. These materials had escaped the notice of professional ethnohistorians and were of little interest to local historians who focused on the lives and institutions of the English settlers. Over the years I gathered records of more than two hundred land transactions, including deeds, deed confirmations and gift deeds, and ninety-seven labor contracts from town repositories in East Hampton, Southampton, Brookhaven, Southold, Huntington, Smithtown, and Oyster Bay. I made copies of the unpublished documents that had been tucked away in the basements of town clerks' offices and transcribed many of them.

In addition to these public records were family account books and ledgers in the Suffolk County Historical Society Museum; the Pennypacker Collection in the East Hampton Public Library; the St. George Manor Archives; the Huntington Library in California; the Emma S. Clark Memorial Library Collections; the Long Island Museum in Stony Brook, New York; the William Floyd Estate Archives; and the Bellport Historical Museum in Bellport, New York. These documents recorded the payments and work records of Native American laborers.

I wrote accounts of the shore whaling era on eastern Long Island in journal articles and in books on the Indians of Long Island, but I never came close to exhausting the sources I had examined (Strong 1983, 1986, 1988, 1989, 1990, 1995, 1995a, 1997). My primary goal here is to open a window on the cultural transition experienced by the Native peoples of Long Island during the decades following the first European settlements on Long Island in the mid-seventeenth century. Most of the 340 whalers who appear in these documents were able-bodied men in their twenties and thirties, born shortly after the first English settlers arrived. They were the first generation to reach maturity in a changing world increasingly dominated by an alien culture. Eight of the whalers were identified as sachems, men who represented their tribal communities in important land transactions. The documents, therefore, provide insights into significant historical and cultural patterns.

This study also examines the shore whaling within the context of Long Island colonial history. The English as well as the Native peoples were experiencing significant cultural changes. The English were in the process of adapting a new identity as Americans while experiencing an unsettling jurisdictional shift from Connecticut and New Haven to the Duke of York's new colony in 1664. The often chaotic changes disrupted local English townships and had a significant impact on their relations with their Indian neighbors. The interaction between the Indian whalers and their English employers provides important insights into the process of acculturation. Each had to make adjustments to the other's cultural norms to protect their self-interest. The English economic system was stacked against the Indians from the beginning, yet they had little choice but to engage because the habitat that had provided them with a comfortable and secure way of life was gradually disappearing.

The standard works on American whaling give little space to the Long Island origins of this iconic American enterprise. Alexander Starbuck's classic *History of American Whale Fishing* ([1878] 1964) and Eric C. Dolin's more recent *Leviathan: The History of American Whaling* (2007) devote only a few pages to the seventeenth-century shore whaling era. A half century before the large whaling ships were launched onto the deep seas in search of whales around the globe, the basic techniques of commercial whale hunting were developed here on Long Island. The whaleboats with six-man crews and the strategies implemented in the killing of the whales were adopted by the nineteenth-century whalers with few changes. Elizabeth Little's research on Indian whalers on Nantucket and Martha's Vineyard (1981, 1988; Little and Andrews 1982) and Daniel Vickers's study "The First Whalemen of Nantucket" (1983) focus on the beginnings of shore whaling near the end of the seventeenth century, nearly five decades after the enterprise began on eastern Long Island. Local historians who wrote about the history of whaling focused on the more romantic period of deep-sea whaling in the nineteenth century (Edwards and Rattray 1932; Bailey 1959; Howell 1941; Willey 1949; Sleight 1931). Andrew Lipman's insightful study of Indians and Europeans on what he calls the "saltwater frontier" in the seventeenth century includes a brief account of Long Island shore whaling. His larger concern, however, is with the response of the coastal Algonquians to the European invasion in the seventeenth century. My more modest intent here is to focus on the origin and development of the contract labor system and its role in the process of accommodation during the early postcontact period.

Acknowledgments

I have accumulated a large debt over my years of researching Long Island Native Americans. My first and largest debt is to the descendants of the Indian whalers, the Unkechaug, Montaukett, and Shinnecock people who have encouraged me to write about their history and have provided me with important insights into their history and culture. David Martine, Shinnecock artist and current director of the Shinnecock Indian Nation Museum, a friend of many years, has shared with me his knowledge of Shinnecock history and has contributed his artwork to many of my publications. Mary Treadwell, Unkechaug elder and director of the Unkechaug Nation Community Development Corporation, another longtime friend, has worked with me on many projects related to the preservation of Unkechaug history and culture. Unkechaug chief Harry Wallace shared with me his knowledge of the Unkechaug maritime heritage. Informal conversations with these three descendants of the seventeenth-century Native American whalers over the years have enriched my understanding of the archival materials.

I have also incurred a large debt to the librarians, archivists, and town historians during my years of researching Long Island Native Americans. Ned Smith, the head librarian at the Suffolk County Historical Society, is first on my list. He helped me locate obscure documents and has generously given me the benefit of his wide-ranging knowledge of local history. I have come to rely on his wisdom and judgment as I struggled to construct a narrative from the primary sources in the collection.

Mary Laura Lamont, park ranger at William Floyd Estate, Fire Island National Seashore, Mastic, New York, led me through the estate archives and shared with me her wealth of knowledge about the Floyd family and the history of Brookhaven Town. She was my co-author on a paper we presented at the Native American and Indigenous Studies Association (NAISA), June 3–6, 2012. The paper served as a basis for an article in the *Long Island Journal of History* (Spring 2015).

Other local historians and archivists have guided me through their collections and shared with me their personal insights gained from long years of working with the primary sources so important to me. The following people, many of whom have become good friends, deserve a special thanks: Barbara Russell, the Brookhaven town historian; Zach Studenroth, the Southampton town historian; Gina Piastuck, director of the Long Island Collection; Steve Boerner, librarian/archivist at the East Hampton Library; Steve Czarnecki, director of the Bellport Historical Museum; Mary Cummings, research center manager, and Emma Ballou, curator, at the Southampton Historical Society; Joshua Ruff, director of collections at the Long Island Museum in Stony Brook; Nomi Dayan, director of the Cold Spring Whaling Museum; Maria Martinez, curator at the Smithsonian; and Julie Green, archivist for the Bridgehampton Museum, who brought to my attention the original copy of the Daniel Sayre letter (1711) in the society collection.

I have also benefited from informed discussions with scholars in my area such as Gaynell Stone, founder of the Suffolk County Archaeological Society; Marshall Becker, professor emeritus at Westchester Community College; Nancy Shoemaker, University of Connecticut; Jennifer Anderson, Stony Brook University; and Laurie Weinstein, Western Connecticut State University. Anderson and Shoemaker read the early draft with a critical eye and made suggestions for changes that significantly improved the manuscript.

I also benefitted from scholars in the marine sciences who read portions of the manuscript and patiently educated me about the characteristics and the natural history of the North Atlantic right whale. Joe Warren, associate professor in the School of Marine Science and Atmospheric Sciences at the State University of New York at Stony Brook, Southampton Campus, and a member of our poker group, read parts of the manuscript and never complained when I interrupted his concentration at poker with questions about right whale behavior. Warren introduced me to the 2014 annual consortium on the North Atlantic right whale (NARWC) at the New Bedford Whaling Museum, where I was able to meet informally with several of the leading experts on this species of whale. One of the most helpful was David Laist, author of *The North Atlantic Right Whales* (2017), who read parts of this manuscript and made useful suggestions. The following year I managed to reciprocate by presenting archival data related to the decline of right whale populations in the latter half of the seventeenth century (Strong 2015).

I must also acknowledge the patient assistance from the people at The University of Arizona Press. Scott De Herrera, the assistant editor, and the series editors, Laurie Weinstein and Allyson Carter, helped me navigate the manuscript through the process of becoming a book. It all began with a casual discussion Laurie and I had at the Mashantucket conference in 2013.

My largest debt, by far, is to my wife, Jane, and our daughters, Lara and Lisa, for their support over the years when the manuscript was taking shape. Jane and Lara read the manuscript and made corrections and suggestions that significantly improved the final draft.

America's Early Whalemen

1

The Whale in Aboriginal Long Island Culture

The North Atlantic Right Whale (*Eubalaena glacialis*)

The words for whale in the surviving Algonquian vocabularies on Long Island vary only slightly. The Montauketts on the far eastern end of Long Island called the whale *potedaup*, whereas the Unkechaug, who live in what is now the town of Brookhaven in central Long Island, called the whale *puttap* (Gardiner [1680] 1980, 15; Strong 2011, appendix). The Unkechaug vocabulary was recorded by Thomas Jefferson when he visited the Unkechaug reservation at Poospatuck in 1791. Roger Williams, in his *A Key into the Languages of America*, said that the Narragansett Indians called the whale *potop-pauog* (Williams [1643] 1973, 181). The Eastern Abenaki called the whale *powdawe* (Rosier 1605, 392).

The species of whale best known to the Algonquian peoples of Long Island would have been the North Atlantic right whale (*Eubalaena glacialis*). There are eight species of baleen whales grouped into four families; the northern and southern right whales are in the *Balaenidae* group (Clapham et al. 1999, 36–37). These magnificent mammals, ranging in length from forty-three to fifty-two feet and weighing as much as seventy tons, must have inspired awe in the Algonquian villagers as they swam slowly by the shore spewing v-shaped water spouts twenty feet in the air from the two blow holes on the top of their heads (fig. 1). The huge heads, which make up two-thirds of their bodies, have several hundred plates of baleen instead of teeth. These plates, about six feet long, made of keratin, a substance similar to human fingernails, hang down from the top of the whale's mouth on both sides of its gigantic tongue (fig. 2). The hair-like fringes on the baleen strips act as a giant sieve enabling the whales to feed on small organisms about the size of a grain of rice called *copepods* (*Calanus finmarchicus*). The baleen plates filter out these tiny creatures as the whales swim slowly along the surface with their huge mouths open (fig. 3). The copepods, their primary food source, flourish in the cold northern waters (Baumgartner, Mayo, and Kenney 2007, 140–43).

The pregnant females parade along the Long Island beaches in November on their way south to give birth in the more accommodating warm southern waters along the coast of Florida and Georgia (map 1). They generally produce a single

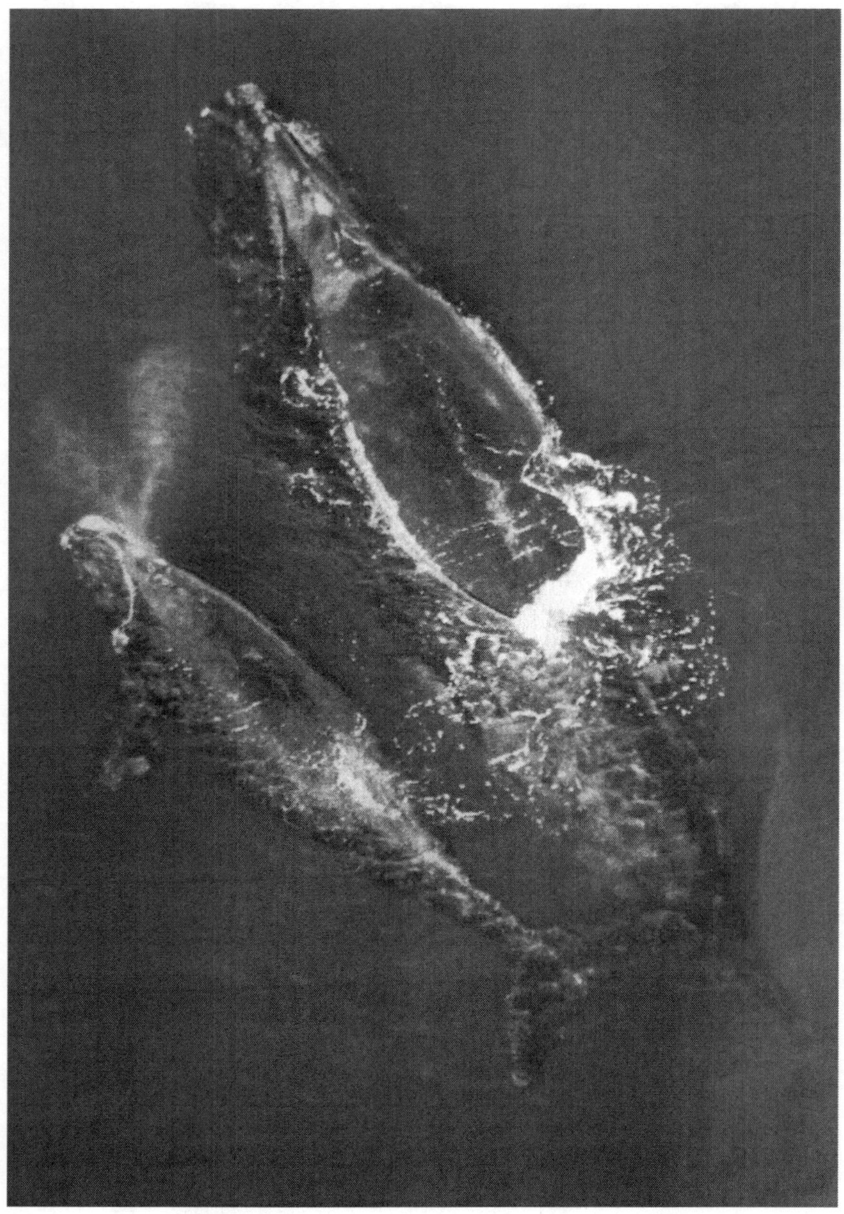

Figure 1 North Atlantic right whale and calf *Eubalaena glacialis*. Wikimedia Commons, public domain.

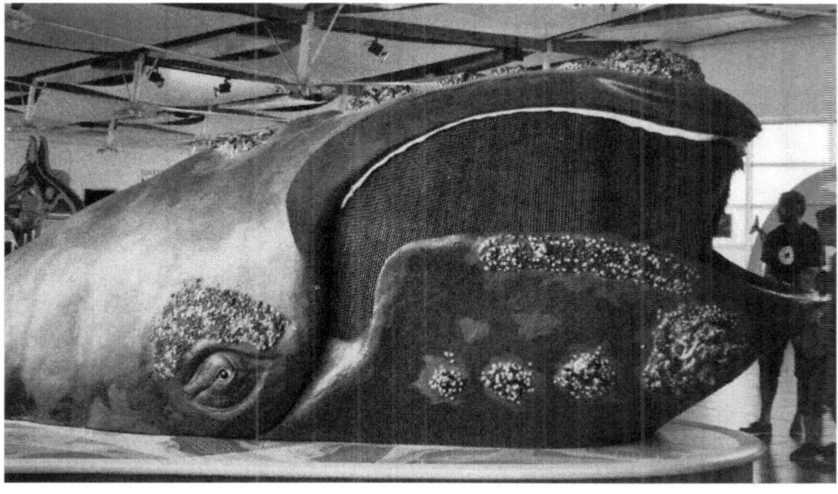

Figure 2 North Atlantic right whale mouth with baleen plates. Wikimedia Commons, public domain.

Figure 3 Baleen plate, courtesy of the Cold Spring Harbor Whaling Museum, Cold Spring Harbor, New York

Map 1 North Atlantic right whale seasonal migratory corridor from the Bay of Fundy, south to calving grounds off Georgia and the Carolinas. Map drawn by Sari Ilona Jekely based on the account of the first year in the life of *Arpeggio*, a right whale calf born in January, 1997, by Scott D. Kraus and Rosalind M. Rolland, "Right Whales in the Urban Ocean," in Kraus and Scott, eds. *The Urban Whale: North Atlantic Right Whales at the Crossroads*, Cambridge, Mass.: Harvard University Press, 31–33.

calf every three to five years after a thirteen-month gestation period. The calves vary in length from about twelve to fifteen feet at birth and grow about three feet a month during the first eight months (Kraus, Pace, and Frasier 2007, 175–82). The calves continue nursing for eleven months. The comforting southern water, however, is devoid of nourishment, prompting the nursing mothers to return north where they can replenish their fat stores (Reeves, Breiwick, and Mitchell 1999, 78–79; Kraus and Rolland 2007, 19–21; Baumgartner, Mayo, and Kenney 2007, 143). The mothers and their calves remain close together as they return to the northern feeding grounds. This pattern of movement along the shores made them vulnerable to the Indian hunters on Long Island.[1]

The right whales have no fixed migration routes. They do not swim on regular paths nor do they travel in large pods or groups (Kraus and Rolland 2007, 19). Adult males are independent travelers who sometimes accompany the females south but tend to move to the locations where they find the largest concentrations of food. The identified areas where they gather to feed are Cape Cod Bay, the Bay of Fundy, the Great South Channel adjacent to Cape Cod Bay, and Roseway Basin off Newfoundland (Kraus and Rolland 2007, 18). Since the degree of copepod concentrations vary in these areas, the whales move from one to another looking for the best meal.

Using a technique called "ram feeding," the right whales swim slowly and steadily near the surface with their mouths open for hours without interruption, making them vulnerable to hunters pursuing them in canoes or small boats. Forty percent of the whale's body consists of a layer of blubber about a foot thick. This keeps the carcass buoyant after death, enabling hunters to tow them ashore. These characteristics made them easy prey for hunters and purportedly led the Basque to name them the "right" whale to hunt. For scientists, however, the naming of the species was not so straightforward. In 1735, Swedish naturalist Carl Linnaeus set forth a system for naming and classifying flora and fauna using Latin terms. The scientists struggled to distinguish between the North Atlantic right whale and its close cousin, the bowhead whale, until early in the twentieth century when general consensus settled on *Eubalaena glacialis*, "true ice-related whale" (Laist 2017, 16–32). The more practical designation given by Basques, however, remains and usually precedes the scientific label.

The number of right whales in the North Atlantic in prehistoric times is subject to some debate. Although everyone acknowledges that the relevant data is sparse, the U.S. Department of Commerce estimated in 1991 that there were at least ten thousand. Studies by Randall Reeves in 1992 suggested a lower number (Reeves, Smith, and Johnson 2007, 43–44, 68–69). Reeves's figure is based on the documented oil and baleen exports from the American colonies in the seventeenth century. These figures, however, may be underestimates because of sparse records and the well-known activities of smugglers during this time. More recent estimates made in 2015, based on food supply and habitat range, concluded that the prehistoric population may have been between fifteen thousand and twenty thousand (Laist 2017, 262).

The estimate for the surviving right whale population in 2007 was about 350 (Kraus and Rolland 2007, 12). The report for 2013, based on the right whale identification database curated by the New England Aquarium, estimated the population to be 522 (Pettis 2014). David Laist, in his comprehensive study *North Atlantic Right Whales: From Hunted Leviathan to Conservation Icon* (2017), notes that "despite the large range of uncertainty in former numbers, there is no doubt that North Atlantic right whales are one of the world's most endangered large whales with a long road ahead if they are to recover former population levels" (Laist 2017, 263).

Images of Precontact Indian Whaling

In 2007, archaeologists excavating a site in the Arctic on the Chukotka Peninsula in Russia discovered an engraved walrus tusk depicting whaling scenes on both sides. Daniel Odess, one of the archaeologists who worked on the site, said that the artifact was embedded with materials that produced three-thousand-year-old radio-carbon dates. It is possible, of course, that the carving itself is much younger, but even so it is good evidence that Native people were hunting whales long before the Europeans arrived (Pringle 2008, 175). A detailed analysis of the engraving by David Laist notes that "the whaling scenes illustrate a fully developed whaling tradition virtually identical to the first historical accounts of Inuit and Thule whaling in the nineteenth century" (78–79).

The hunters were depicted using a harpoon attached to a line held by the men in the umiak. What appears to be a sealskin float or "drogue" designed to slow down and tire the wounded whale was tied to the line. The Paleo Inuit hunters on Unalaska Island in the Aleutians developed a hunting tool that was adopted by the European whalers centuries later (Dolin 2007, 249–50). The tool makers drilled a hole in the middle of the point and attached a line that went back to their boat or to a seal skin drogue. Once the harpoon was plunged into the whale, the shaft detached leaving the point deeply embedded in the flesh. When the whale lunged forward, the tension on the line caused the point to turn perpendicular to the entry wound, lodging it securely in the body. The whale, encumbered by the lines to the boat and to the drogues, soon tired and became vulnerable to the hunters' lances.

Although the evidence for prehistoric whaling in the northern Pacific and Bering Sea is convincing, similar activities along the Atlantic coast of North America remain a subject of debate among scholars. Two intriguing copper

Figure 4 Theodore de Bry, *Curious Method of Catching Whales*, from *Americae* Part 9 (c. 1590). Library of Congress Rare Book Collection, IMG 3279 Plate # AA2.

plate engravings made by Theodor de Bry around 1590 also depict Indians killing whales, but these were not, of course, firsthand observations. One is based on an account of Indian whale hunters off the coast of Florida, written in 1590 by Spanish explorer Jose de Acosta in his *Natural and Moral History of the Indies* (de Acosta 1590, English translation 1880, 148–50) (fig. 4). De Acosta, who never visited Florida, wrote the account based on information given to him, he said, by "reliable men." De Bry published the engraving accompanied by de Acosta's text in Part IX of his *Americae* series. The upper half of the image, entitled *Curious Method of Catching Whales*, depicts Florida Indians in dugout canoes killing right whale calves by pounding stakes into the two characteristic blow holes on their heads. The whales in the engraving are a little less than four times the height of the man seated on the whale's back, suggesting that they were a little less than twenty feet, the size of a right whale calf after a few months' growth.

When a whale swam within reach, the Indians, wrote de Acosta, went out in canoes, stepped onto the animal's back, and drove wooden pegs into its two air holes. When the whale, unable to breathe, lost consciousness, the Indians pulled it ashore by means of a rope that they attached to its tail. They then cut the whale's flesh into pieces and ate the meat. He commented on the "industry and courage of the Indians" in their combat with the great beast. The hunting strategy described by de Acosta is most unusual and perhaps somewhat imaginative, but there is no reason to dismiss the whole account, especially since his description of the right whale's anatomy is accurate.

The engraving in figure 5, entitled *Harpooning Whales*, portrays a quite different and much more plausible strategy for hunting whales. Here the Indian hunters, depicted on a site along the northern New England coast, are harpooning the whales, towing them ashore, and butchering them. The Indians are in dugout canoes similar to the ones in the previous image. In the far-left margin of the engraving stand two European observers. Historian James Axtell, who published the image in his *Beyond 1492*, concluded that the scene was meant to show Indians assisting Europeans (Axtell 1992, 115). The presence of Basque whalers in these waters as early as 1550 is well documented (Proulx 1993, 31). Later accounts by English explorers in 1602 and 1620 reported seeing Indians and Basques working together. In 1602, Captain Bartholomew Gosnold, while at anchor off the coast of Maine, saw six Indians in a Basque shallop with a mast and sail. The Indians were equipped with an iron grapple and a copper kettle (Brereton [1602] 1906, 330). Richard Whitbourne, an

Figure 5 Theodore de Bry, *Harpooning Whales*, from *Americae* (1601–2). Engraving depicting European explorers, possibly in Newfoundland, witnessing Native American whaling practices. Kraus Collections, Library of Congress classification G 159 E 141.

English merchant who served as governor of Renews, a short-lived colony in Labrador, reported in 1620 that he had seen Indians working with Basque whalers helping them kill whales and assisting with the trying out of the blubber (Whitbourne 1620, 1; Proulx 1993, 59).

Accounts of Precontact Indian Whaling

Although the images by De Bry and the reports by Gosnold and Whitbourne suggest the involvement of coastal Native American Indians in whale hunting, they do not give much detail. A report published only a decade later provides more specific information. In 1605, James Rosier; Henry Wriothesley, the third Earl of Southampton; and some wealthy London merchants joined under the leadership of Thomas Arundell, the first Baron Arundell of Wardour, in a venture to establish a colony in North America for English Catholics (Akrigg 1968, 51–52, 158–59). The company commissioned Captain George Waymouth, an experienced navigator as well as an accomplished mathematician and engineer, to look for a location. Waymouth had recently returned from an unsuccessful attempt to find the fabled northwest passage to India. Rosier accompanied Waymouth on the ship *Archangel* to "take due notice and make a full report" of the expedition (Rosier 1605, 357).

The expedition sailed along the New England coast from Nantucket northward to Monhegan Island and the general area of the Penobscot and Kennebec rivers. Rosier did not give the specific location in his public report for fear that rivals might take advantage of the information. He went about his task with care and diligence, noting the flora and fauna and the geographic features, with a focus on the potential for farming and fishing. Rosier and Waymouth were also close observers of the Eastern Abenaki people they encountered. They exchanged knives, bracelets, rings, shirts, combs, looking glasses, sugar candy, and tobacco pipes for beaver pelts, otter skins, furs, and food. From the time of their arrival in May of 1605 until their departure in mid-June, they visited the Indians in their villages and entertained them on board the ship.

In the course of these interactions, Rosier wrote down a vocabulary that Ives Goddard, the Smithsonian linguist, identified as Eastern Abenaki (Goddard 1978, 71). Rosier said the Indians would "fetch fishes, and fruit bushes, and stand by me to see me write their names" (Rosier [1605] 1906, 371). He and Owen Griffin, a member of the expedition who was to lead a small party that would remain behind to plant the new colony, learned enough Algonquian words to communicate with a few of the Indians who had mastered some English. Rosier said that Griffin had reported to him about their form of government, "the ceremonies of their idolatry," and the names of their important leaders, who were called "Bashabes" (Rosier [1605] 1906, 274, 388). Rosier also recorded a great deal of information about their material culture, including the construction of their canoes, their bows and arrows, their clothing, and their body decorations.

Most important for our concerns here was Rosier's description of a whale hunt. His account provides a more detailed context for de Bry's engravings. "One especial thing," he said, "is their manner of killing the whale, which they call *Powdawe*" (Rosier [1605] 1906, 392). His informants told him that they go out in "a multitude of their boats" led by their king and attack whales as long as six fathoms (thirty-six feet) with a bone harpoon fastened to a rope, "made strong with the bark of a tree." Whales this size are depicted in de Bry's engravings. According to Rosier, "they surround [the whale] with their boats and when he rises out of the water they shoot him with their bone tipped arrows until he perishes." Then they drag the body ashore and call their village leaders together with a song of joy. The whale meat is carved up and distributed among the Sagamors who, in turn, "divide the spoils and give every man a share," which they hang up in their houses for preservation. The meat is boiled in a large pot with corn and other ingredients. Rosier's reference to a "bone harpoon" is noteworthy because barbed harpoon points fashioned from bone have been found in several prehistoric sites in New England (Fowler 1972; Moffett 1969).

Nantucket historian Elizabeth Little and David Laist, however, remain skeptical of Rosier's account (Little 1981, 49–51; Laist 2017, 165–71). Both Little and Laist note, correctly, that it does not appear that Rosier was an eyewitness to the hunt. His description, nevertheless, conforms to the early engravings and to other accounts as well as prehistoric artifacts related to whale hunting by eastern coastal Indians. Roger Williams, writing in 1643, reported a protocol of whale meat distribution similar to the one in Rosier's report. Williams said that whales "not above sixty feet" were cut up "in several parcels" and sent "near and far for an acceptable present" (Williams [1643] 1973, 181). The ceremonies and the distribution process following the successful hunt were similar to those described by Rosier. There is an account by Pilgrims describing Native Americans eating the flesh of a stranded whale (Shoemaker 2015, 269). Williams also remarked about the Indians' skilled seamanship in handling canoes beyond the surf. "It is wonderful," he wrote, "to see how they will venture in those canoes" (Williams [1643] 1973, 178). William Wood, another seventeenth-century observer, reported that:

> In their cockling fly-boats [canoes], where an Englishman can scarce sit without fear of tottering, they will venture to sea, where an English shallop dare not bear a knot of sail; scudding over the overgrown waves as fast as a winde-driven ship, being driven by their paddles . . . if a cross wave (as is seldom) turn her keel-upside down, they, by swimming free her and scramble back into her again. (Wood [1634] 1968, 91)

These boats, said Wood, "were made of whole pine trees, being about two foot and a half over and twenty feet long . . ." and carried the hunters as far as two leagues out to sea (Wood [1634] 1968, 46). An account written in 1642 by Thomas Mayhew Jr., a Protestant missionary who lived among the Indians on Martha's Vineyard for fourteen years, recounted seeing Indians off the Nantucket shore hunting whales "in fragile canoes."[2]

Shore whaling by the prehistoric peoples in Labrador and Greenland is well known (Taylor 1988; IWC 35–37, 75–77). This whaling technology, depicted on the engraving from the Bering Sea area, was introduced to the eastern Arctic regions by the Thule people, who migrated eastward across the Canadian Arctic to Greenland and Labrador around AD 1200 (Friesen and Arnold 2008, 527; Pringle 2008, 175). Their skin-covered umiaks, quite similar to the Basque whaleboats, were most effective in pursuing the bowhead whales (*Balaena mysticetus*), who inhabited the waters to the north of the right whale habitat.

Closer to home, Paul Bailey, the Suffolk County historian, reconstructed a coastal whale hunting scene based on local folk accounts from Long Island. "During the winter months the dug-outs were kept on the outer beach, near the surf, and at a warning cry from a lookout posted on a high sand dune, they would be launched through the breakers. Being armed only with stone tipped wooden spears, they endeavored to drive the whale into shallow water, where the women, youths and old men helped dispatch it with knives and hatchets" (Bailey 1957, 83). Another account, written by naturalist Thomas Beale in 1839, described an attack on what he thought was a sperm whale by New England Indian hunters. He states that "we had it proved to us that the Indians who inhabited the shores of North America used to voyage out to sea and attack this [sperm whale] animal" (Beale 1839, 138). Beale, however, does not tell us who offered him the proof, but his account is similar to those reported by Rosier and Mayhew, suggesting that the Indians still adhered to long-standing traditions of whale hunting dating to prehistoric times. The Indians, he wrote, attack the whale,

> . . . from their canoes and pierce him with their lances of wood or other instruments of the same material which were barbed, and which were fastened by a stout warp, or piece of rope, to a large block of light wood, which was thrown overboard the moment the barbed instrument was thrust into its body, which being repeated at every rising of the whale or when they were near enough to do so in a few instances, by a sort of worrying to death system, rewarding the enterprising savage with the lifeless body of the victim, but which in most cases was that of a very young one, and even this, when towed to shore, was impossible to turn over, so they were obliged to content themselves with flinching (flensing) the fat from one side of

the body only. Few, indeed, must these instances have been, when we consider the means that were employed in the capture of so immense an animal possessing such enormous strength by which their barbed spears and lances of wood must frequently have shivered to atoms or drawn from the flesh of the whale by the resistance the blocks of wood to which they were attached must have occasioned, when the animal became frightened into its utmost speed. . . . (Beale 1839, 138–39)

However, as Elizabeth Little noted, it seems most unlikely that the animal in Beale's account was a sperm whale, even a young one, because these whales seldom come close to shore (Little 1981, 54). The account probably came to Beale from New Englanders who were describing an attack on a young right whale.

Antler bone projectile points found in Sag Harbor and East Hampton by Foster Saville, an archaeologist for the Museum of the American Indian, were identified in the museum file as harpoon points because of their size. There was no toggle mechanism associated with these points. The one from Sag Harbor was five inches long and the one from East Hampton measured three inches. Both are in the Smithsonian collections (cat. #150095.000 and cat. #150096.000) (fig. 6). These points were likely attached to shafts propelled by atl-atls, a hunting tool commonly used for spearing large fish and small marine mammals. Numerous atl-atl weights were found on sites in the area. Evidence

Figure 6 Antler harpoon points excavated from a site in East Hampton by Foster Saville.

of a prehistoric whale hunting technology for Long Island, however, is sparse compared to the materials found in the archaeological sites in the Bering Sea area and on the strait of Belle Isle in Labrador.

The Spirits of Deep Waters: Whaling Ceremonies and Opposing Forces

The ceremony with a "song of joy" following a successful whale hunt in Rosier's account parallels an account in David Lion Gardiner's *Chronicles of Easthampton*, written in the nineteenth century. Gardiner, a direct descendant of Lion Gardiner, who settled on eastern Long Island in 1639, drew on Gardiner family material to write a brief history of East Hampton. According to Gardiner, the Montaukett Indians, whose villages were on the far eastern end of Long Island, honored the whale spirit with the sacrifice of the fin and tail of the whale. The Montaukett ceremony shares similarities with rituals observed by other coastal peoples.

The Norse whalers in Skogsvag placed the tails and flukes of minke whales in an upright position in stone circles marking sacred ground. The ceremony included songs honoring the Norse god Njoror, thanking him for his gift (Lindquist 1994, 1: 288–306). Carved images of whales and whale feasts on rocks near the shore marked places in Australia where prehistoric aboriginal whalemen held dances and ceremonies. An image located near Sydney shows a whale feast involving thirty-one figures led by a large man, perhaps a shaman (Russell 2012, 27–28). Archeologist Henry Lourandos noted that "large-scale intergroup communal and ceremonial occasions were held, with up to 1,000 people attending." Another observer reported that runners were sent out across the region to invite people to the feast, where the whale was cut up using "coastal flint, fashioned into knives" (Russel 2012, 25–26).

Closer to home, prehistoric artifacts found at two sites on Long Island appear to be related to the veneration of whales. A cache of six vertebrae from the tail of a whale was found in 1920 by Reginald Pelham Bolton when he was excavating a site on Wright's Island, near Throg's Neck on western Long Island. The bones had been secured and carefully placed together in what appeared to be a ritual context. Another artifact that appeared to have ritual significance was found on the eastern end of the island in Suffolk County. A pestle, carved from the rib bone of a whale, had a distinct black band about an inch wide around the middle and twelve holes carved along the surface (fig. 7). These embellishments likely had a religious significance beyond the obvious association with females and domesticity. The artifacts are now housed in the Smithsonian Archive Center, Suitland, Maryland (cat. #182733.000 and cat. #23/1648).

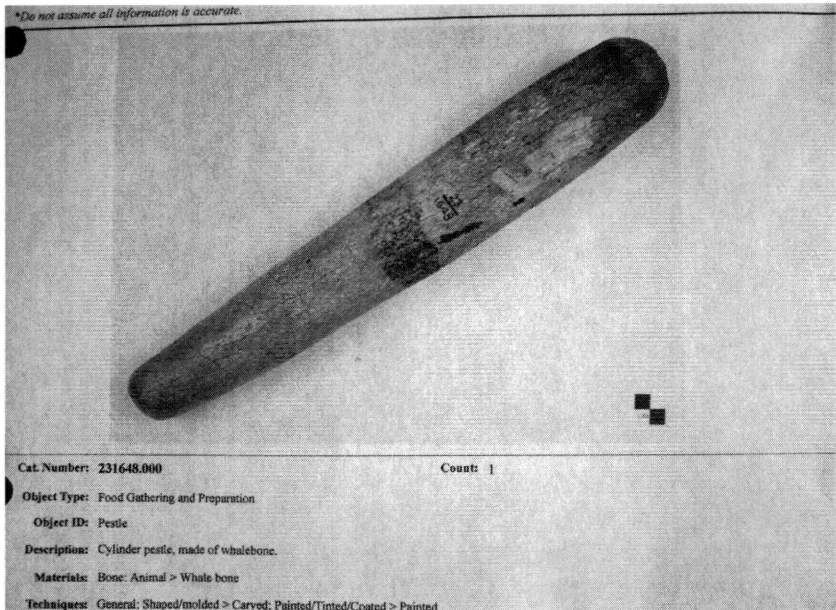

Cat. Number: 231648.000   Count: 1

Object Type: Food Gathering and Preparation

Object ID: Pestle

Description: Cylinder pestle, made of whalebone.

Materials: Bone: Animal > Whale bone

Techniques: General: Shaped/molded > Carved; Painted/Tinted/Coated > Painted

Figure 7 Painted whalebone pestle, Smithsonian collections, Cat.# 231648.000. Black band and drilled holes suggest ritual significance. Courtesy of the National Museum of the American Indian, Smithsonian Institution, Washington, D.C.

According to Gardiner, the Montaukett ceremony continued with a "great and prolonged pow-wow" wherein they engaged in what English observers described as "violent gesticulations, horrid yells, and laborious movements of the limbs and body, with distortions of the features" (Gardiner [1840] 1973, 3). A similar ceremony was likely taking place when Williams observed the distribution of whale meat after the hunt. The purpose of the ceremony, said Gardiner, was to procure the favor of Cawhlutoowit, the good deity, and to keep away Mutcheshesumetooh, the evil deity. Gardiner drew on an account of the Montaukett belief system written in 1761 by Samson Occom, the Mohegan missionary (Occom [1761] 1980, 218).

An effigy carved on a mica tablet may express such opposing forces. The tablet is about seven inches long, tapering from a width of five inches to two inches at the narrow end (fig. 8). A farmer in the town of Brookhaven found the artifact in the mid-nineteenth century. The New York State Museum in Albany acquired the artifact sometime later. Lisa Anderson, the museum curator, estimated that it was made during the Middle Woodland Period (letter to author, May 23, 1996). A serpent with horns and three feathers in the center is surrounded by the tails of whales. The image appears to be a composite

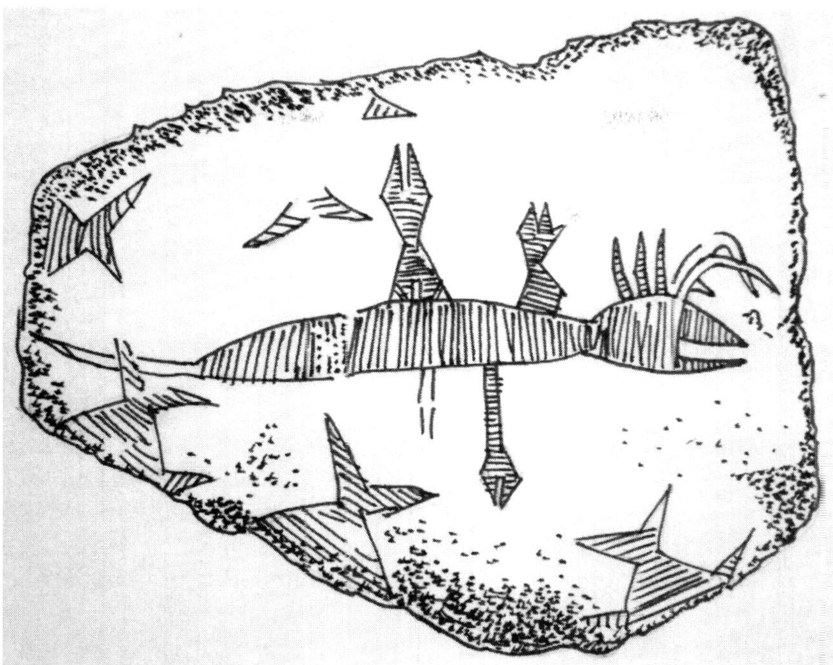

Figure 8 Late Woodland engraved mica tablet found in Brookhaven in the 1840s by a farmer. New York State Museum collections. Drawing by David B. Martine.

being, similar in many ways to other symbolic expressions in prehistoric North American cultures, swimming among a pod of whales.

The presence of feathers and antlers on the water spirit indicates that it was a powerful spirit representing the three universes. The feathers were a symbol of the upper world, the antlers represented the surface world, and the serpent was associated with the underworld. These composite spirit beings were believed to be extremely powerful. In the Cherokee legends, the *Uktena* was such a being, with a snake body, deer antlers, and large wings, believed to live under water in a mountain pool (Hudson 1976, 145).

Kathleen Bragdon, in *Native Peoples of Southern New England*, concluded that this mica etching may have represented the underworld in opposition to the thunderbird spirit associated with the upper world and was linked as well to the powerful Algonquian spirit named Abbomacho, who often appears as a water serpent that can cure disease and heal wounds (Bragdon 1996, 188–89). Belief in a water serpent being was also expressed by the Norse whalers in their mythology. The being, *miogarosormr*, is represented on the Swedish Altuna rune stone and the Danish Hordum stone as an evil sea serpent engulfing the world (Lindquist 1994, 109–11). Miogarosormr appears to be a spiritual being similar to the Montaukett's Mutcheshesumetooh.

The opposition of the two powerful spirit forces was also expressed in the beliefs of the Lenape on western Long Island. In a Lenape legend, the thunder beings captured the great horned serpent who lived under the sea and held it prisoner (Skinner 1914, 71). The thunder beings scraped scales off the serpent's back and gave them to the Lenape, who laid them on the ground in a ceremony that would bring rain. An image of the thunder being in the form of a splayed bird image was found on a pottery fragment excavated by Mark Harrington in a site near the present-day Shinnecock Reservation (Harrington 1977, 56).

Three more artifacts with thunderbird images were discovered on eastern Long Island. A small notched pendant was found near Sag Harbor by William Wallace Tooker, an amateur archaeologist whose collections are now in the Smithsonian Archival Center (cat. #231659.000). The pendant has incised thunderbird images on both faces. Archaeologists excavating an area near the Sylvester Manor house on Shelter Island in 2007 found the other two (Gary 2007, 106–7). One image was etched on a silver coin and the other on a small cobble stone. The coin was well worn and difficult to date, but the faint markings were quite similar to those found on coins produced during the reign of King Philip IV, from 1621 to 1665. Both images, concluded archaeologist Jack Gary, "may have been created by the same hand and at least indicates a continuation of traditional Native American symbolic practice in Sylvester Manor's 17th century contexts."

Spirits of the Deep Waters: Calling the Whales

Whale songs similar in concept to those of the Montauketts and Norse are also mentioned in Passamaquoddy mythology. Glooscap, the creator spirit, sings a magic song to the whales, calling a large female to the shore where he climbs on her back and rides from the cold winter northland south to the warm land of summer. He rewards her with a pipe and tobacco, which she lights and swims away leaving a trail of smoke behind her. "And to this day the Indians, when they see a whale blow, say she is smoking the pipe of Glooscap" (Leland 1884, 33–37). The aboriginal peoples in coastal Australia and Tasmania believed that their shamans would sing to the whale spirit asking for the whales to be sent ashore (Clarke 2001, 21). This belief may be related to natural occurrences. During winter months, when seas were high, large numbers of whales often washed ashore (Russell 2012, 25).

Although the Montauketts believed in a tension between powerful spirits, these spirits were often related to the animals they hunted. Hunting rituals were a fundamental aspect of Algonquian belief systems rooted in their conception of the relationship between the natural world and the spirit world. As anthropologist Kathleen Bragdon noted, "animals in the dark woods and deep waters were transformations of even more powerful beings" (Bragdon 1996, 195). According to Benjamin Basset, who collected folklore from the Wampanoags on Martha's Vineyard, the Indians believed that a spirit named Moshup, who controlled the creatures of the deep, sent the drift whales to them as an act of kindness (Basset 1792, 140; Little and Andrews 1982, 18–19).

Similarly, the Montaukett whale ceremony reinforced a spiritual connection ensuring continuing success in hunting and finding drift whale carcasses on their shores. Although a Montaukett was identified on whaling contracts in 1675 and 1676 as "Moshup," sachem of Montaukett, there is no indication that there was a mythic being called Moshup in the belief system of the Long Island Algonquians (RTEH 1: 373, 407–9). There is evidence, however, that driving the smaller whales into tidal bays was practiced on Long Island.

An account from eastern Long Island makes reference to similar whaling techniques. In a seventeenth-century document, Unkechaug Indians living on the southern shore of Long Island complained to the governor that the English had taken fish from them after the Indians had "driven [them] upon their beaches" (NYCD 14: 720). This suggests a hunting technique that may have been used for small whales and calves as well as smaller sea mammals. References to the "luring" of whales to the shore by the Aboriginal people in southern Australia suggest that they may have employed a similar strategy.

The testimony about the Indians' boat-handling skills by Roger Williams indicates that the Indians were capable of driving the right whale calves toward the shore and killing them with stone and bone-tipped lances. This strategy, called "spear whaling," was used by the Norse whalers in the ninth century. Ole Lindquist, in his doctoral thesis on the evolution of whaling in Norway and Iceland, drew from medieval court records describing whaling methods. The *kvalraqtur*, or whale drive, began out at sea in boats placed at strategic locations and drove small whales into fjords and inlets, where they were attacked with bows and arrows and spears (Lindquist 1994, 2: 309–24; Laist 2017, 89–91).

Conclusions

The whale ceremonies and artifacts, such as the mica tablet with its whale tails, are compelling evidence that the whale was a significant presence in the cultural traditions of the Long Island Indians, a presence inspired by more than the occasional beaching of a whale carcass. Although the historical descriptions of Indian whale hunting by Rosier, Mayhew, Beale, and Bailey and the images of whales that often adorned early maps were not based on eyewitness observations, it seems most unlikely that they were complete fabrications. The

Indians of coastal Long Island were closely attuned to their maritime environment. They hunted sea mammals, fished in the coastal waters, and harvested shellfish. They celebrated the spirits of the deep waters by sacrificing to them the crucial body parts of the most powerful and awesome denizen of their maritime world. Their material culture also reflected this association. Whale bones and fins, for example, were also fashioned into elaborate belts. Adriaen Van Der Donck in his *Description of New Netherland* (1655) described the dress of the Indians in some detail. He reported, "Around the waist they all wear a belt made of leather, whale fin, whalebone or sewant" (Van Der Donck [1655] 2008, 79). Although disagreements continue about prehistoric whaling, clearly the whale played a significant role in the world view of the Long Island coastal Algonquians.[3]

2

Drift Whales

A Contentious Asset

Prior to the arrival of the Europeans, the carcasses of large sea mammals that had died of natural causes or had been stranded in the tidal bays along the Atlantic coast of Long Island were frequently washed up on shore, where the Indians eagerly utilized their remains. Even today, with a much reduced whale population, an average of two to three whales wash up on the Long Island beaches each year (fig. 9). In precontact times, these belonged to the sachems, who controlled the hunting territory where the beaches were located. As the Native peoples became more involved in the English economy, they found that control over their beaches and access to the sacred fins and tails of whales was becoming compromised. When the English arrived, they saw the drift whales as a lucrative source of very scarce capital in their agrarian economy. They were, however, careful to put the commercial asset in a theological context, calling the whales "the providence of God."

The oil had a ready, inexhaustible market in the colonies and in Europe, where it was used for lighting and lubrication (fig. 10). Whale oil was much preferable to animal fat, pine pitch, or fish oil as a source of illumination (Dolin 2007, 35). The baleen strips from the whales' jawbone, a strong, flexible material, was used for buggy whips, corsets, umbrellas, and small boxes (fig. 11). It was the plastic of its day and continued to be in demand as late as 1906, when it was valued at 2,000 English pounds a ton (Conway 1906, 39). These products brought in much-needed hard currency to the local economies on eastern Long Island. The oil was used as a form of currency as well. In 1683, for example, John Miller received a barrel of oil valued at two pounds in payment for a colt (RTEH 2: 123).

Although the settlers who in 1640 established Southampton and Southold on the two "fish-tail" forks at the far eastern end of Long Island were farmers, tradesmen, commercial fishermen, and merchants, with no experience in whaling, they were quite familiar with the commercial potential of the drift whales. The company that founded Southampton had been organized by settlers in Lynn, Massachusetts, shortly after they arrived in 1635 from the rural areas in southern England.[1] Although Massachusetts was a center of Puritan enthusiasm, the Southampton Town records clearly indicate that these immigrants,

Figure 9 Beached whale at Smith Point, Long Island, October 10, 2014. Photo by author.

Figure 10 Whale oil lamps. Courtesy of the Whaling Museum and Education Center, Cold Spring Harbor, N.Y.

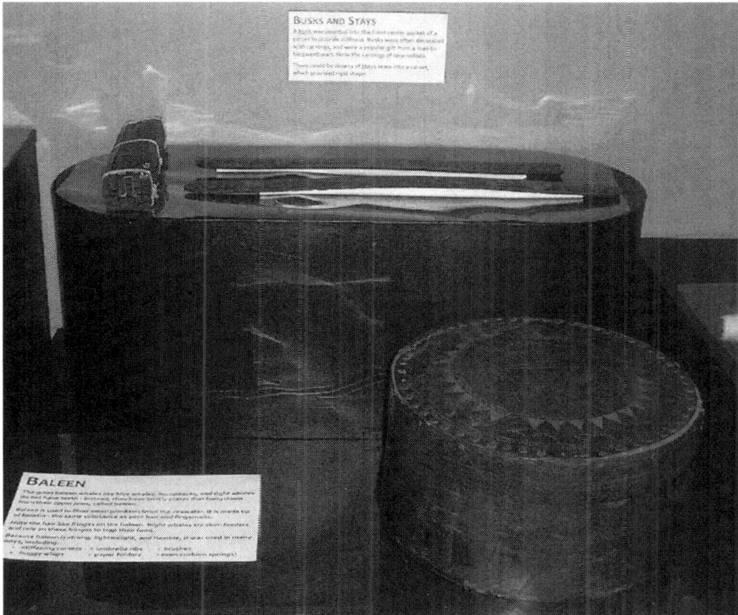

Figure 11 Baleen plates used for corset stays, boxes, and buggy whips. Courtesy of the Whaling Museum and Education Center, Cold Spring Harbor, N.Y.

led by Edward Howell, John Cooper Sr., Daniel How, and Thomas Halsey, were more interested in improving their economic status than in religious piety (Goddard 2011, 20).

The four men were among the largest landowners and taxpayers in Lynn according to the local tax records (Adams 1918, 53). With the exception of these four, the rest came from the "middling" classes eager to improve their status and to increase their land holdings, a motivation shared with most of the migrants from England in the 1630s (Strong 2007, 1–19; Goddard 2011, 18–19; Seed 1995, 20ff; Martin 1991, 133, 138; Breen 1989, 89–98). The acquisition of land was a near obsession because the ownership of property in fee simple was a privilege of the aristocracy back in their homeland. Land ownership became the primary basis of social status in colonial America.

Five years after their arrival in Lynn, the Southampton company "hived out," as such moves were called at the time, and relocated on the south fork of eastern Long Island, where they purchased a tract of land from the Shinnecock Indians and founded the town of Southampton (RTSH 1: 12–14; Adams 1918, 45; Howell 1887, 46–48) (see map 2). The Shinnecocks were one of two Indian communities on the south fork of eastern Long Island. Their neighbors to the east were the Montauketts, whose villages were located at Montauk on

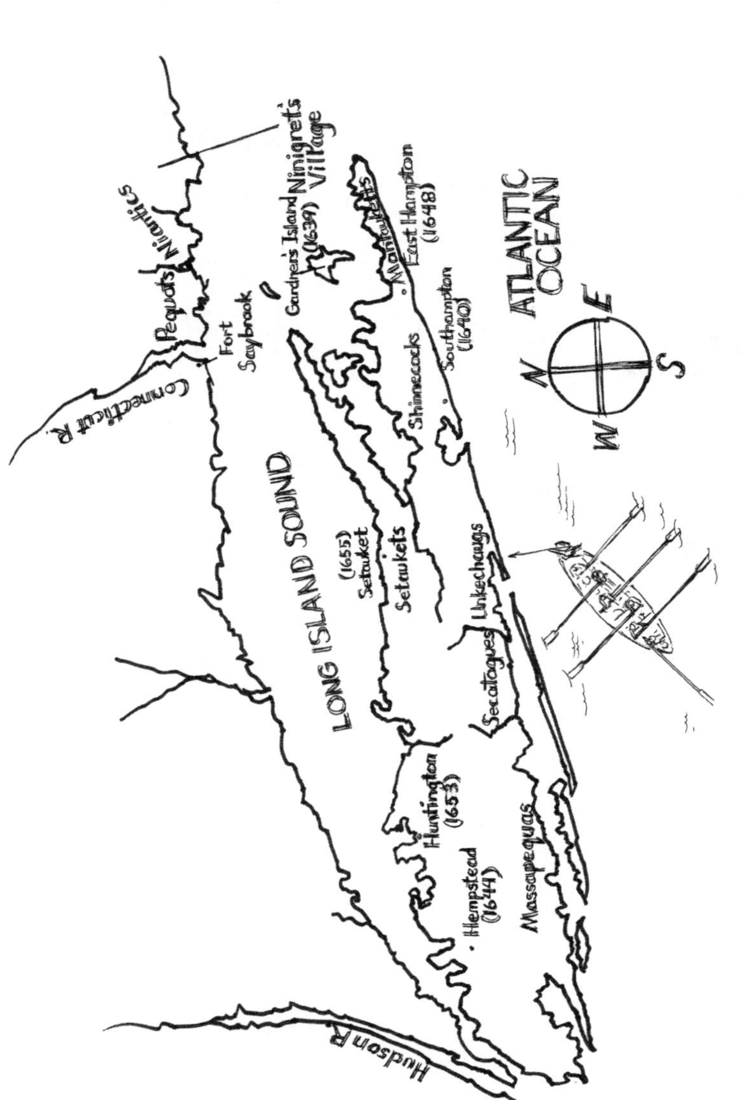

Map 2 Long Island in the seventeenth century. Drawing by David B. Martine, director, Shinnecock Nation Cultural Center and Museum.

the far eastern tip of the south fork. The Southampton settlers had the support of Massachusetts governor John Winthrop Sr., who wanted an English settlement created on the island to strengthen English claims based on the voyages of John Cabot in 1497 against the Dutch, who asserted that all of Long Island belonged to them by right of Henry Hudson's voyage of discovery in 1609.

The first English toehold had been established by Lion Gardiner on an island at the mouth of Peconic Bay, between the north and south forks on the east end of Long Island in 1639, at the invitation of Wyandanch, the Montaukett sachem. After witnessing the crushing defeat of the Pequots by the English in 1637, Wyandanch had come to Lion Gardiner, the commander of Fort Saybrook, at the mouth of the Connecticut River, seeking a political alliance and access to English trade goods. The Montauketts had been tributaries of the Pequots, relying on them for protection from their enemies in exchange for wampum.

Ninigret, the Niantic sachem, whose villages were in Rhode Island, a short distance across the sound from Montauk, had attempted to bring the Montauketts into a tributary relationship, but Wyandanch, impressed by the English victory over the Pequots, preferred an alliance with Lion Gardiner. Ninigret, who never forgave Wyandanch for rebuffing his overtures, frequently raided Montaukett villages. As a result, Wyandanch became ever more dependent on his alliance with Gardiner. With English support, Wyandanch and his Montauketts became one of the dominant tribal communities on Long Island.

The defeat of the Pequots and Gardiner's alliance with the Montauketts certainly made the Southampton company feel more secure in their decision to establish a settlement in the Long Island wilderness. The settlers' primary focus, of course, was on planting and cultivating the land, but they would certainly have heard about the drift whales that were frequently found on the Atlantic shores. John Winthrop Sr. wrote in his journal that "there were three or four cast up . . . almost every year" (Hosmer [1908] 1959, 1: 148). In 1635, "some of our people," said Winthrop, "went to Cape Cod and made some oil of a whale, which was cast on shore." There is no record of the first whale carcass on the Southampton beach harvested for oil and bone, but there is a Dutch account describing a first encounter that may have been quite similar (O'Callaghan 1966, 1: 346). According to an account found in "an old book" kept by Antoine de Hooges, the colonial secretary for Rensselaerswyck, it took place after a heavy storm swept through the area, destroying houses and "nearly carr[ying] away the fort." After the storm abated, a whale was sighted, much to the surprise of the local population, near an island later called Walvish Island by the Dutch. The location, above Albany where the Mohawk River flows into the Hudson, is not a likely place to see a whale, although the large mammals have been known to swim up freshwater rivers.

According to de Hooges, in March 1647 a whale "of considerable size, snow white in color, round in body, and blowing water out of its head" was observed by the people. Shortly thereafter a second whale was spotted. This one was brown, forty feet long, with fins on its back, ejecting water high in the air. The brown whale stranded itself on the island, bringing a crowd of local people to the site. Joe Warren, on the faculty of the School of Marine and Atmospheric Science at Stony Brook-Southampton, made an educated guess based on this sparse data. The white "whale" might have been a beluga or perhaps a pale-skinned porpoise of some kind. The large brown whale he thought was likely a baleen whale, perhaps, a humpback (personal communication, March 18, 2015). Few if any of the farmers and townsmen had any experience with harvesting the oil from a whale, but this did not dissuade them.

They began cutting in much the same way that the Southampton residents would have. They cut out the blubber and "roasted" it to extract the oil. The total mass of blubber soon overwhelmed them. The river was covered with grease, a condition that lasted for three weeks, and the "air was infected to such a degree with the stench, as the fish lay rotting on the strand that the smell was perceptively offensive for two miles leeward" (ibid.). The first "whale" sighted headed south but ran aground some forty miles from the mouth of the Hudson. In that area, noted de Hooges, four more whales stranded themselves that same year. The accounts indicate the frequency of whale strandings along the Atlantic shore as well as the potential for a lucrative source of capital.

Not surprisingly, disputes over the drift whales led to a town ordinance in 1644. The town magistrates ordered that:

> henceforth within the bounds of this plantation any whale or whales cast up, for the prevention of disorder it is consented unto that there shall be four wards in this town, eleven persons in each ward, and by lot two of each ward shall be employed for the cutting out of the said whales, who shall have for their pains a double share, and every inhabitant with his child or servant that is above sixteen years of age, shall have in the division of the other part an equal portion. (RTSH 1: 31–32)

The distribution of the oil and baleen was to be based on the property holdings of the town residents. The selection by lot of men who would do the cutting indicates that few, if any, of the townsmen had experience in the highly specialized skills required for flensing a whale. Although the colonists may have known something about the process of flensing and trying out the whale oil from the English who operated whaling stations on the North Atlantic island of Spitsbergen at the time, the whole operation here was likely by trial and error during these early years.

The town ordinance also established procedures for spotting the whale carcasses. Following any storm, two persons were to be designated as "look-outs" to locate drift whales on the town beaches. The ordinance also stipulated that any town resident who saw a whale and did not report it would either pay a fine of ten shillings or be whipped. The squads quickly arrived to begin the long, arduous, labor-intensive, and unpleasant task of harvesting the oil and baleen. The townsmen were to provide the carts to move the blubber to a location near the town. From a sparse number of references to the trying process, it appears that the townsmen carted away their share and tried out the blubber near their homes. That, of course, would change when commercial shore whaling became established.

In 1648, the town experienced a number of dramatic changes that led to a revision of the drift whaling system established four years earlier. In 1647, the town's first minister, Reverend Abraham Pierson, a staunch Puritan who believed that only church members should vote, was at odds with a majority of the inhabitants who preferred a more liberal approach to religion. Pierson left the community, taking a number of like-minded families with him. He was replaced the next year by Reverend Robert Fordham, who had "hived out" of Hempstead, an English town in western Long Island under Dutch jurisdiction. Fordham brought several members of his congregation with him. Six of these newcomers, John Ogden; Joseph, John, and Isaac Raynor; Thomas Topping; and Fordham's son, Joseph, became involved in shore whaling operations. At about the same time, nine Southampton families hived out and went east to found the town of East Hampton (Adams 1918, 71–73). Such movements, usually led by ministers, were not uncommon because the parish community provided a social network, thereby reducing the dangers and risks of settling in the wilderness.

Ogden was a capable and innovative entrepreneur, a man of many talents. His skills as a builder and a stone architect had been recognized by Dutch governor Willem Kieft, who invited him to New Amsterdam in 1642 to build a stone church, and later by the Southampton freeholders, who asked him to replace the floor and build the pews for the Southampton meeting house (Callaghan 1966, 262; RTSH 2: 206–7). He founded a small settlement of six families called "North Sea" on the north shore of the south fork, a short distance from the village of Southampton. His purpose, in part, was to develop a port facility with warehouses to store the oil and baleen from the drift whales until they could be shipped to the markets in New York, Boston, and London.

The town welcomed Fordham's group because they replaced those who had relocated to East Hampton and they brought in an influx of much-needed capital. Ogden, who had been made a freeman shortly after his arrival, was elected to serve as a magistrate in the fall of 1650 (RTSH 1: 75). The officials ordered that all the inhabitants, including the newcomers, "shall have their equal vote in making a conclusion concerning the whale or whales that may, by god's providence, be cast up within the bounds of the town" (RTSH 1: 53–54). This ordinance allowed the new arrivals who were not original shareholders in the town to have a voice in the regulations related to the harvesting of the whale carcasses. The flensers, however, were again allotted larger shares, and the town constable was authorized to assign men to watch the beaches for the first appearance of drift whales. This ordinance underscores the economic and political importance of the profits from the drift whales. In 1653, only five years after the 1648 revisions in the drift whale regulations were drafted, a more detailed system was established. This time the inhabitants were divided into four squadrons led by Richard Smith, Thomas Cooper, John Howell, and Thomas Topping (RTSH 1: 91–93). These squadrons were assigned to flense the whales on a rotating system from early spring to the following September.

The trying out of the oil from the blubber brought some complaints from the town residents. In 1672, the Court of Sessions for East Riding, an administrative unit that later became Suffolk County, ordered that "whereas the trying of oil so near the street is so extreme noisome to all passersby, especially to those who are not accustomed to the scent thereof . . . and in respect it is very dangerous (if the oil should fire) thatch-roofed buildings or haystacks. Therefore order that no person whatsoever after this present year shall try any oil in this town nearer than 25 poles (about 140 yards) from the main street," adding that the order applied to both East Hampton and Southampton (RCSS 29).

The town crews likely employed a variation of the procedures used by the English whaling crews in their trying stations on Spitsbergen Island in the early decades of the seventeenth century. The stations, equipped with furnaces, storage buildings, and lodging for the workmen there, were described in a 1662 report published by the Royal Society of London (quoted in Conway 1906, 205–7). The whaling ships anchored in the bays off Spitsbergen and launched shallops carrying six men to attack the whales near shore. After a successful kill they towed the whale back to the ship, where the carcass was attached to the gunwales for flensing. The blubber was peeled off as the body turned in the water and was cut into large rectangular "blanket pieces" about six feet long, weighing about two hundred pounds. The blanket pieces were taken ashore and carried by two men on a stretcher-like "barrow" to a wooden platform, where they were laid out and cut into smaller pieces about four feet long and six inches thick. These strips were minced into smaller pieces and dumped into two large pots on a furnace built of local granite blocks.

Although the flensing and trying procedures used on Long Island in the seventeenth century were not recorded in detail, the process in the early twentieth century was described by Everett Edwards, a legendary shore whaler, with the help of his daughter, Jeanette Rattray, in *Whale Off: The Story of North American Shore Whaling* (1932). Edwards's account of the trying operations closely parallels methods employed on Spitsbergen Island, suggesting that there were few changes over the centuries. The information in the 1662 report and in *Whale Off*, therefore, provide a general idea about the methods used by the Southampton crews in the 1640s.

According to Edwards, once the whale was ashore, the first task was to cut the head off and remove the baleen from the mouth. The crew, said Edwards, would then peel the blubber away in large "blanket" pieces from the exposed area of the carcass. Specialized long-handled cutting tools, including blubber spades, boat spades, and bone spades, were used. The razor-sharp, shovel-shaped blades were ideal for severing the head, removing the baleen from the jawbone, and cutting the blubber into strips that could be peeled away using a hawser and tackle or a winch and capstan. The body was turned as the peeling continued until the blubber was entirely removed and cut into large chunks called blanket pieces, a process that could take as long as three days. The blanket pieces, similar in size to those described in the 1662 London report, were about six feet long, two feet wide, and six inches thick. These pieces were cut into smaller "horse" pieces about two feet long and three inches wide. These pieces were then carted to the try works. Here the pieces were minced into slabs about a quarter inch thick and tossed into the kettle pots on the furnace.

As the oil boiled out of the blubber, the pieces of skin, called "fritters" or "cracklins," were skimmed off with a long-handled sieve and thrown into the furnace to keep the fire going. There was no need for additional wood once the process began. The oil was ladled from the 250-gallon boiling pots to a cooling vat with a small bailing bucket attached to a long handle. After a period of time, the oil was transferred to wooden casks and taken to the nearest port for shipping to market. The profits from these shipments drew the attention of the colonial officials. Their concern was expressed in the fall of 1668 when colonial authorities, suspecting that the east end towns were finding ways to avoid paying the taxes "due to his royal highness," asked for an accounting of the drift whale carcasses (Christoph and Christoph 1982, 202).

There were some variations in the designs of the trying furnaces, but the function was the same. Here, too, Edwards's account closely parallels the descriptions in the Royal Society report from Spitsbergen. He described the trying furnace he built as follows:

The fire was made in a homemade furnace, built so: Set two rows of stone six inches high, the kettle's width apart; set the two kettles on them, close together. Brick up outside of the kettles to one-third their height, and cement them airtight. Build a brick chimney at one end, tight against the second kettle. Scoop out the earth underneath the stones, to make room to build the fire. (Edwards and Rattray 1932, 94)

Edwards's furnace is different from the replica furnace constructed on the grounds of the Southampton Historical Museum (figs. 12 and 13). This structure represents the furnaces built on the decks of the nineteenth-century whaling ships. The seventeenth-century shore whaling furnaces were very close in design to the nineteenth-century furnaces built on the decks of the whaling ships. The trying process, regardless of differences in furnace design, would have been similar, taking several days or longer.

The East Hampton proprietors followed Southampton's approach in processing the drift whales. Property owners all received shares of the oil and baleen based on the amount of land they owned. Several of them had served on the whaling squads in Southampton. In 1650, as the founding families were still arriving, East Hampton created two squadrons to cut up and try out whale oil (RTEH 1: 8). Any Indians who brought the town information about the location of a drift whale "shall have five shillings," and any town resident who "do bring ye first tidings of it he shall have a piece of whale three foot wide." Three years later the town issued a more detailed procedure for harvesting the whale carcasses.

Not all of the town residents, however, were happy with the communal approach. The two whaling groups had to be supervised by overseers "to see that every man do his work." Those who shirked their duties were fined five shillings

Figure 12 Replica trying furnace with iron trying kettles. Courtesy of the Southampton Historical Museum, Southampton, N.Y.

Figure 13 Whale oil skimmer held by Mataukus Tarrant, Shinnecock Nation.
Courtesy of the Southampton Historical Museum, Southampton, N.Y.

(RTEH 1: 54). The anticipated profits from whale oil and bone also led to
conflicts on occasion. In 1653, Widow Talmadge, a strong-willed woman, was
not satisfied with the share of oil and baleen. The town ordered that "the share
of the whale now in controversy . . ." shall be divided between the two parties
(RTEH 1: 54; Breen 1989, 100–105).

The dispute undoubtedly played a role in the decision of the town to establish a more detailed "whale code" revising the 1650 regulations. The new
regulations stipulated that only those residents who owned thirteen or more
acres could receive shares. In January 1663, the town again revisited the drift
whale issue, adding a third squadron of eleven men to process the drift whales.

Clearly whale products were becoming an increasingly important economic concern on eastern Long Island. Although drift whale harvesting was a communal enterprise, some members of the community were able to avoid the more menial chores. Reverend Thomas James, who had arrived in East Hampton in 1651 at Gardiner's invitation, and Lion Gardiner, who had moved into the village from his island, avoided serving on the squads by providing a quart of liquor to each of the flensers (RTEH 1: 199).

The oil and baleen were exported to European markets, bringing the Long Island communities into a rapidly developing international economy. As historian T. H. Breen noted in his study of East Hampton, the local communal activity was ironically providing the launching platform for a preindustrial capitalist system (Breen 1989, 100–105). Expressions of entrepreneurial capitalism, of course, had always been a force in European colonialism and was often in direct conflict with town governments. The scramble for Native American land on Long Island, for example, began with the arrival of the Lynn settlers in 1640. Private individuals such as Lion Gardiner, Richard Smith, John Scott, John Ogden, and Richard Woodhull took advantage of the anemic town enforcement powers in order to expand their personal land holdings. Their scramble for personal wealth had often found them at odds with the towns, the Indians, and each other. The lucrative profits from the drift whales soon drew them into yet another unseemly scramble, this time for control of beaches outside the town boundaries.

Violence on the Middle Ground

Richard White, in his classic study of the early contacts between the Algonquian peoples and Europeans, describes the "middle ground" as a cultural space wherein both sought to protect their interests and to pursue their own goals (White 1983, 1991).[2] The diplomatic and economic interactions brought the two groups into the same physical space, but for the most part they remained apart in their respective communities until the development of the whaling operations brought them together. The procedures for cutting out the blubber by assigned squads indicates that the colonists did not rely to any significant extent on Indian labor at first. This is not surprising because relations between the Indians and the newly arrived settlers remained tenuous as the communities regarded each other with wary eyes. In April 1641, only four months after the Southampton settlers purchased the town plot, an entry in the records reflects the settlers' fears. They prohibited the selling or lending to the Indians of "either guns, pistols, or any other instruments of war *viz* powder, shot, bullets, matches, swords or any other engine of war whatsoever"(RTSH 1: 22). The following year the town ordered every man to bear arms, keep watch, and to participate in military training exercises (RTSH 1: 27).

In May 1643, concerned about the possibility that minor incidents might lead to violence, the town ordered that damage to persons or property by Indians should be immediately reported to the magistrates before any precipitous action was taken in retaliation (RTSH 1: 28). In some cases, however, it was the Indians' property that was damaged. The English often allowed their hogs to roam freely, resulting in damages to shellfish sources and Indian planting grounds (RTSH 1: 77, 91, 98). English cattle grazed on the open meadows rather than in enclosed pastures. As a result, the cattle competed with the deer for subsistence, thereby reducing an important food source for the Indians. The Indians sometimes "hunted" and killed the cattle grazing on the open meadows. Fears that such minor incidents might escalate into violent confrontations that could threaten the small community were among the concerns that led the town to place itself under the jurisdiction of Connecticut in 1645 (RTSH 1: 31).

On two occasions violent conflicts between the Indians and the settlers had long-range political, economic, and cultural consequences. In 1649, Thomas Halsey's wife was murdered, allegedly by a Shinnecock. Mandush, the Shinnecock sachem, refused to turn over the suspects to the English, resulting in an armed standoff between the settlers and the Shinnecocks. According to Thomas Halsey and John Gosmer, the town magistrates, the Indians were "gathered in a hostile posture" (RCNP 9: 143, 10: 98). As the crisis deepened, the English invoked Gardiner's alliance with Wyandanch by asking the sachem to intercede on their behalf. Wyandanch came to Southampton and, according to testimony by Thomas Halsey and Thomas Sayer, negotiated a settlement with Mandush.

The Shinnecock sachem was well aware that an armed conflict with the English might bring on his people the fate of the Pequots. His only real option was to accept some form of accommodation that would best serve the interests of the Shinnecocks. Wyandanch proposed that the Shinnecock become his tributaries and turn over the accused men to him, thereby avoiding a humiliating capitulation to the English. Such an arrangement was in accord with traditional customs, although in this case the English were the dominant agency. According to Gardiner, Wyandanch took the men to the Connecticut Court in Hartford where they were hung (Gardiner [1660] 1980, 144–45). As tributaries, the Shinnecock had to give Wyandanch the authority to dispose of their tribal lands.

Although there are many questions about the legitimacy of transferring Shinnecock lands to Wyandanch under these circumstances, clearly Mandush was forced to make these concessions under extreme duress. Mandush's family was divided over this settlement, but those who opposed the imposition of Wyandanch's authority over them remained silent at the time, awaiting a chance to challenge the arbitrary loss of authority over their lands. The English went ahead and anointed Wyandanch "the Grand Sachem" of all Long Island and used this fictional title as a convenient vehicle for alienating Indian land on eastern Long Island (Strong 2001, 19–27). Wyandanch pressed local sachems to sell their lands to purchasers that he endorsed. Deeds from Long Island sachems without Wyandanch's endorsement were open to challenge.

Eight years later an incident between the Southampton settlers and the Shinnecock again disrupted the peace. This time there was an organized rebellion, not a single act against one person. A group of Shinnecocks, joined by at least one African American slave, burned buildings in Southampton belonging to two leading members of the English community, Edward Howell and Robert Fordham (Strong 2012, 159–72). It is noteworthy that in both incidences the targets were members of founding families. In the latter, Reverend Robert Fordham, the wealthiest man in Southampton, was targeted. The selection of these prominent freeholders suggests that the attacks may have been a calculated strike against those who personified the imposition of English domination over the Shinnecock.

In a panic the Southampton magistrates distributed gunpowder to forty militiamen and sent to the Connecticut Court in Hartford for help (Strong 2012, 165). The court dispatched Captain John Mason and a small troop of men to Southampton. Mason's troop was small, but his reputation was large; he had been one of the two English officers responsible for the massacre of more than seven hundred Pequots during the Pequot War, many of them burned alive in their fort at Mystic, Connecticut (Cave 1996, 150–51). Four Shinnecocks were arrested without incident and taken to Hartford for trial. Then Mason met with John Ogden, John Gosmer, and Thurston Raynor, the town magistrates, to evaluate the damage. They concluded that the Shinnecock should pay an exorbitant fine of seven hundred pounds. A look at the estate inventories in the Court of Sessions records gives a sense of how exorbitant this was. The market value for a farm with twenty acres of land and three buildings ranged from 40 to 70 pounds, depending on such variables as the quality of the land and the condition of the buildings (RCSS 20, 34, 63). The only collateral the Shinnecock had was their land, and that was now under the authority of Wyandanch. Not surprisingly, two of the magistrates, John Ogden and John Gosmer, along with Lion Gardiner, would soon benefit from their role in settling the conflict.[3]

Contentious Assets

For the most part, during the first two decades after settlement, contacts between the English and the Shinnecock involved land transactions and occasional trade. The Shinnecock exchanged animal pelts, venison, feathers, corn, and baskets for English tools, clothing, and alcohol. Even in times of tension, when Indians were prohibited from entering the English village, exceptions were made for women and "ancient men" who were allowed to come with their goods for trade (RTSH 1: 57). This narrow window was gradually widened for female domestic workers and male laborers who built fences and tended livestock. Indians were given corn and bread for their labor (RTSH 1: 89). These connections established a fragile network of communication that gradually created a platform of relationships amid the contentious postcontact climate. Peter Thomas, in his study of cultural change in New England, called these networks "bridging mechanisms." They would later provide a vehicle for the recruitment of Indian whalers (Thomas 1985, 139–44). Drift whale harvesting, however, continued to rely on local English labor well into the 1660s.

The cultural differences were also evident in the differing perceptions of whales. In 1648, when the English negotiated with Wyandanch, the Montaukett sachem, and sachems from Southampton, Shelter Island, and Southold for the right to establish the town of East Hampton on land to the east of Southampton, the Indians were careful to protect their rights to the fins and tails of the whales. The English, who had little interest in those parts of the whale, agreed that the Indians "are to have the fins and tails of all such whales as shall be cast up. . . ." (RTEH 1: 2–4). Within a relatively short time, however, the Indians came to recognize the commercial value of the rest of the whale bodies.

The English had little interest in harvesting drift whales that came ashore on isolated beaches some distance from town until the late 1650s, when the communities expanded and developed infrastructure making it possible to transport the barrels of oil to places of embarkation for foreign markets. The Atlantic beach areas outside the town boundaries now became of primary interest to the towns and to private entrepreneurs. In the spring and summer of 1658, Thomas Topping and Lion Gardiner secured leases for the use of meadowlands west of the Southampton Town boundary at Niamuck (canoe place), a narrow strip of land between Peconic Bay and Shinnecock Bay. Although their primary interest at the time was in sources of feed for livestock not access to drift whales, the leases would later be expanded southward to the Atlantic beaches where the whales washed ashore. Both leases ignored the Unkechaug sachems, Tobacus and Winecroscum, under the presumption that Wyandanch as "Grand Sachem" had absolute authority over the dispossession of Unkechaug lands. There would be consequences.

Topping's lease dated May 29, 1658, was to run for ten years. John Cooper and Lion Gardiner witnessed the transaction (DSBD 2: 152). The tract was located near what is now the village of Quogue, on the western bank of Quantuck Creek. The meadows and wetlands here were identified in the lease as being "commonly called or known by the name of Potunk or Ketchaponack or both. . . ." Lion Gardiner, who undoubtedly played a role in bringing Topping together with the Montaukett sachem, signed as a witness.

A month after Gardiner had assisted Topping in obtaining his lease, he met with Wyandanch and negotiated a lease for a tract of grazing meadows beginning west of the Southampton Town boundary at Niamuck and running westward to "where it is separated by the water of the sea coming in and out of the ocean sea" (RTSH 1: 170–71). The western boundary was the Cupsage inlet, "the old gutt," west of the mouth of Seatuck Creek, on the eastern border of Topping's lease. Gardiner gave Wyandanch "a considerable sum of money and goods" and a yearly rent of twenty-five shillings paid on demand every October "forever."

Gardiner knew that whales frequently drifted ashore on the beaches south of the meadows, but Wyandanch told him that the whales belonged to the Indians by an ancient right "granted by our fathers." The sachem also wanted continued access to the flag grass and bull rushes for mats and wigwam construction. The meadows and beaches purchased by Topping and Gardiner in the summer of 1658 included the western section of the Shinnecock hunting grounds and stretched west to the eastern section of the Unkechaug territory. Neither community was in a position to challenge Wyandanch and the English at that time, but that was soon to change.

In the fall of 1658, the scramble for access to drift whale carcasses on beaches outside of town boundaries began. On November 13, 1658, Gardiner approached Wyandanch with a request for access to drift whales at Neapeague Beach, an area lying east of East Hampton in the heart of Montaukett hunting grounds. Wyandanch, perhaps in an effort to strengthen his alliance with Gardiner and with East Hampton, granted Lion Gardiner and Thomas James, the East Hampton minister, rights to beached whales on very generous terms (RTEH 1: 150; Breen 1989, 109–10). There was no mention of "ancient rights" to the drift whales. The reverend was second only to Gardiner in terms of power and influence on eastern Long Island.

Wyandanch divided the whale carcasses equally between the two influential East Hampton men. There would be no charge, he said, for the first whale carcass, but for all those thereafter they would pay him or his children and successors "what they shall judge meet and according as they find profit by them." These liberal terms, in sharp contrast to the agreement a few months earlier, placed Wyandanch in a position to call on English assistance should rival sachems challenge his authority. It was a wise move, because his fears were well founded. Ninigret, the Niantic sachem, raided Montaukett villages on several occasions, and Uncas, the Mohegan sachem, frequently expressed deep personal animosity toward Wyandanch (Strong 1997, 206–10; RTSH 5: 18–19).

A month after Gardiner secured the rights to drift whales east of the East Hampton bounds, he turned over the tract on the south shore of Brookhaven to John Cooper Jr. of Southampton. It appears that Gardiner was acting as a surrogate for Cooper (RTSH 1: 170). Cooper, whose family was one of the more prosperous in Southampton, agreed to take over the yearly payments to the sachem because he and his father wanted the grazing land for the horses and cattle they raised for Caribbean trade. The planters on the islands were in constant need of livestock to replenish their stock of animals who succumbed to the heat and tropical diseases.

Cooper also knew that control of the southern meadows would put him in a good position to benefit from any change in Wyandanch's restrictions on access to drift whales. He had seen how the sachem had changed his policy on whale rights when he granted Gardiner and James access to the drift whales at Neapeague the month before. Cooper was also aware that Montaukett power and influence had been steadily deteriorating. Disease had taken a heavy toll, and the threat from Ninigret's Niantics was increasing (Strong 2001, 27–28). Cooper soon found, however, that the scramble for the beaches would bring him into conflict with his Southampton neighbors as well as with members of his own family.

In April 1659, John Richbell, an Oyster Bay merchant, joined the scramble for rights to drift whales. He met with Tackapousha, the Massapequa sachem whose lands ran along the shore from what is now Jones Beach to the western boundary of what would become the town of Huntington (DSBD 2: 67–68; Strong 1997, 230). Tackapousha had formed an alliance with the Dutch gaining their support for his influence over the Indian communities on western Long Island and for his control of the Atlantic beaches west of Huntington (Strong 1997, 236–38). For the sachem this was strictly a business deal; there was no diplomatic advantage to granting a concession to Richbell, who played no major role in the Oyster Bay town government. Rather than allowing Richbell to set the fee for the whales, Tackapousha charged him six pounds' worth of wampum for each whole carcass and a proportionate sum for incomplete remains. Richbell was also obliged to pay Indians who brought him word about the presence of a drift whale a shirt or one shilling in wampum.

A month after Richbell secured whale rights from Tackapousha, John Ogden purchased a large tract of land west of the Southampton bounds from Wyandanch with Gardiner's assistance. The parcel stretched from the Peconic River in the north and to Cooper's meadowlands in the south. The lease included specific language exempting Cooper's lease and meadowlands previously leased to Thomas Halsey and John Gosmer. There was also a clause reserving hunting, fishing, and fowling rights and access to berries and other plants for the Shinnecock villagers in the area. The cash, however, went to Wyandanch and his descendants, who were to receive a yearly payment of twenty-five shillings. There was no mention of access to drift whales. Ogden apparently shared Cooper's hope that Wyandanch's position on that issue might change in the future. Lion Gardiner, of course, along with his son, David, signed as witnesses (RTSH 1: 162).

The agreement did not mention the meadowland at Potunk that Topping had leased from Wyandanch the year before. The omission is puzzling because Gardiner and John Cooper had both signed as witnesses. They were well aware that Topping's lease was to run for ten years. There is no record of an objection by Topping, but events three years later revealed that he had merely been biding his time.

In June 1659, the shift in Wyandanch's policy finally did occur, undoubtedly influenced by Tackapousha's decision to profit from his beaches. Wyandanch and his son, Wyancombone, sold Gardiner the right to harvest the drift whales that came ashore on a stretch of beach beginning at the western end of Southampton Town and running westward to "a place called Kitchaminchok," located in Moriches Bay, south of the present-day village of East Moriches (DSBD 2: 85–86). Wyandanch, who died sometime that year, may have had concerns about his health. He included Wyancombone in all of his negotiations in 1659, perhaps because he hoped that his son would be in a better position to protect the family legacy, a futile hope as it turned out.

The tract ran parallel along the southern boundary of the lease that Gardiner had turned over to Cooper the previous year. Wyandanch set a twenty-one-year term for the agreement to begin in 1659. He charged Gardiner five pounds sterling "or any good pay" for a whole whale, but "if it be a half whale, a third part or otherwise they shall pay according to proportion." The sachem, who had embraced the capitalistic market system with considerable acumen, demanded payment within two months after the blubber had been stripped and carted "home to their houses." The two months clause also indicated that Wyandanch had learned how the "whale design" worked. He understood that it took about that amount of time before the cash would be available. The contract was quite detailed, stipulating that the agreement would continue in force beyond the twenty-one-year term if less than five whales came ashore during "the term above said." It is noteworthy, however, that Wyandanch had not abandoned the traditional beliefs about the importance of the tails and fins of the whales. "We reserve," he said, "the tails and fins for ourselves."

Gardiner actually had no interest in harvesting drift whales so far from his home in East Hampton. He turned over his lease to John Cooper as he had done the year before, giving Cooper control of the meadows for his livestock and access to drift whales on the Atlantic beaches. Cooper now had a lucrative, diversified source of income. The contract, however, would be challenged seven years later by John Ogden in a dispute that ended up in a lengthy, contentious court battle argued by two of the most prominent lawyers in the newly established colony of New York.

A month after Cooper obtained control of the beaches, Anthony Waters, one of John Cooper's neighbors in the North Sea settlement in Southampton, approached Gardiner, asking for his help in negotiating with Wyandanch for access to the beaches west from Cooper's western boundary at Kitchaminchok and running westward to a place called "Enaughquamuck" ("the far end of the fishing place") (DSBD 2: 85–86; RTSH 2: 34–36; Tooker 1911: 61–62). The location is uncertain, but it was probably somewhere south of the Mastic Peninsula near Pattersquash Island in Moriches Bay. Gardiner agreed to help Waters as he had Cooper.

Wyandanch and Gardiner included Tobacus and Winecroscum, the Unkechaug sachems, in the negotiations because the area was within the bounds of their hunting territory. The sachems sold Gardiner "the bodies and bones of all the whales that shall come upon the land, or come ashore," again reserving all the tails and fins for themselves. They charged Gardiner five pounds sterling "or any good pay" for every whole carcass and a proportionate amount for partial carcasses. The Unkechaugs may have given Gardiner a better price than Richbell got from Tackapousha for reasons of diplomacy. The payments, once again, were due "within two months after they have cut and carried the whale home to their houses. . . ." It is noteworthy that the blubber was to be tried out near their residences as had been the practice when the townsmen harvested the drift whales on the town beaches.

Tobacus and Winecroscum were called to testify before three English witnesses: Zerobabel Philips, Joseph Raynor, and Thomas Halsey, all prominent Southampton freeholders. They swore that they had acted "voluntarily without compulsion." In another addendum, Gardiner turned over the lease to Anthony Waters, as he had done the year before to John Cooper. Waters agreed to pay Wyandanch the fee agreed on in the lease (RTSH 2: 36). This agreement left the Atlantic beaches from the Southampton Town border west to an area in Moriches Bay near Pattersquash Island south of the Mastic Peninsula under the control of John Cooper and Anthony Waters.

This was to be the last transaction made by the Montaukett sachem. According to Lion Gardiner, the sachem was poisoned in the fall of 1659, but he offered no further details, and his account is not corroborated in the colonial records (Gardiner [1660] 1980, 146). There were many obvious suspects among the sachems on Long Island, including Uncas, the Mohegan sachem, and Ninigret, Wyandanch's old nemesis. In the previous decade, beginning with the sale of the East Hampton tract in 1648, Wyandanch had been directly involved with twenty negotiations involving deeds, leases, and confirmations, most of them during the last three years of his life. Most of these transactions had involved land in the hunting territories of other sachems (Strong 1996, 68–69, n. 12). Any one of these men could have been responsible, but it is also possible that Wyandanch's death may have been the result of natural causes. According to Lion Gardiner, smallpox took the lives of two-thirds of the Indian population on Long Island from 1659 to 1662.

Wyandanch's death marked the decline of what Francis Jennings called "the deed game," wherein the English gained control over the Indian lands (Jennings 1975, 128–45). The relations with sachems now shifted to negotiations over unresolved specifics in the land transactions. The language in the deeds was often unclear about boundaries as well as such specifics as the access and control of beaches where whales most frequently washed ashore. The contentions over drift whales now embroiled the sachems and their supporters.

3

Sachems, Entrepreneurs, and Conflicting Sovereignties

To many, whale oil must have seemed like the root of all evil. The baleen and oil generated conflicts at every level of colonial society and within Native American kinship systems. While shore whaling was still in its infancy, the conflicts over access to beached whales continued to disrupt the affairs of the English towns and the Native communities. The origins of the shore whaling enterprises, the subject of the following chapter, are best understood within the larger context of these conflicts.

The death of Wyandanch left only three surviving members of his immediate family: his widow, Wuch-i-kit-taw-but; his son, Wyancombone; and his daughter, Quashawam. The English anointed Wyancombone the heir apparent to the title of Grand Sachem. In February 1660, the young sachem endorsed a deed to land in Huntington wherein he claimed that he had been "ordained" Grand Sachem by both the English and the Indians (RTH 1: 20). Gardiner and Ogden were in agreement about the succession, but they were soon embroiled in a contentious dispute over who would control the young "Grand Sachem." Both men claimed they had been given that authority by Wyandanch before his death.

The stakes were high. Whoever had influence over the young sachem had an advantage in the scramble for the remaining Indian lands on eastern Long Island as long as the fictive title of "Grand Sachem" could be maintained. The following August, Gardiner and three prominent East Hampton residents, Thomas Baker, John Mulford, and the Reverend Thomas James, attempted to purchase the remaining Montaukett lands. John Ogden moved quickly to block their purchase, claiming that he was Wyancombone's guardian and that Gardiner would be the "ruin" of the young man and his people (Strong 2012, 177–81).

The death of Wyandanch also led to tensions between rival sachems. Ninigret saw an opportunity to renew an old rivalry between his Niantics and the Montauketts. He unleashed several raids against Montaukett villages during the spring and summer of 1660, forcing the frightened Montauketts to seek refuge inside the bounds of East Hampton. In January 1662, Gardiner, Thomas James, and John Mulford took advantage of the Montauketts' plight by pressing Wyancombone and his mother, Wuch-i-kit-taw-but, to give them a tract of land as a gift of "thanks" for protecting them from Ninigret. The tract, called Hither Woods, lay between East Hampton on the west and the Montaukett homeland on the east (Smith 1926a, 25–29). The text, written as if Wyancombone himself were speaking, affirmed that Gardiner and his son David were his "two guardians," appointed by his father.

The gift of land, said Wyancombone, was given freely and "without any money" or other payment to "our beloved friends and neighbors of East Hampton." When it came to the rights to drift whales, Wyancombone made a significant change in an earlier agreement his father had made with Gardiner and James. In 1658, Wyandanch had granted Gardiner and James access to all of the drift whales, but this time half of the drift whales went to the town residents and the other half were to be divided between Gardiner and James. It appears that the town officials would not go along with the seizure of Montaukett land unless the residents got a share of all that went with it, including the whales. In fairness, the East Hampton residents probably felt that it was the whole town that gave refuge to the Montauketts and had risked an attack by Ninigret.

Issues related to drift whales would soon set neighbor against neighbor, divide families, and encourage the rise of factions within the Shinnecock community. On April 10, 1662, Thomas Topping made the first move, followed by John Ogden five days later. Topping, who had purchased a small parcel of meadowland adjacent to Cooper's beach tract in 1658, now saw an opportunity to challenge the validity of Gardiner's purchase from the sachem that same year. Topping, whose purchase ironically had been endorsed by Gardiner and Cooper at the time, sought to claim the rights to all the beaches in Gardiner's 1658 purchase as well as the whole tract purchased by John Ogden from Wyandanch in 1659.

Topping's purchase was a transparent effort to challenge the legitimacy of Wyancombone's inherited authority. Topping, aware that Algonquian sunksquaws held the same authority as the male sachems, sought out a Shinnecock sunksquaw named Weany (Williams [1643] 1973, 201). Her supporters included Cobish (Goabes), the husband of Mandush's widow. Weany and Cobish apparently felt that Wyandanch's death freed the Shinnecock from any obligation to honor the land transactions made by the Montaukett sachem. They sold Topping all the land from Canoe Place (Niamuck) to Seatuck Creek (RTSH 1: 167–68).

Topping made sure that the access to drift whales was explicit in his agreement. He was to receive one half of all the profits from the whales as well as "the herbage and feed that shall be or grow thereon." In exchange Topping agreed to pay fourscore fathoms of strung wampum (480 feet), or other equivalent pay, at or before the first day of the following December. The purchase was witnessed by Thomas's two young sons, John and Elnathan, and his son-in-law, James Herrick. It appears that he could find no one outside of his family who would endorse his action, and even that unity would not survive.

On April 15, 1662, John Ogden, apparently unaware that his 1658 purchase was now claimed by Topping, traveled to East Hampton and met with Wyancombone; his mother, Wuch-i-kit-taw-but; and the two Unkechaug sachems, Tobacus and Winecroscum, in the presence of Lion Gardiner and East Hampton freeholder Thomas Talmadge (DSBD 2: 156–57; Strong 2011, 56). Ogden was interested now in the beach lands lying to the west of Southampton. He and Gardiner had apparently resolved their differences because Lion Gardiner signed as a witness to the transaction. The negotiation was based on the presumption that the authority of the Grand Sachem remained in effect and gave the stamp of validation to such transactions. The primary role of the Unkechaug sachems, however, does suggest that the "house of Wyandanch" was in decline. The agreements made while he lived, for example, had relegated local sachems to a secondary position.

Ogden purchased the rights to "all the whales that shall be cast up upon the beach," but Tobacus and Winecroscum reserved "to ourselves the fins and tails." Ogden agreed to pay five pounds in wampum at six pence per bead, provided it be a whole whale. The payment was due two months after the whale "is cut out and carried home." The bounds of the beach ran from the western boundary of the lease Gardiner turned over to Anthony Waters in 1659, "namely at a place called by the Indians Compawamuck." Curiously the western boundary of the 1659 tract was identified as "a place called 'Enaughquamuck.'" A likely explanation is simply that they are orthographic variations of the same place. The western boundary of Ogden's lease is identified as "a place commonly called by the Indians Poetstack." The location is difficult to determine with any precision, but it may have been an area south of Bluepoint near the outlets of Namkee Creek and Whalebone Creek. Namkee Creek marks the western boundary of the Unkechaug hunting grounds. A map in the Brookhaven town historian's office, made in 1670 by Robert Ryder, school teacher in Setauket, shows an inlet across from Bluepoint with a whaling station on the eastern bank (map 3).

Wyancombone died shortly after his endorsement of Ogden's purchase. His death was probably caused by one of the epidemics that sporadically swept through many Indian villages in the years between 1659 and 1664 (Strong 1997, 234–35). The following October, Anthony Waters, perhaps concerned about the uncertainty of land claims to the Atlantic beaches, turned over his interest in the beach area to Thomas Cooper, John's younger brother (RTSH 2: 36). The conflicting land claims had created quite a muddle and it affected

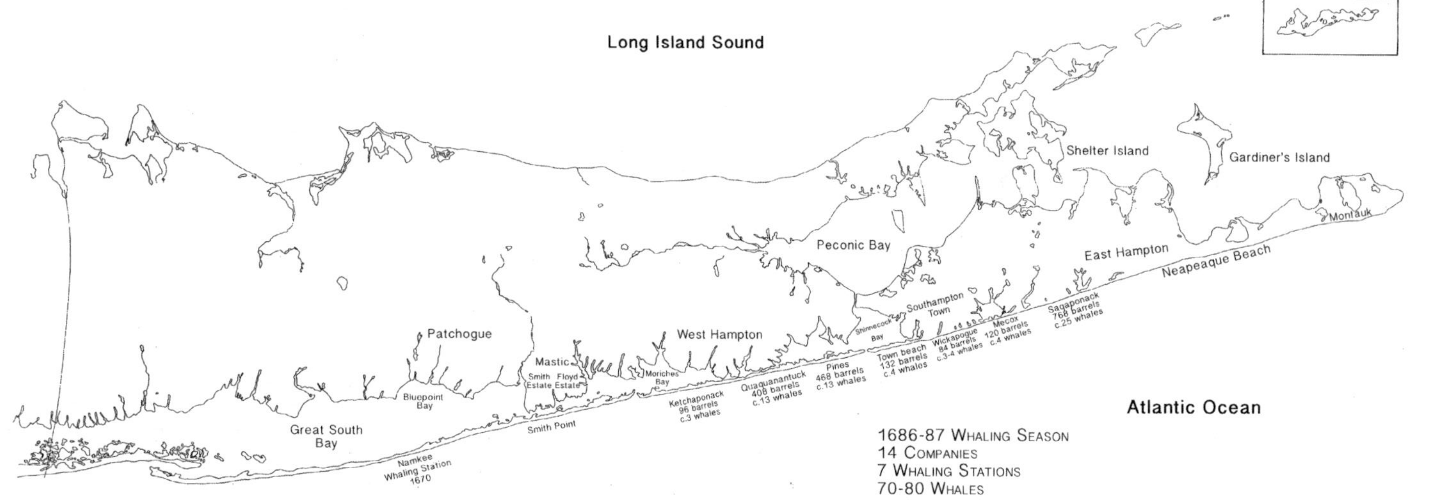

Map 3 Whaling stations on eastern Long Island, based on the report of the 1686–1687 season in Pelletreau (1903, 2: 496). Digital map by Jeremy Dennis, Shinnecock Nation, Long Island, N.Y.

nearly all of the prominent stakeholders on eastern Long Island. The Setauket freeholders, for example, looked on Ogden's purchase with alarm. Not only was it on beach land they wanted to bring under their control, but it also brought them into a potential conflict with the Unkechaug sachems with whom they had previously established a good working relationship (Strong 2013, 36–63). Topping's move, of course, angered Ogden, Cooper, and other Southampton entrepreneurs who had purchased or leased land through Wyandanch.

On January 14, 1663, Cooper, in an attempt to reinforce his claim to his beaches now claimed by Topping, followed Ogden's footsteps to East Hampton to meet with Wuch-i-kit-taw-but and Lion Gardiner (RTEH 1: 199–200). Wuch-i-kit-taw-but is identified here as a sunksquaw, indicating that she had taken over leadership of the Montauketts following the death of her son. She testified that the year before she had sent two of her advisors, Checanow and Tobias, to mark out the boundaries of the beach land that Wyandanch had granted to Cooper and that she had marked them again this winter. She added that she expected to receive payment for the drift whales as stipulated in the previous agreement. Gardiner signed below the sunksquaw.

Insight into the turmoil related to the issue of drift whales was revealed dramatically at the town court session that opened in Southampton a day after John Cooper's visit to East Hampton. Cooper brought suit against three of his fellow town residents: Joseph Raynor, Richard Howell, and Samuel Dayton, and his own younger brother, Thomas, accusing them of taking a whale off his beach at Ogden's Neck, south of present-day Quogue (RTSH 2: 27–28). All of these men would later invest in whaling companies. The jury found for John Cooper and charged the defendants with court costs. Such court actions, usually involving charges of trespass, were a means used in the seventeenth century to establish property ownership. The absence of reliable surveys and the conflicting purchases from Indians brought landowners into court seeking a decision by a public agency that would determine the boundaries of their property.

Court actions could also bring testimony from relevant parties and enter it into the official record. This is what Thomas Topping did at the same court session where Cooper filed his suit. Topping brought in a Shinnecock woman, identified as "Pametsechs' squaw," probably Weany, to testify that the Shinnecocks had granted him the rights to drift whales in an effort to deflect any action against his purchase by Cooper. He wanted to establish that the Shinnecock were the true proprietors of the land in his purchase. The Shinnecocks testified that their territory extended west to a place they called "Masspootupaug," an area near Apocock Creek about two miles east of Seatuck Creek. Their testimony affirmed that they were the owners of the tract that Topping had purchased (RTSH 2: 27; Tooker 1911, 113–14). Cooper must have listened to the woman's testimony with some dismay, knowing full well that it would soon be used against him.

Sure enough, the following June, Topping sued Cooper, charging him with illegally seizing a drift whale on his newly acquired beach property and demanded twenty pounds in damages (RTSH 2: 30). The exact location is not recorded, but it was undoubtedly on an area of beach that Gardiner had purchased from Wyandanch and transferred to Cooper in 1658. The case was still pending the following September in what must have been a crowded court docket. In August of 1663 Topping received more support, this time from Robert Seelye, whose land claim was in conflict with a deed endorsed by Wyandanch. A veteran of the Pequot War, Seelye was a prominent resident of the north shore town of Huntington, west of Setauket, and had an interest in a tract of land that had been purchased from a local sachem without Wyandanch's endorsement. His deed was contested by John Scott, an aggressive entrepreneur whose purchase of the same tract had been signed by the Montaukett sachem. Seelye, therefore, shared Topping's interest in undermining the legitimacy of the Grand Sachem's authority.

Seelye told Topping that five sachems and many Indians met before him at his home in Huntington and testified that "the Montaukett sachem hath no prerogative over their land . . . but the right of land is in those sachems that do inhabit in their respective places" (RTSH 5: 18–19). According to Seelye, the Mohegan sachem Uncas told him that even when Indians overcame an enemy, "it was not their fashion to take away their lands." Uncas, of course, had been an implacable enemy of Wyandanch and his family, but the testimony of the Long Island sachems carried considerable weight. Seelye asked Topping for a response and offered to come to Southampton when necessary to give him his support. Topping's response, if there was such, has not survived. There the matter rested for the next six months. During that time both Lion Gardiner and Wuch-i-kit-taw-but died. Quashawam, daughter of Wuch-i-kit-taw-but and sister of Wyancombone, was now the only surviving member of the Grand Sachem's family.

John Ogden, who was struggling to develop a shore whaling operation without much success (see next chapter), and, perhaps discouraged by the conflict and uncertainty about land claims and the unsettling rumors that an English fleet was on its way to seize the colony of New Netherland from the Dutch, left Long Island and moved to New Jersey, where he helped to found Elizabethtown. He sold his tract of land to John Scott, who in turn sold it to the town of Southampton on February 2, 1664 (RTSH 1: 175–76). Ogden, however, did not give up his claims to the Atlantic beaches as evidenced later by yet another court battle. Both Southampton and East Hampton now had a direct interest in maintaining the succession of Wyandanch's authority. They moved quickly to take action that they hoped would bolster the legitimacy of Montaukett hegemony over Shinnecock lands. Their urgency was fueled in part by speculation about King Charles II's plans for Long Island. There was talk of dramatic changes in the existing relationships between Connecticut and the eastern Long Island towns.

On February 11, 1664, John Howell, Joseph Raynor, and James Herrick of Southampton, accompanied by Thomas Baker of East Hampton, met with Quashawam, whom they anointed sunksquaw over the Shinnecocks and the Montauketts (RTSH 2: 36–37). The presence of Thomas Topping's son-in-law in the group suggests that he had broken with his wife's family and now supported the legitimacy of the Wyandanch family authority. Topping was now faced with anger from his neighbors and tension within his own family. The squabble among the English spilled over into the Shinnecock community. Cobish, for example, was apparently having second thoughts about his involvement with Weany's sale of land to Topping. He would later shift his support from Weany to the nuclear members of Mandush's family. These interactions reflect what historian Susanah Shaw Romney described as "the complicated interface between personal ties and empire . . ." that found expression in "territorial and political ambitions in the seventeenth century" (Romney 2014, 270).

In the midst of all this turmoil, decisions were being made at court in London by officials who had little knowledge or much interest in the concerns of contending parties on eastern Long Island. Plans had begun to take shape in November of 1663 that would radically change the political landscape on Long Island, much to the dismay of the freeholders in Southampton and East Hampton (Ritchie 1977, 14; NYCD 2: 400–401, 507–8). On March 12, 1644, King Charles granted his brother, James, the Duke of York, a patent for a huge tract of land that included all of Dutch New Netherland and the Connecticut towns of Southampton, Brookhaven, and East Hampton on Long Island. The Long Islanders, uncertain about the Duke's plans for their towns, supported any move that might keep them under Connecticut's jurisdiction.

The Connecticut Court responded to this threat by authorizing a committee to expand the boundaries of their Setauket township. The committee met in Setauket and negotiated purchases of land from Tobacus and from the Setaukett leaders, Mahue, Massetewse, and the Setaukett sunksquaw (RTBH Hutchinson, 10–12). The acquisitions extended the Setauket town boundary on the north and south shore. The acquisitions on the south shore in particular drew the attention and concern of two Southampton men, John Cooper and Richard Howell, who feared that they might lose control of the areas where their whaling activities were located. They were undoubtedly not pleased to have a rival township intrude itself into their relations with the Indian sachems, but they feared the uncertain future under the Duke of York. It is not surprising, therefore, to find that the two men gave their support to the Connecticut purchase, signing as witnesses, a decision they later regretted.

A New Sovereignty: The Duke's Colony, 1664

In August, less than two months after the purchases by Connecticut, a fleet under the command of Richard Nicolls captured New Netherland. The Duke of York established the colony of New York and appointed Nicolls the first governor. In February 1665, Nicolls called a meeting of representatives from the Long Island towns to meet with him at Hempstead, where he pressed them to ratify a framework for governance of the new colony. The code, called the "Duke's Law," was written in large part by Matthias Nicolls, a lawyer (unrelated to the governor) who came with the invading fleet for this purpose. The governor also brought two other distinguished barristers, John Rider and John Sharpe, to assist in setting up a unified system of jurisprudence (Hamlin 1939, 73–74, 150). The two men were frequently called on to argue cases involving disputes over access to and possession of drift whales. Matthias and the two barristers were instrumental in establishing a Court of Assizes (from the Latin word *assidere*, to sit beside). The court was empowered to try major civil and criminal cases and to hear appeals from the local town courts (Christoph and Christoph 1983, xi).

The response from the eastern towns to this legal framework was cool to say the least, but the Duke's Laws were ratified after a month of acrimonious debate. Southampton sent Thomas Topping and John Howell and East Hampton sent Thomas Baker and John Stratton (a.k.a. Stretton). All of them, except Baker, later became investors in shore whaling. The towns of Setauket, Southampton, and East Hampton reluctantly accepted the somewhat heavier administrative hand of the new colony. Nearly a half century later, a New York colonial governor complained that the east end towns, "from whence the greatest quantity of whale oil comes, act as though they do not belong to this colony. They are full of New England principles," he lamented (NYCD 4: 1058). In particular, of course, the independent-minded townsmen chafed at the imposition of colonial taxes. Richard Nicolls, the victorious commander who was appointed governor of the new colony, demanded that every sixteenth gallon of whale oil from the drift whales be paid to the colony (NYCD 5: 474). The governor was careful to exempt whaling companies that killed whales at sea from the tax, hoping to encourage the growth of such operations. The tax on drift whales proved nearly impossible to collect because there was no practical way to keep track of the occurrences. Local town justices, of course, could not always be depended on to report them.

In October 1665, once the legal system was in place, the governor moved to resolve the disputes over land claims (DSBD 2: 123–27). He first called Quashawam and several sachems, who are unfortunately not named, to a meeting that included Thomas Baker and the Reverend Thomas James, representing East Hampton, and Thomas Topping and John Howell, representing Southampton. Nicolls first addressed the lingering disputes over the grazing rights for English livestock on the Montaukett lands. He made no mention of Quashawam's authority over the Shinnecock and made it explicit that "there shall be no superior sachem upon Long Island, but that every sachem shall keep his particular propriety over his people as formerly." The governor had declared there was no longer a Grand Sachem, but he did not address the legitimacy of the deeds authorized under that title prior to 1664. The titles to the lands contested by Topping and the town therefore remained unsettled. Nicolls was astute enough to realize that he needed to bring the dispute to closure and, in the process, assert his authority over both the towns and the private entrepreneurs.

He was soon to have more such opportunities to enforce colonial rule than he may have wanted. The establishment of a central authority encouraged many to bring their complaints over the heads of the local town governments. Among them were Indians who complained about "diverse trespasses" on their lands by Englishmen. The following June, Nicolls issued an executive order warning all persons in the colony that they were to honor the agreements made by the sachems and town representatives the previous fall (NYCD 14: 583). Anyone who willfully broke any part of the covenant would answer to the governor.

Indian affairs remained a challenge for Nicolls, who had no personal experience with Indians to draw on. He was forced to rely on the local settlers who themselves had arrived on Long Island only two decades before him. The governor recognized that their advice might well be biased against Indians, but he had no choice. Nicolls turned to influential men from the local towns to serve as his advisors on Indian affairs and hoped for the best. In July 1666, he appointed Thomas Topping and William Wells of Southold to form a Commission on Indian Affairs that included the men he had met with the previous October: Howell, Baker, and James, and added John Mulford of East Hampton (DSBD 2: 49–50).

The commission, said the governor, was to bring order and good management of all affairs between Indians and the English and to investigate the complaints brought by Indians and Englishmen about "diverse trespasses and abuses done" in instances where there is no remedy except the Court of Assizes. The committee was to assess damages and award reparations in a timely manner. They were empowered to call persons before them and to administer fines when necessary. Unfortunately, although there are occasional references to the commission, no detailed record of their activities has survived.

Minor incidents involving Indians and English were usually settled at the local level. In one such case, John Cooper accused Jeffrey Indian of stealing goods from him. The court, on December 5, 1666, ordered Jeffrey to return Cooper's goods and pay a fine of twenty-five shillings. It is possible that Jeffrey had taken the goods as an advance payment for the whaling season and had not shown up. He did sign up to hunt for Cooper several years later (RTSH 5: 20; SBD 36–38). Another incident involved an Indian named Harry, who also later went whaling. Thomas Halsey Jr. had loaned a gun to Harry in violation of the law prohibiting the distribution of guns to Indians. The Southampton Town constable seized the weapon and fined Halsey, who pledged to "stand between harm and damage and his man" (RTSH 5: 20–21).

Major disputes involving land claims between town governments and private entrepreneurs, of course, required the governor's personal intervention. The conflict over the lands west of Southampton was one such dispute. It involved the controversy stemming from Topping's purchase of the lands west of Southampton that Ogden and Cooper had bought from Wyandanch. The governor asked the parties to present their papers and arguments before him prior to the October 1667 session of the Court of Assizes. The governor appointed two Southampton men, John Howell and Henry Pierson, to review the papers and arguments from all parties and to recommend a resolution to the rather tangled affair. All of the parties agreed to abide by the governor's determination.

The Mandush family and the Southampton men, led by Thomas Halsey Sr. and Thomas Sayre, prepared their arguments supporting the town's case against Topping. Mandush's daughter, who is not named, argued that Weany had no right to sell Topping the parcel because it was owned by all of the Shinnecocks. She further added that the Shinnecocks had sold the land to "our ancient and loving friends, the townsmen of Southampton" (RTSH 1: 169). There was no mention of Quashawam nor of the Montauketts. Halsey and Sayre based their argument in support of the Wyandanch legacy on their own recollections from nearly two decades earlier, when Mandush agreed to transfer the authority over his lands to the Montaukett sachem (RTSH 1: 158).

In anticipation of the governor's examination, the Mandush family, led by Mandush's son, daughter, and widow, now married to Cobish, issued a statement on September 17, 1666, denying Weany's right to sell Shinnecock land to Thomas Topping. They asserted their proprietary rights to the lands in question. Mandush's widow sharply disagreed with her husband, Cobish, who had supported Weany. The family testified that the "interest and propriety unto the said land belongeth totally or principally to us . . ." (RTSH 1: 169). The tract had been sold by them to "our loving friends, the townsmen of Southampton," and if the governor supported their claim to proprietary rights, the Southampton townsmen "shall pay unto us, as the said honor [the governor] shall determine."

The governor's determination, issued the following month, was a compromise in which everyone got something, but the big winner was the governor himself, who brought recalcitrant town officials and a wealthy private entrepreneur to heel and avoided provoking either of the Shinnecock factions. Topping was required to turn over his deed to the town but received a payment of five pounds sterling and an allotment in the undivided town lands. He was ordered to pay the Mandush family the same amount of wampum, fourscore fathoms, that he had paid to Weany, who apparently kept her wampum. Nicolls affirmed Cooper's right to the beach area and the drift whales. Nicolls, however, had little time to congratulate himself before Cooper reignited the controversy a year later.

The governor's action at the time, however, convinced many that there were some clear advantages to having a central colonial authority. Setauket, seeing an opportunity to finally gain control over the Atlantic beaches, asked Daniel Lane, the local mill owner and one of the few freeholders who could read and write, to draft a letter to Governor Nicolls asking for a patent that included the lands on the southern shore (Barstow 2004, 204–5). Lane, who had represented Setauket in 1665 at the Hempstead conference, knew the governor and was familiar with the workings of the colonial government. Nicolls responded a month later by issuing a patent on March 7, 1667, that created an entity called the Town of Brookhaven. It was the largest township on Long Island, including an area west of Southampton stretching from "north to the sound and south to the sea or main ocean" (RTBH Hutchinson, 18–19).

Three months later the new town assembly, concerned about Cooper, Waters, and the other Southampton men who had often harvested drift whales on the beaches within their newly acquired patent, instructed Lane to "speak to his honor, the governor, concerning the whales at the south, that come within our bounds to be at our disposal" (RTBH Hutchinson, 25). Under the protocol established when Southampton and East Hampton were founded, the towns owned the whale carcasses that drifted ashore on beaches within their patents. Brookhaven was calling for the governor to issue a finding that the same protocol applied to them. Cooper was alarmed and moved quickly to protect his leases. A few weeks later, before the governor could respond, Cooper and the Southampton "adventurers," as private entrepreneurs were often called, made a preemptive strike.

Cooper, Raynor, and Ogden called on Winecroscum and Tobacus to reaffirm their rights to drift whales on the beaches that were now within the Brookhaven patent. Tobacus declined, probably because he wanted to establish a good relationship with the new town authorities. Winecroscum, however, was more amenable. On July 8, 1667, Cooper pressed the Unkechaug sachem to make a declaration before John Mulford, the justice of the peace for East Riding (what is now Suffolk County). The sachem agreed and testified that some years before he had sold John Cooper of Southampton the rights to "all the whales that shall be cast up from time to time forever," on an area of beach running from the western boundary of Southampton Town to Kitchaminchok (DSBD 2: 246).

Winecroscum told Mulford that "though some English hath desired to buy whales of him," it was only John Cooper Jr. who had purchased the rights to whales. The sachem said that Cooper had paid him for a whale that had been "cast up" at *Cupsewag* (Cupsage), an inlet across from the mouth of the Carman River in Moriches Bay. He further noted that John Ogden, Joseph Raynor, and John Cooper's brother, Thomas, all Southampton freeholders, were present when the whale was cut up. The absence of a statement from Tobacus, however, set the stage for what became a lengthy conflict between Brookhaven and Southampton.

Eleven and One-Half Barrels of Oil: *Cooper v. Ogden*, October 1667

Cooper now moved to further strengthen his claims to the beaches in Brookhaven by bringing suit against John Ogden at the annual Court of Assizes in October 1667. It was a tactic he had employed in the Southampton Town court three years earlier when he sued his own brother. Fearing that Winecroscum's endorsement might not be enough to protect his claim to the beaches within the Brookhaven patent, he accused John Ogden of a theft that had occurred five years earlier. He claimed that Ogden owed him the market value of eleven and a half barrels of oil (ca. 23 lbs.) that Ogden had allegedly taken from a drift whale on his beach at Kitchaminchok. This beach area lay to the west of the tract that Governor Nicolls had awarded to Cooper in 1666.

Underscoring the economic importance of whale oil, the case was tried in the highest colonial court by the two most prominent barristers in the colony. Cooper hired John Sharpe and Ogden hired John Rider. Nicolls must have taken some satisfaction as he witnessed the legal system he had introduced at work resolving an acrimonious dispute without his intervention. Unfortunately, the court records for this period were badly damaged in a fire in 1911 that nearly destroyed the New York State archives, making it difficult to follow the details of testimonies. Nevertheless, the surviving text provides important insights into the role played by whale products in colonial New York.

John Sharpe presented as evidence the agreement of June 8, 1659, wherein Gardiner had turned over to Cooper his rights to the drift whales on the beaches from the western boundary of Southampton Town west to "a place called Kitchaminchok" in Moriches Bay (DSBD 2: 85–86). Rider countered, pointing out that the lease was not dated. However, a date of June 8th had been inscribed at the top of the deed, apparently by the clerk. The gaps in the damaged transcript make it impossible to follow the arguments with certainty, but it appears that Rider challenged Cooper's lease on these grounds. If the lease was invalid because it lacked a date, then Cooper had no exclusive right to the whales on that beach.

Sharpe argued that the absence of the date was simply an oversight and that Cooper's exclusive right to the beach was common knowledge. In a calculated move, Sharpe swore in John Ogden's son-in-law, Robert Bond, as the first witness for the plaintiff. Bond's appearance must have embarrassed Ogden and most certainly influenced the jury. Bond testified that he "well remembers Lion Gardiner's conveyance of his interest in the whales of the plaintiff . . ." (Christoph and Christoph 1983, 52–53). Other witnesses affirmed Bond's testimony. A Montaukett identified only as "the little sachem," perhaps Wyancombone's son, also supported Cooper's claim, saying that the beach land had belonged to "the Great Sachem Wyandanch" and that it was sold to the plaintiff.

John Rider then introduced what the transcript describes only as "another deed." Unfortunately, no further mention of this document has survived in the damaged records. Rider called on Edmund Shaw and Joseph Raynor, who testified that the whale was cast up on Ogden's beach (DSBD 2: 156–57). Rider, of course, knew that Raynor, who had been sued by Cooper in the town court in 1663 prior to the establishment of the colony of New York, may have harbored some ill will toward John Cooper. He took the risk, but it probably worked against his client. The jury apparently suspected some bias against Cooper because they found Raynor's testimony unconvincing. Cooper won the case and Ogden was ordered to pay Cooper forty pounds, double the value of the oil, and the court costs as well.

Ogden was not a man to give up easily. He had faced down Lion Gardiner a most formidable foe, and brought the same resolve to his dispute with Cooper. He appealed in the next session of the Court of Assizes in October 1668 (Christoph and Christoph 1983, 76–78, 90). Most of the men who testified the year before were again called to the court. John Sharpe, who once more represented John Cooper, called in Anthony Waters to testify. Waters, who had sold his beach lease to John's brother, Thomas, in October 1662 affirmed that Wyandanch owned the beach land and stated that no one had ever challenged his lease (RTSH 2: 36). Rider called in Edmund Shaw, Richard Howell, and Joseph Raynor and introduced a deposition from John Jessup (taken in East Hampton by Justice John Mulford) supporting Ogden. Richard Howell's testimony was suspect because he, along with Raynor, had been sued by Cooper in 1662.

John Sharpe took a second deposition from Jessup; this time, however, it was made in front of the Southampton constable. Jessup's second deposition, according to the transcript, "seemed to contradict his previous statement," and now supported John Cooper. There is no explanation in the transcript for the change in Jessup's testimony, but it is likely that the Southampton officials who favored John Cooper may have intimidated Jessup. John Sharpe again won the day. The court ruled that Cooper's title "is to be preferred."

The importance of the case prompted the court to appoint a commission to investigate the financial accounts of Ogden and Cooper. The commission reviewed the previous "several trials and hearings had between them about the beach and oil," and reported a week later. They ordered Ogden to pay Cooper an unusually large sum of 63 pounds and 14 shillings and, in addition, to pay the costs of both trials (Christoph and Christoph 1983, 90–91). The fine was more than a year's wages for a laborer and enough to purchase a small farmstead with twenty acres of land.

Contested Beaches: Brookhaven, Southampton, Oyster Bay, and Huntington Scramble for Drift Whales

When the Brookhaven magistrates learned that Tobacus had not testified before Mulford, they saw an opportunity to attack Winecroscum's testimony. Daniel Lane, who had established a trusting relationship with Tobacus, was chosen to meet with the sachem. In 1664, Lane had been involved with four major negotiations between Tobacus and Setauket and had been the one designated to bring the payment for one of the transactions to the sachem (Strong 2011, 55–63). Tobacus once even asked Lane to draft a letter to Governor Winthrop for him, appealing for the governor's support against a possible attack from Ninigret, the Niantic sachem. Lane convinced Tobacus that his interests were best served by allying his people with the town of Brookhaven, whose boundaries now officially incorporated all of the remaining Unkechaug lands, rather than with the "adventurers" from Southampton.

Tobacus and three of his followers, Purche, Massetus, and Ahutous, were invited to a "full town meeting" on March 23, 1668, to discuss access to the whales on the town beaches. Winecroscum, who was not invited, apparently had been overruled by Tobacus, but he remained loyal to the sachem. He later joined other Unkechaugs in a statement declaring that Tobacus was "our sachem and governor" (RTBH Hutchinson, 69–70). Tobacus agreed the town should have "all the whales that come within their patent bounds." He stipulated, however, that the town had to pay the Unkechaugs five English pounds in wampum for each whale and three pounds for "the party that brings news that is certain for each whale," and to give the Indians ten fathoms of wampum for carting the blubber and baleen "to the place appointed by the said inhabitants" (RTBH Hutchinson, 24–25).

At the same meeting, after repudiating the 1659 and 1662 agreements with Gardiner and the Southampton entrepreneurs, the town set forth a plan they hoped would put the final stamp on the matter. They organized a procedure for harvesting the drift whales that was similar to the precedents set earlier in Southampton and East Hampton. Organizing the town into four squads, they drew lots to determine the schedule for the squads. Samuel Dayton went first, followed by Richard Woodhull, who had been a member of the Southampton squads when he lived there, and then by Henry Perring and Joshua Garlick. Their task was to cut out the blubber and "get it fit for carting" to the middle of town to "be divided equally according to their allotment, and if there be any man that cannot or will not go to the cutting out . . . they are to lose their part of that whale to the rest of the squadron" (RTBH 1924, 150). The division of the whale oil and baleen was determined, as it was in the other towns, on the contribution that the individual "undertakers" had made to the purchase of the land from the Indians and other financial costs related to the establishment of the settlement. Newcomers to the town, of course, could buy shares in the common lands (Goddard 2011, 19).

When Cooper, Raynor, and the Southampton men continued to take whales from the Brookhaven beaches in spite of the town's agreement with Tobacus, Brookhaven appealed to the governor, charging that "some other persons not belonging to our town, without our leave or consent, do pretend a privilege upon the beach lying to the south and within [our] bounds aforesaid and have actually cut up and carried away some parts of a whale . . . contrary to the privileges of [our] town upon pretense of an agreement made with some Unkechaug Indians." In April 1668, Nicolls, who must have been losing his patience with Cooper and some of the Southampton men, ruled that "the inhabitants of the town of Setauket (alias Brookhaven) aforesaid and no other without their consent, shall or may cut or carry away any whales or great fish which are or hereafter may be cast upon any part of the land or beach within the bounds and limits of the said patent" (NYCD 14: 605). This was one of the last rulings made by the governor before he retired and returned to England. His replacement, Francis Lovelace, was interested in promoting his fortune through trade. He was, therefore, much more friendly to private entrepreneurs than Nicolls had been.

The Southampton men were quick to take advantage of the change in emphasis in the governor's office. The following fall, represented by Joseph Raynor, Richard Howell, and Anthony Waters, they appealed Nicolls's ruling to Francis Lovelace, telling the new governor that Nicolls had been badly misinformed by the Brookhaven officials (NYCD 14: 607–8). The men referred to their agreements with Winecroscum and Tobacus, which they noted had been made in 1659 and 1662, long before Setauket had obtained their patent, and had been confirmed recently by Winecroscum. These leases, they continued, "had been formerly purchased by the companies or some one of them and a valuable consideration given for the whales that should be cast up thereupon for the space of a certain term of years and not yet expired." Lovelace agreed that the lease should remain in effect even though there had been a change in the town's legal status. He suspended Nicolls's ruling and ordered the Setauket officials to "permit and suffer the [company] to enjoy what they have purchased. . . ."

Lovelace, however, pressed the towns for "the king's share" of drift whale profits. In 1671 he sought information about occurrences on town beaches in a memorandum "to see what drift whales have happened" on the beaches of Rockaway, Huntington, and Southampton, and "to enjoyne the respective justices to make a strict inspection for the future into that affair" (NYCD 14: 661). Not surprisingly, the lack of a response to his memorandum confirmed Lovelace's suspicions about the east end towns. In the spring of 1672, he expressed his frustration: "Whereas I am given to understand that there hath been great abuse by neglect of ye office of several towns upon Long Island in not making enquiry into or securing his Royal Highness his part of Drift whales or great fish cast upon the beach or shore according to the directions in the law. . . ." Then the governor ordered that the local Indians and others be asked to report the occurrences of drift whales on the town beaches (NYCD 14: 664).

The scramble for whale oil profits also set town against town in other parts of Long Island. The same spring that Lovelace issued his pronouncement, a conflict broke out between the residents of Oyster Bay and Huntington over the harvesting of drift whales. Joseph Finch of Huntington complained that Oyster Bay residents had cut up a drift whale on a Huntington beach and tried out the oil. The governor, however, was as concerned about getting the royal tax as he was about Finch's complaint. He ordered an inquiry into the matter to find a fair resolution for the two parties and to secure the "Duke's interest." Finch was awarded fifteen barrels of oil, "out of which he had to pay the colonial tax, and the remainder went to pay Oyster Bay" (NYCD 14: 665–66).

Although the conflicts over drift whales never entirely abated, attention, energy, and innovation had shifted to the shore whaling enterprises in the 1660s. Most of the Southampton adventurers involved in the drift whale enterprise had turned their eyes to the waters beyond the shore.

4

Origins of "Ye Whaling Design" on Long Island

English Whaling in the Early Seventeenth Century

When the English settlers on Long Island contemplated hunting whales from their eastern shores, they had some sources of knowledge for reference. Their Indian neighbors were skilled at navigating small boats and dispatching animals with spears, and English entrepreneurs based in London had recently begun whaling operations off Spitsbergen Island east of Greenland. Jonas Poole, commissioned by the English Muscovy Company in 1611 to initiate a whaling operation there, turned to the Basque whalers for help.[1] Poole, whose ship the *Margaret* carried six experienced Basque whalers, instructed his crew members to watch the Basque carefully as they pursued and killed a whale (Conway 1906, 42–43).

Two years later an English fleet of seven vessels carrying twenty-four Basque whalemen hunted whales off Spitsbergen. These men had highly specialized skills: harpooners; whaleboat captains, who directed the attack on the whale; steersmen, who stood in the stern with the twenty-foot-long oar; and the flensing men, who butchered the whale and supervised the trying process (Conway 1906, 52–53). It was a coordinated team effort that could easily fail unless everyone did his job in a timely manner. The necessity for teamwork and the basic tool kit remained the hallmarks of shore whaling until the practice ended in the early twentieth century.

The stalking and killing techniques used on the open sea from a galleon were essentially the same as those employed by the shore whalers. Poole's men saw the Basques launch small, sturdy shallops called "catcher" boats, carrying from four to eight men from the ship, to pursue the slow-moving right whales (Proulx 1993, 31–32). Surviving descriptions of the details of these boats vary because the Basque often altered the design to fit different situations, but one account describes them as "sharp at both ends, about twenty-seven feet long" (Proulx 1993, 32; Scammon 1968, 224). John Brereton, in his 1602 *Relation*, reported seeing a Basque shallop with a mast and a sail (Brereton [1602] 1906, 330). The Long Island shore whaling operations used a similar design that the English adapted from among the Basques' innovations. The boats were

Figure 14 Whaleboat, Sag Harbor Whaling Museum, Sag Harbor, N.Y. This boat has had extensive rebuilding, but it may be one of the oldest-known boats according to William Ansel (Ansel et al. 2014, 150–51).

twenty-eight feet long and six feet across at the center, tapering to a point at both ends, and had a portable mast and sail (Edwards and Rattray 1932, 56). The pointed ends enabled the whalemen to launch the boat without turning it around (fig. 14).

From Canoes to Whaleboats

The dugout canoes of the Long Island Indians were also pointed at both ends, but there the similarities end. In a canoe the paddlers sat looking forward so they could all see where they were going; in a whaleboat, however, only the man in the stern with the steering oar looked forward, while the rest sat looking backward. This alone required a significant change in mindset for the Indian whalers; moreover, they had to make this shift under extremely difficult conditions, as whale hunting on the coastal waters in open boats from November through April was treacherous and arduous. It was not a good time to be out on the cold winter waters where a man overboard can survive only a few minutes before hypothermia takes its deadly toll.

Figure 15 Drawing of whaling crew attacking a whale on 1722 map of Gardiners Island.

The Reverend Charles Wooley, who visited New York from August 1678 to July 1680, described a whale hunt in his *Two Years Journal in New York* (Wooley [1701] 1968, 38–39): "Two boats with six men in each make a company, viz . . . four oarsmen or rowers, a harpooner and a steersman" (fig. 15). As soon as the harpooner plunges the harpoon into the whale, "he makes all foam, with his rapid violent course." Unless the three-hundred-foot warp attached to the harpoon runs free, continued Wooley, the boat is likely to be overturned, throwing the crew into the freezing waters. Nathaniel Huntting describes such an event in his journal: "This day a whale boat being alone, the men struck a whale and she coming under the boat in part staved it, and though the men were not hurt with the whale, yet before any help came to them, four men were tired, and chilled, and fell off the boat and oars to which they hung and were drowned" (quoted in Breen 1989, 202).

The seventeenth-century accounts, however, do not give any details about the positioning of the crew members in the boat or their roles in the hunt. There was undoubtedly some ongoing situational experimentation dictated by the particular talents, physical strengths, and experience of the individual members, but the basic duties during the hunt probably changed very little from the methods employed by the Basque, English, and Dutch whalers in the northern waters. The Native Americans would have been familiar with the harpoons and lances and comfortable with the motions of the whaleboat on the open water, but they had to adjust to a new way of navigating. They had to depend on the man standing in the stern with the steering oar to guide the boat as they propelled it forward.

The descriptions of whaleboat crew responsibilities by Everett Joshua Edwards in *Whale-off* (1932) are quite similar to the accounts written by such deepwater whalemen as William Davis in *Nimrod of the Sea* (1874). A successful crew had to bond into a tightly knit team because their lives and fortune depended on each other. Misjudgment or failure to perform assigned tasks put all at risk as they attacked a dangerous quarry on the open sea. Timing and discipline were crucial. Every man had to follow an exacting, coordinated pattern of movement. Each position on the boat had specific duties that had to be done in concert with the other positions (fig. 16).

No detailed accounts of specific tasks assigned to members of the shore whaling crews during the seventeenth century have survived, but descriptions from the nineteenth and early twentieth centuries indicate that hunting methods changed very little over time (Dolin 2007, 95–96; Edwards and Rattray

Figure 16 Whaleboat and crew. Drawing by David B. Martine, Director, Shinnecock Nation Museum and Culture Center, Southampton, N.Y.

1932; Dakin 1963; Ansel et al. 2014, 26). The "mate" or "boatheader" was the man in charge who trained the crew. The boat was propelled by five oarsmen, all facing the "boatheader," who stood in the back (stern) of the boat, looking forward as he steered the boat toward the whale. He was usually the one who gave the orders and directed the hunt. With great dexterity he manned the massive steering oar, which was attached to the boat through a grommet on the stern post and varied in length from twenty to twenty-eight feet.

The second in command was the "boatsteerer," who pulled the "harpooner's oar" and sat on the port side on the front thwart, his fourteen-foot oar mounted on the starboard side. His task was to make sure that all the equipment was in place on the boat prior to launching. He had to be strong enough to hurl the heavy weapon into a moving target with great force. In front of him was the bow oarsman, who pulled a sixteen-foot oar mounted on the port side. The next man, who sat in the thwart across the widest part of the boat, pulled the eighteen-foot midship oar on the starboard side. The third man, the tub oarsman, sat on the next thwart and manned a sixteen-foot oar on the port side. The fifth rower pulled the "stroke oar" in the stern mounted on the starboard side. His oar matched the fourteen-foot harpooner's oar. The length of the oars was determined by the width of the boat at the point where they were mounted. This arrangement, according to Davis, preserved the balance when the harpooner had peaked his oar and stood in the bow to cast his harpoon into the whale (Davis 1874, 159). The longest oar (the midship) and the shortest oar (the stroke oar) pulled against the two sixteen-foot oars on the port side pulled by the bow oarsman and the tub oarsman.

The boatheader steered the boat as close to the whale as he could. At his signal, the harpooner peaked his oar by securing it in a cleat in front of his seat (fig. 17). He stood up, turned around, and placed his left leg in a notch in the forward thwart and, timing his cast with the movements of the whale and the boat, drove his harpoon, with the line attached, as deeply into the whale as he could. The harpoon had a two-foot-long iron shank ending in a double barbed point at the end of an eight-foot haft made of thick, rough-cut oak or hickory to facilitate the grip (fig. 18). The harpoons used by Ogden probably evolved from the Indian and Inuit spears into what the Dutch called "darting" or "harping" irons with barbs and flues. The toggle iron, a barbed point mounted on a haft with a pin, was not developed until the mid-nineteenth century, when an African American blacksmith named Lewis Temple fashioned an iron toggle based on the Inuit design (Dolin 2007, 249–50).

The harpoon haft was attached either to a three-hundred-foot warp coiled in a wooden tub or to wooden drogues (blocks of wood or seal bladders designed to slow the whale down) (Dolin 2007, 49–50). The purpose of the harpoon was not to kill the whale but to slow down and mark its movements (Little

Figure 17 Whaleboat crew attacking a whale. Drawing by David B. Martine.

1981, 43–47). The function and position of the second boat probably was determined by whichever one made the first successful strike with the harpoon. Once the harpoon was in place, the harpooner took up his oar and the boat pursued the whale, waiting for it to tire and slow down. Then the harpooner and the boat header would change places, not an easy maneuver in the best of circumstances. The boat header had to be proficient at casting the fifteen-foot lance with great precision, aiming for a critical spot where it could penetrate the lungs, causing death (fig. 19). The bow oarsman on the port side was responsible for getting the lances ready for the boat header and for putting up the mast, if needed. The midship oarsman had only one job: he rowed.

Willits Ansel, the whaleboat expert at Mystic Seaport, has commented on the difficult choreography performed by the boat header and the harpooner when they changed places, a counterintuitive move that has puzzled scholars (Dolin 2007, 95–96; Ashley 1926; Ansel et al. 2014, 21). Ansel noted that when an old whaleman was pressed to explain the reason for the two men to change places, he replied that they were two different jobs and required two different skills. Perhaps, suggested Ansel, it was a matter of status. The boat header, who was the commanding officer, was given the honor of making the kill. According to Edwards, this maneuver was performed by his crew in the nineteenth century. It seems unlikely, however, that an Indian crew in the seventeenth century would have made such a change. The Indian hunter with the greatest skill with a spear would most likely have cast the harpoon as well as the lances.

Figure 18 Harpoon held by Mataukus Tarrant, Shinnecock Nation. Courtesy of the Southampton Historical Society.

Possibly, the boat header may have been an Englishman who was experienced in steering the small sloops used by fishermen to catch perch and other small fish along the coast. These skills would be most useful when the whaleboat was under sail. In his history of East Hampton, T. H. Breen noted, however, that Englishmen would have been very reluctant to participate in whale hunting because they were independent-minded men who disdained working for wages (Breen 1989, 168). Only two whaling contracts make references to the presence of Englishmen in the whale hunt. The first was a contract negotiated by John Cooper's brother, Thomas, in 1679 (SHTA Liber A2: 123). Thomas agreed "to go to sea with them [the Indians] lameness and sickness excepted." Thomas, who was fifty-one at the time, had understandable health

Figure 19 Whaling lance held by Mataukus Tarrant, Shinnecock Nation. Courtesy of the Southampton Historical Museum.

concerns; he was elderly by seventeenth-century norms. The second contract was negotiated by Benjamin Conkling two years later in March 1681 (RTEH 1: 95). The Indians agreed to sign the document on the condition "that English with their boats go to sea and attend the said design."

Court records entered in January and March 1675, referring to the theft of whale parts, indicate that Simon Hellyer (Heller), an East Hampton resident, may have been in a whaling crew (RTEH 1: 375–77). While suggestive, this information does not allow us to draw any conclusions, as no contracts negotiated by whaling company owners for the services of English crew members have surfaced.

When the thrashing death throes subsided, the harpoons and lances were secured, warps were attached to the carcass, and the arduous task of pulling it to shore began. It was a job that could take hours, followed by the cutting and trying process, which could take several days. Some accounts note that hunting crews waited for the carcass to float ashore, but this is unlikely to have been a common strategy. The wind and tides posed the risk of the carcass drifting for some time and coming ashore in an inconvenient location. A long delay might also cause the blubber to spoil.

Getting Started: John Ogden's Proposal

As early as 1632, the Dutch were making plans to expand their whaling operations from Spitsbergen and Greenland south along the Atlantic coast to the
mouth of the Delaware Bay. David De Vries, the Dutch entrepreneur who
founded the colony of Swanendael on Delaware Bay in 1630, envisioned the
development of a whaling operation from that settlement. De Vries noted that
many whales had been seen along the shore from December through March,
clearly a reference to the North Atlantic right whale (De Vries [1655] 1968,
15–16). He brought a sloop with harping irons to the colony, but the plans
were disrupted when an Indian attack wiped out the settlement a year later
(Jacobs 2007, 70). Whales were regular visitors along the Long Island shores
throughout the seventeenth century, drawing the interest of Dutch and English
entrepreneurs. Jasper Dankerts, an agent for a Dutch religious sect seeking a
location for a settlement in the colony, kept a journal of his observations from
1679 to 1680. He included a pen and ink drawing of New York Harbor near
Sandy Hook showing six whales and two smaller animals, probably porpoises.
The bay, he said, "swarms with fish, both large and small, whales, tunnies and
porpoises" (Dankerts and Sluyter 1867, 100) (fig. 20).

The English soon began making their own plans to take advantage of this
lucrative resource. Early attempts at whaling made by Captain John Smith in
1614 and 1627 had been discouraging. He reported that he had spent "much
time in chasing them, but couldn't kill any" (quoted in Laist 2017, 171). In
1647, a Mr. Whiting received permission from the Connecticut Court to form
a company licensed to hunt whales for seven years, but there is no further mention of his endeavor in the Connecticut records (RCC 1: 154). The Dutch in
New Amsterdam revived their interest in 1652, when the officials in Holland
wrote to the New Netherland governor, Peter Stuyvesant, telling him that "the
whale-fishery might at some seasons of the year be carried on." If it could be
done profitably, they continued, "it would be very desirable" (NYCD 14: 195).
Although the responses to the appeal are not detailed in any documents, apparently some limited activity took place because four years later Hans Jongh,
a soldier and tanner, asked the council in New Amsterdam for oil or "some
of the fat of the whale lately captured" (quoted in Starbuck [1878] 1964, 11;
NYS.MSS vi: 354).

On September 30, 1650, John Ogden, who had arrived in Southampton
only two years before, was one of the first on record to make serious plans for
a "whale design." He petitioned the Southampton Town officials for permission to organize a shore whaling company. The town granted him an exclusive
license to "kill whales on the south sea" for the next seven years (RTSH 1:

Figure 20 Whales in New York Harbor. Drawing by Jasper Dankerts [Danckaerts]. From Dankerts and Sluyter, *Journal of a Voyage to New York, 1679–80*, translated by Henry C. Murphy. In *Memoirs of the Long Island Historical Society*. Brooklyn, N.Y.: Long Island Historical Society, 1867. Plate II.

70–71). Ogden used his influence as a town magistrate at the beginning of the next year to overturn the prohibition against making harpoons for the Indians (RTSH 1: 30).

There was, however, some skepticism about the success of Ogden's "whale design," as these seasonal operations came to be called. Town officials set forth conditions similar to those imposed on Mr. Whiting by the Connecticut courts in 1647, requiring him "not to delay but do [be] somewhat effectual in the business within a year after this present day," adding that if his company did "not kill in the design" a whale or whales within the space of two years, "his liberty is annulled. . . ." They also warned him not to interfere in any way with the right of the town to the drift whales (RTSH 1: 70–71).

Ogden was certainly aware of the challenges he faced. Not only did he know about the flensing, trying, storing, and shipping procedures used on drift whale carcasses for nearly a decade, but he may well have had some knowledge of the hunting methods and equipment used at Spitsbergen. Ogden's fellow investors at the time are not named, but later documents indicate they may have been his son, John; John Oldfield; Richard Woodhull; and Richard Shaw from East

Hampton (RTSH 2: 2; 1: 71). Oldfield, a neighbor from North Sea, had been invited to settle there with the understanding that he would pursue his trade as a tanner, a highly valued skill in colonial villages (Howell 1887, 435).

In August 1654, Ogden and his North Sea neighbor, Richard Woodhull, petitioned the town for "the liberty of striking whales . . ." on the same terms as before (RTSH 1: 71). Apparently the 1650 license was no longer in effect. Either the company had been unable to launch its boats within the first year or had failed to kill any whales, as required, over the two succeeding seasons. There is evidence, however, that Ogden had managed to successfully kill some whales between 1654 and 1658. In December 1658, an unsigned petition to the Southampton Town magistrates, written in the first person plural, asked for the "liberty to bring the whales we strike ashore on your land, and make them out into oil without molestation" (RTSH 1: 126).

William Pelletreau, who transcribed the town records, inserted a footnote indicating that the petitioner was probably John Ogden. The petition also asked that any whales bearing "our marks by lance or harping iron" that washed ashore on the town beaches be granted to Ogden's company, adding that the company would respect the town's right to all drift whale carcasses. Ogden requested an exclusive seven-year term, as he and Woodhull had been granted in 1650. His plan, he said, was to begin operation in the spring of 1659.

There is no further reference to the petition nor to a whaling operation until the spring of 1660, when an unidentified whaling company entered a charge of trespass against John Ogden's company (RTSH 2: 2). The case was put to arbitration with the agreement of both parties, but there is no mention of the outcome in the records. The conflict may have been related to the challenges of killing the huge mammals and securing their carcasses. Wounded whales often escaped only to die later and drift ashore. Claims made by a rival whaling company to the carcass were often difficult for courts to resolve unless the irons with identifying marks were found in the body. It was also possible that a whale may have been attacked by two companies without success. When a carcass carrying the irons of both companies later washed ashore, the court then had to decide which irons caused the fatal wounds (Barstow 2004, 227–28). Despite such problems, Long Island entrepreneurs were willing to take the risks, spurred on perhaps by the development of whaling operations to the north.

In 1662, Felix Christian Sporri, a doctor who was visiting Rhode Island, wrote a fairly detailed account of a crew killing a whale in Narragansett Bay (Bridenbaugh 1974, appendix V, 144–45). "There are small fishing boats," he wrote, "each containing six or seven men." The first boat moved up beside the whale and launched a harpoon into its body and then killed the whale with lances. He described the harpoon as a spear with a double-edged point about nine feet long, fastened to a rope running out forty or fifty fathoms (240) to

300 feet). Once the whale was fastened to the first boat, the second boat came alongside and struck the whale with another harpoon. "When he felt this new wound, he turned his head down and raised his tail out of the water and beat about with such violence that it was terrible to behold." The whale swam off with both boats in tow until he tired. Then the boats closed in and hurled numerous lances into the body until a spout of blood shot out of the blow hole, signaling the whale's imminent death.

"They towed him ashore," continued Sporri, "greatly pleased, for they had earned more than a whole farm would bring us in an entire year." The whale, he said, was "fifty-five feet long and sixteen feet high; it had only two fins; the tail was broad." According to Stony Brook University marine scientist Joe Warren, Sporri's description suggests the animal was most likely a right whale (personal communication). Sporri's report is significant because it indicates that Rhode Island whalers were engaged in whaling very early on and were reaping great profits. It also demonstrates how dangerous and difficult the killing of a leviathan on the open water in small boats could be. Sporri, unfortunately, does not say anything about the ethnicity of the men in the boats.

Whether or not influenced by news of whaling in New England, several companies were clearly operating in Long Island waters by the late 1660s. In Southampton, John Cooper was preparing for the 1668–69 season by requesting a license to provide Indians with gunpowder in exchange for joining his whaling crews (NYCD 14: 608–9). Samuel Maverick of East Hampton wrote to Governor Nicolls in October of 1669 reporting that twelve to thirteen whales had been killed on eastern Long Island during the season from November 1668 to March 1669 (NYCD 3: 183). Three years later an entry by Governor Lovelace's council, in response to a petition from the eastern Long Island towns, noted that they had been engaged in whaling for the past twenty years, "but could not bring it to any perfection till within these 2 or 3 years past . . ." (NYCD 3: 197). Maverick and the governor were probably referring to whales taken by three whaling companies established in Southampton and one in East Hampton. Two Southampton companies were led by Josiah Laughton and John Cooper and a third by John and Richard Howell, Zerobabel Philips, and Joseph Raynor, all of whom had been involved in the harvesting of drift whales. The lone East Hampton company was owned by Jacob Schellinger.

Unfortunately no primary records of these ventures have survived. The three Southampton companies are mentioned in two 1670 contracts, and Schellinger's company is described in a secondary source (SHTA Liber A2: 85; RTSH 2: 56–57). According to Alexander Starbuck in his classic *History of American Whale Fishing*, Schellinger negotiated with a party of Montaukett Indians to hunt whales in 1668 (Starbuck [1878] 1964, 12). Schellinger, a wealthy merchant from Holland, had come to New Amsterdam in 1652 and married Cornelia, the widow of Jacobus Loper and mother of two sons, James and Janneken. The Schellinger family moved from New Amsterdam to East Hampton shortly after the English formed the colony of New York in 1664.

Schellinger and his fellow investors, who are not named, agreed to pay the crew of Montaukett Indians to hunt whales three shillings a day from November 1668 to April 1669. This was a shilling more than the standard fee for one day of labor, although exceptions were sometimes made for skilled artisans such as carpenters (Anderson 1991, 143–44). The Indians agreed "to attend diligently with all opportunities for the killing of whales or other fish " and Schellinger and his partners agreed to provide the boats and equipment. These ventures were not very well documented. Not until 1670, when the first whaling contracts were entered into the town records, was an informed understanding of shore whaling possible.

Prior to his whaling operation in 1667–68, mentioned above, John Cooper, one of Ogden's bitter rivals in the quest for access to drift whale beaches, briefly turned his attention to shore whaling prospects elsewhere. He accepted the invitation of Peter Carteret, the assistant governor and secretary of Albemarle County in North Carolina (RTSH 2: 50–53), who in the spring of 1667 asked Cooper to help him develop a whaling industry in the newly formed colonial outpost that would serve to diversify their tobacco-based economy. Cooper formed a company with Nicolas Stevens, a merchant from Boston, and Humphrey Hulse from East Hampton. Stevens and Cooper entered an agreement into the town records that called for Stevens to secure a ship with "all manner of tackle, rigging, sails, and anchor," recruit a crew of thirteen men and a boy, and serve as "the master for this present voyage, to take care of all things about this design, and give an account at the end of the voyage."

The cost of the operation would be shared by the investors, but no further mention of the ambitious operation is made and most likely nothing ever came of it. Albemarle County was a settlement of scattered plantations with an unstable government run by a few aristocratic proprietors at the time. It was described in a granting document as "not yet cultivated or planted, and only inhabited by some barbarous people with no knowledge of Almighty God"; furthermore, the county had no deep water port (Rankin 1962). If the operation was launched, the investors would surely have lost a great deal of money. In the fall of 1667, Cooper turned his attention to whaling opportunities at home. Long Island entrepreneurs, however, were still struggling to develop and sustain successful operations.

The Economics of Whaling

The companies generally involved the better-off among the Southampton Town residents, men such as John Cooper; Richard, John, and Arthur Howell; Joseph Raynor; Thomas Topping; and James Herrick. The companies, however, were not exclusive. Small contributions from farmers and tradesmen were also welcome. John Oldfield, a member of John Ogden's company in 1654, was, as noted above, a tanner by trade. The whaling contracts usually listed only one or two leading investors, referring to the others as "their associates." These men came from closely related families, forming a kinship system that controlled whaling operations on Long Island for nearly a century.

Historian T. H. Breen described the East Hampton community as "a group of families—really a complex network of local clans," whose names frequent the whaling contracts: Gardiner, Mulford, Dayton, James, Osborn, and Stratton (Breen 1989, 166). They had the financial resources and experience with harvesting drift whales that would serve them well in the emerging shore whaling operations. The whaling contracts entered from 1670 to 1685, along with the reports of Long Island companies operating in the 1686–87 and 1710–11 seasons, include the names of 104 investors, many of whom were connected by blood or marriage. While these kinship connections served them well in terms of political, economic, and social control, they did not assure complete dominance and civic tranquility. Disputes frequently led to civil suits within and between families. It has often been said by local historians that the prominent Long Island families were either in church marrying each other or in court suing each other. On occasion Indians were able to take advantage of strife among the elites to advance their interests.

The timing was right in the middle of the century for the whale design. Breen noted that a major factor in the development of privately owned companies was the political stability in England following Cromwell's victory in the English Civil War. The stability encouraged an expansion in trade that made it possible for eastern Long Island to engage in the global market. The people wanted manufactured goods from England and Europe that could not be purchased with the profits from agriculture alone. The demand stimulated entrepreneurial activity and expanded market opportunities. The capital returns from the export of whale products could finance the importation of goods that had previously been considered luxury items such as linens, pewter and silverware, furniture, curtains, glassware, and porcelain. The availability of English manufactured goods also brought changes in Native American material culture.

A very rough estimate of the "start-up" costs of a whaling operation is possible with the help of commodity prices and property evaluations in the Southampton and East Hampton town records, the Suffolk County probate records, and New York colonial documents. These sources provide a general picture of the financial challenges involved. The precise market value for such commodities as clothing and tools, of course, varied depending on the quality of the items and market fluctuations. The prices of basic staples such as corn, however, remained fairly stable throughout this period. When fluctuations appeared, an average figure was used.

The equipment required is documented in accounts of shore whaling from the seventeenth to the early twentieth centuries. There were few significant innovations made in the basic tools and hunting strategies. The first expense was the purchase or construction of whaleboats. Accounts of whale hunting by Samuel Purchas in 1612 (Dow 1985, 7–8), a description of a whale hunt on Narragansett Bay in 1662 (quoted in Dolin 2007, 391–92), and a journal account by Charles Wooley in 1678 (Wooley [1701] 1968, 38–39) all describe the use of two boats, each with a six-man crew. Although this strategy was most likely used by Long Island whalers as well, whaling documents indicate that many Long Island company owners, perhaps lacking the manpower to form two six-man crews, may have dispatched only one boat. It is also possible, of course, that companies employed whalers who were not under contract, suggesting the company owners deemed it necessary to secure only the more skilled hunters.

A successful whaling operation depended on at least one well-constructed, reliable whaleboat. Cooper's probate listed two whaleboats valued at four pounds per boat (RCSS 73–74). Notations in an account book by Richard Macy of Nantucket indicated two men could construct a whaleboat in about three days (Little 1981, 41). The 1672 estate inventory for Roger Smith of East Hampton listed a "whale craft" evaluated at three pounds (RCSS 52).

Unfortunately there are no surviving descriptions of the whaleboat construction techniques used in the seventeenth century. A general understanding, however, can be gleaned from related sources. Macy's notations described a whaleboat constructed with overlapping cedar planking. The design and construction techniques differed little from those used by the Vikings in the tenth century. The Viking plank fishing boat excavated at Skuldelev, Norway, was a bit larger than the seventeenth-century English whaleboats. The Norse boats were thirty-six feet in length and eight feet in width at the center (Graham-Campbell 2013, 37–50). The wedge-shaped planks were cut very thin to make them light enough for portage. Paul Dudley of Boston, writing in 1753, said that the cedar boats used by whalemen "were so light that two men can conveniently carry them, and yet they are twenty feet long, and carry six men" (Dudley 1753, 262–63). The whaleboats varied in length from twenty to about thirty feet.

The standard size for whaleboats on Long Island in the early twentieth century was twenty-eight feet long by six feet across (Edwards and Rattray 1932, 55). According to Edwards, the boats were equipped with a mast stored in the bottom of the boat. A second set of oars, replacements for those broken or lost at sea, probably added as much as two pounds to the cost of the boats.

The iron tools required a considerable capital outlay. The irons, the warps, and much of the equipment had to be purchased from New England or imported from England. Iron, a scarce commodity in the Atlantic colonies, was available from Saugus Iron Works near Lynn, Massachusetts, from 1646 until 1676 and thereafter from sources in the southern colonies at considerable expense. The forging and fashioning of the harpoons was no easy task. Few blacksmiths had the skills or experience required to make the harpoons, lances, and other iron tools for whaling. Ogden had an advantage here: his sister, Hannah, was married to Robert Bond, a Southampton blacksmith and one of few, if not the only one, on Long Island who had the necessary skills (Howell 1887, 422). This was yet another example of the family connections that played a significant role in the development of the whaling industry on Long Island. Ogden's relationship with Bond, however, was not always cordial. In 1667, his son-in-law testified against him in a dispute with John Cooper over beach rights in 1662 (see previous chapter).

John Cooper's probate record included harping irons valued at eight pounds, ten shillings. He must have had at least seventeen lances because the market price for one lance was ten shillings (RCSS 106). The Unkechaug Indians who hunted for John's brother, Thomas, in 1678 demanded that he provide "two sufficient boats, and two warps and two hand warps, and eighteen good irons" (SHTA Liber A2: 123). The warps required to hold fast the harpoon to the whale, tow the whale to shore, and turn the whale during the butchering process were expensive. Cooper's one coil warp (ca. 1,200 feet) was valued at fifteen pounds, as much as two horses in their prime (RCSS 73; Ansel et al. 2014, 60, 64).

Cooper also owned flensing tools (cutting knives, spades, pikes, and gaffs) that cost four pounds and two shillings. The trying process required a furnace, iron kettles, wooden barrels, a small shed, and a cart. A cart could be constructed for about three pounds and a supply of four thousand barrel staves cost twenty-five shillings six pence (Marshall 1962, 122; RCSS 73–75). Barrels, costing about three shillings six pence each, were put together as needed during the trying process. If an adult whale were tried out, the company might need as many as sixty barrels at a cost of nine pounds.

The two-kettle furnace, which could probably have been constructed in two days by two men, cost an estimated nine shillings for the labor. The wages for unskilled labor averaged about two shillings a day, but a mason could ask for about six pence more. The tools and the 250-gallon iron try pots were extremely expensive. A ten-gallon iron kettle, for example, was valued at one pound and ten shillings (RCSS 63). The large trying pots might cost as much as twenty or thirty pounds. Some company owners, such as John Cooper, John Ogden, and the Reverend Thomas James, would have used the ones they had constructed for their drift whale operations. Others may have rented or leased the trying stations used by the towns to process drift whales. By 1687, however, fourteen companies had established their own trying stations on the Atlantic shore from West Hampton to Montauk (Pelletreau 1903, 2: 495–96) (figs. 21, 22, 23, and 24).

The cost of two boats and oars (twelve pounds), harping and flensing irons (twelve pounds, two shillings), and barrels, based on the average harvest by fourteen companies in 1687 (156 barrels), would cost about twenty-four pounds. The cost of two carts (four pounds), a furnace and iron kettles (twenty to thirty pounds), and rope (fifteen pounds) would require an investment of about ninety pounds, more than a year's salary for the Reverend Robert Fordham (Howell 1887, 101). Although most of the costs were first-time only, a whaling company was a major investment, a substantial sum for members of a community with an economy based primarily on agriculture.

The capital necessary to launch a whaling company would be equivalent to the price of a house and lot in the 1670s. The majority of settlers lived in houses averaging from twenty to thirty-two feet in width by twenty feet in length, costing from fifteen to thirty-five pounds (Barstow 2004, 304). Joshua Garlick, whose son was an investor in a whaling company in 1679, left a house and lot in East Hampton to his sons valued at thirty-five pounds (RCSS 83). Samuel Dayton sold his house and ten-acre lot to Benjamin Gibbs for twenty-four pounds, sixteen shillings, and three pence (RTBH Book A: 38). The few affluent settlers, of course, lived in more expensive abodes. In 1671, Thomas Terry's house and lot were appraised at fifty pounds, and Thomas Topping, who

Figure 21 Indian crews flensing whale. Drawing by David B. Martine.

Figure 22 Indians mincing blubber. Drawing by David B. Martine.

Figure 23 Indians bailing oil into cooling vat. Drawing by David B. Martine.

Figure 24 Shore trying station. Drawing by David B. Martine.

died in 1681, left to his descendants a house and twenty-acre lot worth one
hundred pounds (RCSS 34, 110). For a company sending out a single boat,
the cost would have been almost the same as the purchase price of Thomas
Terry's homestead.

Profits and Risks

The cost of financing was daunting, but a successful whaling season could
easily cover that and bring in a substantial profit. The market price for whale
oil fluctuated, depending on quality and demand. The Suffolk County probate
records and the town records from 1675 to 1682 show the price of a barrel
ranging from one to two pounds (RCSS 65, 71, 127; RTBH Book A: 39, 40).
Each barrel was required by the colonial authorities to contain thirty-one and
a half gallons of oil. The coopers who made the barrels had to be licensed and
were held accountable should any attempt be made to alter, even slightly, the
capacities of their barrels. They had to put their individual marks on each barrel
(Braginton-Smith and Oliver 2008, 51).

Estimates about the number of barrels produced by a right whale vary according to size of the whale. In 1678, Charles Wooley wrote, "A whale about
sixty foot long having a thick and free blubber may yield or make 40 to 50
barrels of oil, every barrel containing 31 or 32 gallons at 20 shillings a barrel,

if it hath a good large bone it may be half a tun or a thousand weight, which may give 25 pounds sterling old English money" (Wooley [1701] 1968, 38–39). The price for a barrel of whale oil cited by Wooley is much lower than most of the evaluations in the eastern Long Island town records and estate inventories. The Southampton estate inventories more commonly cite a price of two pounds (40 shillings).

Wooley's estimate of the number of barrels produced, however, is close to numbers cited in contemporary and modern accounts. Lord Cornbury, who was governor of New York and New Jersey from 1701 to 1708, reported to the Commissioners for Trade and Plantations in London that, "a yearling will make about forty barrels of oil; a two-year-old 'stunt' whale will make sometimes fifty, sometimes sixty barrels of oil; and the largest whale that I have heard of in these parts yielded one hundred and ten barrels of oil and 1200 weight of bone" (NYCD 5: 59–60). Estimates by modern marine scientists Randall Reeves, Jeffrey Breiwick, and Edward Mitchell range from thirty-four to fifty-three barrels of oil and about 680 pounds of baleen from mature whales (Reeves, Breiwick, and Mitchell 1999, 4–5, 28, 29).

To determine the number of whales killed each season prior to the decline of shore whaling after the 1730s, Reeves and his colleagues turned to the British customs records of whale oil and baleen imports that began after the 1696–97 season. These accounts list barrels of oil and pounds of baleen imported from New York, New England, and Pennsylvania each year. Reeves employed a conversion ratio of forty-four barrels per whale to estimate the number of whales killed each season from 1697 to 1734. His results showed that the number of whale catches sometimes varied sharply from season to season. In 1706, following the 1705–6 season, for example, no oil was shipped from New York and only eighty-eight barrels from Pennsylvania and New England combined. The total number of whales killed along the Atlantic shore from Maine to Maryland was the equivalent of two adult whales. The next year, however, was quite different. The New England ports shipped 4,180 barrels taken from an estimated ninety-five whales along with 1,012 barrels from New York.[2]

The occasional off year did not deter entrepreneurs from launching a whale design. During the 1681–82 season, fifteen companies employing 192 Indian whalers hunted whales along the Long Island shores from Mastic to Montauk. The next season eleven companies sent out 132 whalers and the following season ten companies dispatched one hundred whalers to pursue whales off the Long Island shore. The numbers dropped to seven companies in 1684–85, the last season for recorded contracts.[3] Two surviving official reports, however, record fourteen companies for the 1686–87 season and nine in the 1710–11 season. These two reports are significant because they list the number of barrels taken by individual companies.[4]

In 1686–87, fourteen whaling companies brought in an average of 150 bar-rels each from an estimated total of seventy to eighty whales (Pelletreau 1903, 2: 496). The companies, operating out of seven locations from Ketchaponack to Wickapogue (map 3), harvested 2,148 barrels of oil, and East Hampton reported having an additional 1,456 barrels "on hand," waiting to be shipped to market in New York or Boston. The total for the two towns came to 3,604 barrels. According to Reeves's calculations, over eighty whales were taken by these companies. It was by far the most successful whaling season on record for eastern Long Island, injecting an estimated seven thousand pounds in currency or credit into the local economy (Pelletreau 1903, 2: 495–96).

In 1711, Daniel Sayre wrote a letter to George Clarke, the colonial secre-tary in New York, to report that a total of 304 barrels had been taken by nine companies during the 1710–11 season (NYS.MSS 54: 188; Adams 1918, 232). Some companies did very well. Josiah Topping brought in eighty-four barrels and Hezekiah Howell and Samuel Mulford each tried out forty-eight barrels, but John Mitchell and Thomas Stevens harvested only six and seven barrels, respectively. The average for the companies was about thirty bar-rels. Investors in all but the latter two companies more than recovered their start-up costs.

Assuming the number of companies remained the same over the next decade, the number of whales killed increased only slightly. Although the numbers varied from season to season, the revenue from whale oil most cer-tainly played an important role in the economic development of eastern Long Island. The hard currency flowed into both colonial coffers and the local economies. The companies had to buy licenses from the governor and pay taxes on the oil and baleen (Pelletreau 1903, 2: 496). On December 25, 1711, for example, Governor Robert Hunter issued a license to ten Southampton men with the stipulation that they pay a twentieth part of all the oil and baleen taken that season (LPSS Book 10: 299).[5] The profits from baleen are seldom recorded, but the price of a pound of baleen was fairly stable, ranging from seven to nine pence per pound (RTBH Book A: 39, 40; Book B: 61). The baleen, therefore, would bring in an additional fifteen to twenty pounds sterling per adult whale.

Once the equipment was purchased, the next step was to find a crew to hunt the whales and to process the oil and baleen for shipping. Few Englishmen had the skills necessary to hunt whales in open boats, nor were they willing to venture out beyond the surf during the winter months when the right whales swam along the Atlantic shore. The Indians, however, were not only accustomed to navigating small boats on the open waters but were also adept at hunting sea mammals with spears. As historian Andrew Lipman noted in *The Saltwater Frontier*, shore whaling was not a colonial invention, it was a "joint creation" of two cultures. He also noted that European efforts, beginning with John Smith in 1614, had failed to launch a sustained shore whaling enterprise. Not until the English turned to the young men from the Unkechaug, Shinnecock, and Montaukett villages was a successful whale design established (Lipman 2015, 222–35).

5

New Needs, Old Traditions

The Cultural Impact of "Ye Whale Design"

Cultural Connections: Trade and Labor

Although much has been made of the cultural differences separating the pre-contact peoples and the European settlers, there were some common under-standings. In the seventeenth century, currency was scarce in the English colonies, resulting in a barter system based on the exchange of agricultural goods, labor, and products manufactured locally (Anderson 1991, 164–65; Braulein 1976, 24–25). Salaries, taxes, and debts were often paid in commodities. The town of Southampton, for example, paid the Reverend Joseph Taylor a yearly salary of one hundred pounds in summer wheat, Indian corn, whale bone, and oil (RTSH 2: 82). Unlike the aboriginal exchanges, however, the colonial economy involved a paper credit system based on the market value of goods, labor, and land. A laborer who built fences for three days might be paid in corn or pork assessed at equal value. It was this aspect of the colonial system that put the Indians at a distinct disadvantage. The English market valuations would have been somewhat of a mystery to the Indians, who undoubtedly viewed them with some suspicion.

The English barter system, however, was similar in some aspects to the recip-rocal exchange of goods in Native American economies. Prior to the arrival of the English on Long Island in 1640, the Native peoples had a subsistence-based economy similar to that of most coastal Algonquian peoples. Their concept of trade was based on gift giving and reciprocity (Bragdon 1996, 130–39; Mauss 1967; Sahlins 1972). People in subsistence-level social systems traded with other communities by exchanging goods of equal value. They also understood that labor as well as goods could be a part of this exchange system. The giving of time to help construct a wigwam or to mind children, for example, were valued gifts in this context (Lenkeit 2001, 103–4). What they did not fully comprehend, at first, was credit.

The Indian involvement in the English economy gradually increased in the 1660s and became more common after 1664, when eastern Long Island was absorbed into the new colony of New York (Lohse 1988, 396–403). As the English population grew, the farmers fenced in more land and introduced new crops and livestock. This expansion created a growing demand for domestic and field labor. As more Indians began working for the English farmers, additional avenues of communication between the two cultural communities opened. These developing relationships had a considerable impact on Native American political systems. Sachems were no longer needed to act as cultural mediators, and they no longer controlled access to European goods. There were also more bilingual speakers, both Indian and English, by the end of the seventeenth century. Arthur Howell of Southampton and Meneges (a.k.a. Tom Indian) from Unkechaug, for example, were bilingual. Both men are identified on documents as "translators."

Coat Men and Clothmakers

The Indians were recruited into the whaling operations with the lure of European goods. Coats, not beads and shiny trinkets, were one of the most frequently requested items beginning with the first contacts in the late sixteenth century (Welters 1993, 16). The European traders were called "coat men" or "clothmakers" by the Indians (Axtell 1988, 135–38). Coats were a symbol of status among Indians and proved to be essential for the success of diplomatic negotiations as well as for the purchase of Indian lands. The important role of coats in facilitating diplomatic negotiations is well documented for the coastal Algonquians from Maine to Virginia.

Historian John De Forest recounts numerous instances in New England following the Pequot War wherein coats facilitated the purchase of Indian lands or sealed a peace treaty. In 1639, for example, when the English negotiated for the purchase of Milford, Connecticut, they "laid down before the sachem six coats, ten blankets, one kettle and a quantity of hoes, hatchets, knives, and looking glasses" (De Forest 1852, 166–67). Two decades later, Connecticut gave six coats to Robin Cassasinamon and his assistants "to reward them for their services in governing the Pequots" and persuading them to do missionary work among the Indians (De Forest 1852, 273). An alliance between the Piscataways and Maryland was affirmed in 1676 with barrels of corn, powder, and shot and over one hundred coats (Rice 2014, 742).

In December 1640, the English company from Lynn, Massachusetts, purchased the land for the village from the Shinnecock for sixteen coats and sixty bushels of corn. The corn was apparently part of the negotiation because the Shinnecock supplies were running low in mid-December, but it was the coats that made the deal. Coats also played a major role in the purchases of East Hampton and Brookhaven. In 1648, the first purchase of land for the East Hampton settlement included twenty coats, twenty-four mirrors, twenty-four hoes, twenty-four knives, twenty-four hatchets, and one hundred steel drills ("muxes") for wampum making (EHTR 1: 3). Seven years later Setauket sachem Warawakmy asked for ten coats, twelve hoes, twelve hatchets, fifty muxes, six kettles, one hundred needles, ten fathoms (sixty feet) of wampum, ten pounds of lead, seven chests of powder, one pair of children's stockings, and twelve knives for the northern half of what is now the town of Brookhaven (RTBH Hutchinson, 1–2). Although the list of European goods in demand had grown, the one consistent commodity was the coats.

In 1657, two years after Warawakmy's settlement, Wenecoheague, another Unkechaug sachem, sold most of the southern half of the town for trade goods including twenty coats, twenty hatchets, forty muxes, ten pounds of powder, ten pounds of lead, six pairs of stockings, six shirts, "one Trooper's Coat made of good cloth," twenty knives, and one gun (RTBH Hutchinson, 2–3). The reference to a "Trooper's Coat" is the only such mention in the Long Island records, but it is likely similar to the coat described by Marshall Becker in his research on matchcoats in the Indian trade as a "tailored matchcoat" (Becker 2005, fig. 738). It is noteworthy that Wenecoheague had raised the ante, doubling the numbers of coats and stockings.

A generation later the coats were an equally important incentive in the recruitment of Indian whalers. In the first contract entered into the town records, two Shinnecock Indians, Towsacom and Philip, agreed to hunt whales for company owner Josiah Laughton for three seasons beginning with the 1670–71 season (RTH 1: 56–57). The company was based at Mecox, about a mile east of Southampton village. The men wanted three coats apiece at the end of each season, a total of eighteen coats overall. Two of the coats kept them warm and the others brought them personal status and influence in their village community. In keeping with the traditional custom of gift exchange, they would distribute the coats to their relatives, friends, and prominent members of their community.

At the end of the 1670–71 season, a Shinnecock whaler named Artor raised the price to four coats per season in his contract with John Cooper, which was to run for ten years, eventually netting Artor forty coats (SBD 77). Artor, of course, had no personal use for so many coats, but, like Towsacom and Philip, he knew the social benefits that came with being a "coat man." Coats were used to barter for Indian labor in many other areas as well. In 1683, for example, the town of East Hampton authorized the payment of a coat valued at one pound for the services of a "ginman," who kept the town livestock pound (RTEH 2: 122–23).

The frequent references to coats in the surviving documents seldom describe them in any detail. English style coats with lace cuffs, buttons, and lining were highly valued and often seen in seventeenth- and eighteenth-century paintings of Indian sachems who donned them for the occasion, but these were not likely to have been distributed in large numbers in the Indian trade. The trooper's coat mentioned in the 1657 purchase of southern Brookhaven was one of the few to be found in the Long Island records. Such coats were often given to a prominent sachem who was in a position to aid the English. For example, Massasoit, the Wampanoag sachem, was given a red coat trimmed with lace, which he immediately put on in the presence of his men. He was said to have been pleased in his appearance and was, according to the English observer, "delighted to behold himself, and his men also to see their king so bravely attired" (Mourt [1622] 1993, 65; Welters 1993, 16).

As Laurel Ulrich has noted in *The Age of Homespun*, the coats more commonly used in the trade, called "Indian coats," were much more modest. These garments were brightly colored lengths of duffel or "trucking" cloth, six feet long and three feet wide, that were worn as a shawl across the shoulders (Ulrich 2001, 55). William Wood, writing in 1634, observed that the Indians used a piece of broadcloth as a coat by day and a blanket at night. He also noted that they carefully examined the material by "interposing it between the sun and them[selves]," to make certain that the weave was tight enough to keep out the cold (Wood [1634] 1968, 65). Robert Plot, writing about English textile production in the 1670s, said that the reds and blues "are colors that best please the Indians of Virginia and New England" (Plot 1677, 184). Plot also noted that Indians often cut holes in the cloth for their arms. Historian James Rice describes the coats given to the Piscataways by the governor of Maryland in 1676 as "bolts of high quality trading cloth" (Rice 2014, 742).

The coats listed in the probate inventories and account books for Long Island investors ranged in price from one to two pounds (RCSS 41, 59, 177, 312). Two small, unlined notebooks with entries dated 1686–90 (RFAC 1) and 1720–32 (RFAC 2), kept by Richard Floyd, who owned a large estate that included the eastern half of the Mastic Peninsula in Brookhaven, contained a wealth of information on trade goods taken by whalers on credit during the seasons.[1] He gave coats to ten of the thirteen Unkechaug Indians on his whaling crews. Meneges, for example, received three coats, one large coat with a lining valued at one pound and fifteen shillings, one at one pound and four shillings, and the third at one pound even (Strong and Lamont 2015, 21; RFAC 1: 2). The other coats were valued at one pound or had no price listed. These coats were probably English-style with sleeves more appropriate for whaling.

In response to the demand for coats, large numbers of ready-made coats for men and boys were shipped to the northern colonies. In 1682, nine hundred of such coats were imported into Philadelphia for a land purchase from the Lenape (Becker 2005, 769). In the mid-seventeenth century, heavy woolen coats were imported for the Indian trade by Boston merchants (Montgomery 1984, 159, 228). These garments, used by seamen, may have been distributed to the Indian whalers. The demand for European clothing also included shirts, britches, and stockings made of cotton and wool that gradually replaced traditional dress made from animal skins (Becker 2005).

Laurel Ulrich argues that the Indians abandoned traditional forms of dress because the animal pelts were too valuable as trade items, but she does not indicate what the Indians were purchasing with their pelts (Ulrich 2001, 55). Daniel Gookin, the superintendent of the Praying Indian towns in Massachusetts from 1660 to 1672, wrote that the Indians were selling their furs to the Dutch and English and then "buy of them for clothing a kind of cloth called duffel or trucking cloth, about a yard and a half wide" (Gookin [1674] 1972, 152; Welters 1993, 18). The entries in the whaling contracts confirm that the Indians on Long Island were also eager to obtain English-style clothing. These whaling contracts make it clear that the Indians were exchanging their hard labor as whalers for European clothing. The cloth apparel was easier to clean, to adjust to the contours of the body, and to accommodate the changing seasons (Lohse 1988, 397).

Whatever the motivation, it is clear, as Marshall Becker has concluded, that 1640 marks a time of transition from animal skin mantles to cloth (2005, 732). The references to coats from 1640 to about 1670 describe them as six-foot-long, five-foot-wide, brightly colored "trucking cloth" or "duffel" (Ulrich 2001, 55). Daniel Denton, an English resident in Hempstead on western Long Island, noted in 1670 that Indians were also replacing animal skins with broadcloth garments while maintaining the traditional forms and designs. "They hang it upon their shoulders," he said, and put a half yard of the same cloth "betwixt their legs and bring it up before and behind, and tie it with a girdle about their middle" (Denton [1670] 1968, 13).

Shoes and stockings also appear on the deeds and labor contracts. In some cases they asked for the tools to fashion their own apparel. In 1670, the Shinnecock whalers Towsacum and Philip Indian, in addition to the coats, stockings, shot, powder, and six bushels of corn, asked for a pair of shoes for each of them or a "block neck" (wooden foot-shaped form) to make them (RTSH 2: 55–57). The Indians who were skilled leatherworkers were beginning to make their own European-style footwear. This suggests that many Indians may have been wearing European-style clothing on a daily basis by this time. If so, it marks a change from the 1640s when the Indians in John Eliot's Praying Towns were the only ones observed wearing English-style clothing daily (Welters 1993, 18). Cultural historian Linda Welters proposes the mid-eighteenth century as the time of changeover from traditional Indian dress to English-style apparel in southern New England (Welters 1993, 25). The data from eastern Long Island, however, indicate that as a direct result of the whale design, this transition occurred much earlier here.

Another category of highly prized English goods were metal items (Lohse 1988, 396). Iron tools evoked a particular sense of awe. Indians, marveling at the array of English tools, at first thought of them as expressions of spiritual power (Axtell 1985, 11–12). Knives, hatchets, awls, fishhooks, hoes, and kettles appeared to have a special essence. They were more durable and convenient to use: the knives and hatchets, for example, held their edges. This sense of awe abated, of course, as the Indians became more familiar with the Europeans and their manufactures, but their dependence on these items never lessened. Archaeological sites in western New York reveal that as early as 1675 about 75 percent of the objects used by the Seneca were of European origin (Axtell 1981, 255). The whaling contracts and ledgers indicate that the percentage of European items in use by the coastal Algonquians would have been even higher by that time.

Women valued the iron and copper kettles as highly as the men did the coats, and they undoubtedly made that clear to the men (fig. 25). That was certainly the case with a company of ten Shinnecocks who signed up with John Howell, his brother Richard, and Joseph Raynor on the same day that Towsacum and Philip signed on with Laughton. Led by Paquanaug and Poireo, the Shinnecocks wanted, in addition to the goods they had received in the past (before contracts were placed on record), one iron pot for each man at the end

Figure 25 Iron pot from Montaukett burial site at Pantigo, East Hampton. Courtesy of the National Museum of the American Indian, Smithsonian Institution, Washington, D.C.

of the season (SHTA Liber A2: 85). The other goods probably included items similar to the ones paid to Towsacum and Philip. The wording in the contract suggests that the Indians had come to understand how the English capitalistic system worked. They reminded Howell and company that John Cooper gave his whaling crew iron pots, and they wanted equal pay, "such like the pots John Cooper gives to his Indians." The Shinnecock men, therefore, brought thirty iron pots into their village over a three-year period. The number of pots introduced over a relatively short time by the Indian whalers must have made a significant impact on their material culture as well as on methods of food preparation.

The coats, kettles, and tools were "one time" items, but three items always in high demand were gunpowder, lead shot, and alcohol, all of which had to be replenished as soon as they were consumed. The Shinnecock wanted powder and shot because they were still relying on wild game to supplement their food supply. The guns also gave them a sense of security against threats from potential enemies, but it increased their dependency on the European economy. The Indians had to keep returning to the English sources of shot and powder (Lohse 1988, 398–400). By the 1670s, guns were readily available in Indian communities as a result of the fur trade. Attempts to curtail the spread of firearms, gunpowder, and shot to Indians had never been very successful. Not only was the gun more effective than the bow and arrow for hunting, it was a fearsome weapon of war. The ownership of a gun immediately elevated an Indian's status and served as a symbol of independence and manhood (Brown 1980, 98–99; Lohse 1988, 396–97). During the latter half of the seventeenth century, the flintlock gradually replaced the more cumbersome matchlock, which required a lighted fuse and a flash pan to fire (Brown 1980, 68–79).

The prohibitions on the distribution of powder and shot to Indians were trumped by the economics of the whaling business. In October 1668, John Cooper, who was in the early stages of organizing his "whale design," requested an exemption from the colonial ordinances prohibiting the payments in powder to Indians. He argued that it would "be helpful and assisting to him in his design of killing whales and making oil, which is work tending to the public good and desires encouragement" (NYCD 14: 608–9). Towsacum and Philip, for example, were paid eighteen pounds of shot and three pounds of powder. Governor Lovelace complied with a provision limiting Cooper to a half barrel of powder a year and requiring that he give a report to the Court of Sessions.

The Deadly Medicine

The goods desired by the Shinnecocks, Unkechaugs, and Montauketts provide insights into the cultural transitions they were experiencing. A common stereotype, of course, focuses on the role of alcohol, an ideal commodity in a market system. It was quickly consumed, and the customer's needs remained unsatisfied. As soon as the last drop from the jug was drained, the customer was back for more. This inelastic demand curve enabled the company owners to recruit and manipulate Indian labor. The destructive impact of this product on Indian life and culture is well documented (Mancall 1995; Murray 2000, 24–28, 109, 110; Heath 1989). The alcohol trade, said historian Daniel Mancall, played a significant role as an enabler in the process of empire building in North America and in bringing Indians into the transatlantic market economy (Mancall 1995, 30–31).

Attempts to regulate alcohol consumption were no more successful than the efforts to limit the flow of guns into Indian communities. Even though the English feared that Indians under the influence might pose a threat to English persons and property, they recognized the advantages that the alcohol trade gave employers. Rum and cider were ubiquitous on Long Island, with a steady flow of rum from the West Indies into the Long Island market. The planters in Barbados wanted flour, whale oil, bacon, candles, and horses from Long Island and paid for them with rum, sugar, molasses, cocoa, and cotton (NYCD 5: 57). The English themselves consumed surprisingly large amounts of alcohol on a daily basis. Protocols enforced by social sanctions in European society, however, limited patterns such as binge drinking, which sometimes disrupted Native American communities. Although long historical experience with alcohol in European cultures had mitigated some of the destructive impact of drinking, alcohol abuse remained a significant social problem for the English as well (Rorabaugh 1979, 122–46).

The consumption of alcohol by whites during the colonial period was estimated by historians to have been about three pints a week, or approximately seven shots a day (Rorabaugh 1979, 7–8; Mancall 1995, 14). The estate inventory of Josiah Barthallomew, following his death in 1687, listed a "1 gill pot, a 1/2 gill pot and a wooden beer bowl," and a hogshead containing seven gallons of rum among his possessions (RCSS 306–7). The Royal British Navy gave a daily rum ration of one half pint or eight shots to the seamen. Unfortunately, the Floyd ledgers do not provide specific information about the daily alcohol consumption of the Indians, but some general patterns can be discerned. Eighty-five of the alcohol distributions recorded in the Floyd ledger for 1686 through 1690 were for rum and only twelve for cider (RFAC 1). Thirty-one of the rum portions were distributed in units of one or two gills (1 gill = 5 ounces), only slightly larger than the amounts set by the royal navy. The rum, probably distributed in "gill pots," was likely consumed during the workday. Small green glass bottles with a ten-ounce capacity have been found in a seventeenth-century Montaukett burial site in East Hampton. The entries in Richard Floyd's whaling ledger reveal the use of alcohol as an incentive to recruit and manipulate Indian labor (Strong and Lamont 2015).

The alcohol of choice was rum. Although most of the rum was distributed in small amounts, some ledger entries record larger portions ranging from one to three quarts. These amounts must have been carried off in containers much larger than the small green glass bottles found in the Indian graves (see below). The alcohol would likely have been distributed as a gift exchange or for trade to both Indians and non-Indian customers. Daniel Mancall in *Deadly Medicine*, his classic study of Indians and alcohol in the colonial period, observed that by the mid-eighteenth century "a fair number of Indians, many of them women, also became distributors of alcohol" (Mancall 1995, 57–61). He also noted that the participation of Indians in the liquor trade undermined the perception held by English officials that the Indians were consuming all the rum themselves.

Among the Indians working for Floyd who appear to have been entrepreneurs in the liquor trade was an Unkechaug Indian named Pemshan, who took five quarts of rum and a gallon of cider (RFL 1: 19v; Strong and Lamont 2015, 29). From the listing in the ledgers one can conclude that these items had been taken over a period of time prior to the date of the entry. The accounts in the ledger list the items and, in most cases, the cost on separate lines under the Indian names. Pemshan was a man of some stature in the Unkechaug community because he participated in important confirmation agreements for two tracts of land on the north shore in Brookhaven in 1687 (RCSS 152–54, 289–90). In a second account book from the 1720s, Floyd recorded that an Unkechaug named Surroot took rum in quart containers (RFL 2: 5, 7, 16).

Alcohol had quickly come to play a major role in the Indian trade. There were, however, serious related consequences that could not be ignored. Alcohol abuse could result in the disruption of both Indian and English families and communities. Southampton required a license to sell alcohol. In May 1658, one of the earliest applications came from John Cooper, asking permission "to operate an ordinary selling liquor and food with lodging for outsiders only" (RTSH 1: 120). When his son, John Jr., launched his whaling operation a decade later, he would have had no trouble securing alcohol to recruit Indian whalers. The Duke's Laws, which went into effect after the English established the colony of New York in 1664, required a license to sell alcohol to Indians. A number of entrepreneurs soon applied for such licenses.

In 1667, Governor Nicolls granted William Wells, the high sheriff, a one-year license to trade liquor to the Indians on the east end of Long Island "for their relief" (NYCD 14: 596). That last phrase is most ironic. This grant marks a shift in colonial policy about the regulation of alcohol. The economic advantages gained by bringing Long Island Natives into the labor force was eclipsing concerns about occasional outbursts of violent, alcohol-induced behavior by Indians. The long-term disruptive impact of alcohol abuse on family structures in Indian communities was of even less concern to a majority of the English.

In June 1669, John Laughton petitioned for permission to sell alcohol to Indian whalers. Governor Lovelace, Nicolls's successor, granted him a license to "dispose of or sell some small quantity of liquor and powder to the Indians that they may be more helpful to him in the whale fishing wherein he is a partner" (Paltsits 1910, 2: 459). John Laughton's partner was his brother, Josiah, who filed a contract for the 1670–71 whaling season. Although John is not named as an investor in the contract, he signed as one of the witnesses. John's liquor license was limited to one year and restricted to a total of three ankers (about thirty gallons) of liquor and thirty pounds of powder. John renewed the license for a third time in August 1671 (Paltsits 1910, 2: 470).

Concerns about the possibility that alcohol consumption by Indians might lead to violence against the English prompted Governor Lovelace to address a complaint from English residents in the eastern Long Island towns about "diverse abuses committed by Indians amongst themselves and sometimes amongst Christians, occasioned by their inordinate and excessive drinking of strong liquors whereof blood shed hath often ensued and frequently great danger of murder to be committed" (Paltsits 1910, 2: 463). Apparently, the ordinance in Duke's Laws prohibiting the "sale, truck, barter, giving any strong liquors to any Indian directly or indirectly, whatsoever . . ." was often ignored. The law carried a fine of forty shillings for the first pint and so on proportionately for greater or lesser quantities (Lincoln 1894, 1: 41). Lovelace ordered that the towns "cause laws prohibiting the abuse of selling liquor to the Indians to be put into execution." Lovelace, however, included a clause that revealed the triumph of economics over concerns about the public order. The ordinance, he said, did not apply to Indian whalers. They were exempted from the restrictions.

Although there are frequent reports about the abuse of alcohol by Indians, there are few references in the Long Island town records about alcohol-related acts of violence, suggesting that the fears expressed to Lovelace may have been inspired by stereotypes about Indians. The "working misunderstanding" underpinning the alcohol ordinances continued throughout the colonial period. Four years after Lovelace issued his ruling, his successor, Edmund Andros, addressed the issue by prohibiting the distribution of alcohol, powder, and shot. Although there was no exemption for whaling, the account books by Richard Floyd and William Smith document the continuing use of alcohol to recruit and manipulate Indian labor. There is a tendency unfortunately to view an Indian who has any involvement with alcohol as a hopeless alcoholic. The following case study reveals the superficiality of that perception.

Meneges and the Deadly Medicine

Meneges, called Tom by the English, was an experienced whaler who had hunted whales for four seasons from 1681 to 1685. He had also been appointed by his people to represent them in important Anglo-Indian affairs for three decades. Meneges was viewed as a man of good character, respected by both the English and the Unkechaug people. During King Philip's War, he served as an emissary between the Unkechaug and the English. However, he did, on one occasion, fall victim to the deadly medicine, and, according to his employer's ledger, he regularly consumed rum and cider. If one looked only at those documents, it might serve to reinforce a familiar stereotype of the "drunken, unreliable, and undisciplined" Indian. Fortunately, we have a larger historical and cultural context that provides a better understanding of Meneges and his times.

Meneges first appears in the colonial records in September 1674, when he was among the seven men called on by Tobacus, the Unkechaug sachem, in a negotiation for the sale of the south meadows on the Mastic Peninsula to the English (RTBH Hutchinson, 32–33). The following April Meneges agreed to "plant, weed and till an acre of Indian corn" for John Biggs of Brookhaven in exchange for a musket that was to be delivered in the first week of May. Meneges would not have possession of his gun for long. In June King Philip, the Wampanoag sachem, launched a bloody conflict that engulfed the New England colonies for two years. A month later the colonial authorities ordered that the Indians' guns be seized and held but that no other action be taken against them (NYCD 14: 692).

The procedure for sequestering the Indians' guns is not well documented, but the town likely handled it just as Southampton had in the late winter of 1668, when fears related to a confrontation between the Montauketts and the town of East Hampton spread to Southampton. The town seized twenty-two guns from the Shinnecock and distributed them among thirteen residents. Isaac Willmans took nine of them, Thomas Halsey took two, and the other eleven men each took one gun (RTSH 5: 23). It is quite likely that Richard Woodhall kept most of the Unkechaug weapons. The small number of firearms surrendered suggests that many did not comply with the ordinance.

That August, Andros sent a message to Woodhull, the Brookhaven magistrate, praising him for his successful actions in seizing the Unkechaug weapons and urging him to remain vigilant (NYCD 14: 695). For the Indians the action had significant political and cultural impact. Guns were essential hunting tools as well as weapons to protect their sovereignty. The order was an affront to a man's individual identity and a threat to the Unkechaugs' tribal independence, leaving them helpless in an unpredictable and often hostile world. Andros then left to consult with officials in New England about the progress of the conflict with King Philip.

As the tension mounted, Thomas Biggs, whose brother John had employed Meneges and promised him a gun, felt that stronger action should be taken. Unfortunately, the relationship between the brothers on this issue is not recorded, but it appears that John had a good relationship with the Unkechaugs. He later employed two sachems, John Mahue and Gie, to tend his crops (RTBH 1924: 113, 23, 54). Thomas wrote a letter to the lieutenant governor, Anthony Brockholes, who was serving as governor during Andros's absence, "relating some apprehensions" about the "ill designs" of the Unkechaug who had not returned to their villages and were "not as comfortable as they ought" with the order to disarm. In an attempt to reassure the English, the Unkechaug sachem, Tobacus, sent Meneges, who must have been known to Thomas, with a message of peace to Brockholes. Brockholes told Biggs that he had met with Meneges and ordered Biggs to keep careful watch, but to take no further action until Governor Andros returned from his meeting with the English officials in New England (NYCD 14: 695). A month later, Brockholes released the weapons to the Unkechaug in time for the fall deer hunt. The weapons of the Montauketts as well as the Manhansetts on Shelter Island, who were suspected of aiding the Narragansetts, remained impounded (NYCD 14: 697).

The governor's decision did not please Thomas Topping, who agreed with Thomas Biggs. In the fall of 1675, Topping, who was serving as the constable for Suffolk County at the time, wrote a letter to the governor decrying the devastating loss of "English blood by the cruel damned pagans." He voiced what was undoubtedly a widely held fear that the war might spread to Long Island and added ominously that he and many others were "sorry that the Indians here have their guns returned to them" (NYDH 2: 263–64).

When Andros returned in mid-September, he spoke to their concerns by issuing an order reminding people of the prohibitions on trafficking strong drink, guns, powder, or shot to the Indians (NYCD 14: 700). Four months later, in mid-January 1676, following King Philip's devastating attack that nearly wiped out the settlement of Springfield, Andros ordered that the Unkechaug and all the Indian communities on Long Island surrender their weapons and prohibited them from leaving their villages without specific permission from the local magistrates (NYCD 14: 711). In April, as the tide turned against Philip, a delegation of Unkechaugs and Indians from western Long Island met with Andros, pledging their loyalty and presenting him with a gift of wampum (NYCD 14: 718). The governor reciprocated with gifts of coats, tobacco, and tobacco pipes and promised to return their guns in time for the fall hunt. It is quite likely that Meneges, one of the few who could communicate in English, was with the Unkechaug delegation.

Meneges's involvement in these affairs had brought him into a close, perhaps paternalistic, relationship with Woodhull. In 1677, Meneges, who identified himself as "Mr. Woodhull's Tom," took a barrel of whale oil "in a tight cask" and five shillings worth of baleen to John Tooker (RTBH 1924, 50). He acknowledged the receipt of two coats as his payment. On another occasion the next year, he and an Unkechaug named Pauwas took another barrel of "good marketable oil in a good stanct [strong] cask" from John Tooker to Richard Smith Jr. (RTBH 1924, 52). In August 1678, Meneges, again identified as "Mr. Woodhull's Thomas Indian," affirmed that he had exchanged ten days of labor for John Tooker for a trucking cloth coat (RTBH 1924, 56). The references to Indians in the possessive reflect the pattern of paternal attitudes that were becoming the norm only two decades after the arrival of the Brookhaven freeholders in 1655. In another entry, for example, the town acknowledged that "Thomas Biggs either himself or his Indian" shall serve as the keeper of the town cattle pound (RTBH 1924, 160–61).

The next mention of Meneges in the records comes in October 1681 shortly before the opening of the 1681–82 whaling season. John Robinson, a twenty-seven-year-old owner of a mill in Cold Spring, Huntington Town, operated a mill that ground corn and sawed wood. He reported under oath before the town magistrate that Meneges, Pauwas, and two other Indians had broken into his house, frightened his wife and child, drunk his rum, ate his venison, smoked his tobacco, broken his windows, tread on his linen, and ransacked his home during an all-night debauch. According to Robinson, Pauwas came to his house demanding his gun, which Robinson had impounded against an unpaid debt (RTH 1: 316–17).

Meneges, probably either a friend or relative of Pauwas, had worked with him, transporting whale oil for Woodhull. He came either with Pauwas or soon after (the testimony is not clear on this) to support Pauwas in his confrontation with Robinson. The two Unkechaug men demanded that Robinson return the impounded gun to Pauwas. Robinson said that when he refused, they forced their way into his house and ordered him to fill a pail of rum for them. When they finished, two more Unkechaug Indians, Ahunshun (Ahuncham) and Memicksieys arrived and forced Robinson to roll out a barrel of rum that he had been storing in a back room. Ahunshun was a member of a prominent Unkechaug family who controlled extensive hunting territory around Moriches (Pelletreau 1903, 2: 259–60). His cousin, John Mahue, and another relative, Worishon, were later engaged in several land transactions in southern Brookhaven. What brought them all to Cold Spring in Huntington is not clear.

Robinson charged that Ahunshun and Memicksieys cocked their guns and pointed them at him and asked him to give them some venison and tobacco. While they were drinking, Robinson said that he hid an anker (ten gallons) of rum outside his house but that they found it. Robinson took his wife, Jane, and their baby out the back door and fled to a neighbor's home. The party lasted all night according to an Indian named Whatnews, who said he passed by the next morning and saw the Unkechaug men in the house. When Robinson returned, he said he found the house in shambles and some of his goods stolen, but declined to give an account of the damages.

Jane Robinson also gave her account of the incident to the magistrate. Her story differed in two important details. Pauwas, she said, had brought a broken gun for Robinson to repair. Her husband had replaced the stock and was holding it until Pauwas paid for the repair. She said that Meneges and Pauwas came together and asked her to show Meneges the impounded gun so that he could see how it was broken. This was an important fact that Robinson had not mentioned, with good reason. It was a violation of the Duke's Laws "to amend or repair guns belonging to any Indian" without a license from the governor upon penalty of ten pounds (Lincoln 1894, 1: 40–41). Jane also testified that David Scudder, the son of Henry Scudder, one of Huntington's founding families, had been present in the house when Meneges and Pauwas arrived. According to Jane, he left before the Indians began drinking, but he had been there long enough to observe the discussion about the repair of Pauwas's gun. The court transcript, however, does not include testimony from him.

Jane had more to say about the guns. She described a struggle between Pauwas and her husband over the gun. Meneges and Memicksieys, she said, intervened and helped Pauwas take the gun and two others from Robinson. The number of guns suggests that Robinson, who undoubtedly had mechanical skills, may have had a side business repairing guns for Indians. That would explain why the Unkechaug Indians from Brookhaven had come to Cold Spring on the western border of Huntington. The amount of rum stored in the Robinsons' home suggests that he may also have been in violation of the laws restricting the sale and distribution of liquor to Indians.

It is difficult to ascertain what was actually going on in the Robinsons' house. It is possible that if indeed he was engaged in illicit dealings with the Indians, he would not have reported the incident at all. The presence of David Scudder and the observations by Whatnews, however, would have raised suspicions from the magistrates. It is clear, nevertheless, that the abuse of alcohol was a factor. It was the sort of story that fueled stereotypes of Indians. It is important, therefore, to note that this one episode should not define Meneges and the others. Meneges's involvement with the negotiations during the crisis caused by King Philip's War was evidence that he was respected by his own people as well as by Woodhull, Brockholes, and the English.

The incident at Robinson's house did not deter Isaac Raynor from signing Meneges on to his whaling crew two month later, for the 1680–81 season.

Meneges was joined by Lenard, Toech, and Wamabaho (SHTA Book D2: 49). This season was Meneges's first, but Toech, Lenard, and Wamabaho were experienced whalers. Raynor provided the boats and equipment and gave them a half share of the catch. The next season Meneges went to sea for Henry Pierson, who offered the usual half share agreement, but there was one significant difference. Pierson included a clause requiring the crew members to continue whaling for him until their debts were cleared and imposed a fine of ten shillings for absences on the hunt and during the cutting and trying of the blubber (SHTA Book D2: 73). None of the crew members from the previous season joined Meneges this time. Whalers regularly changed companies and Meneges's name does not appear on a contract for the 1682–83 season, perhaps because he had found himself in debt to Pierson. In April 1683, he signed up for the 1683–84 season with a Brookhaven company owned by John Jennings under the same terms as he had accepted with Pierson (RTBH Book B: 169–70). This time his crew included Gy (Gie), an Unkechaug sachem, and Goodger, another prominent kinsman.

Meneges did not participate in the 1684–85 season. During the summer of 1684 he was among the Unkechaug representatives engaged with the town of Brookhaven over planting rights on Little Neck in Setauket (RTSH 5: 301–2). Meneges, his friend Pauwas, Goodger, and seven other Unkechaug men met with John Thompson and Richard Floyd and confirmed a former agreement giving the Unkechaug the use of the tract for a period of seven years. Jennings, Meneges's former employer, witnessed the transaction. Meneges, in spite of the incident at the Robinson homestead, had become a familiar and respected presence in Anglo-Indian relations on eastern Long Island.

In 1685, Meneges returned to the sea under contract to Joseph Tooker of Brookhaven. In the document he identifies himself as "Menegusth otherwise known as honest Tom Indian." The agreement stipulates that "the said honest Tom is to have a half share" and the said Tooker will provide the boat and equipment (RTBH Book B: 246). Meneges may have decided to come back to whaling because Tooker's contract made no mention of fines and had no clause extending the contract until all debts were paid. This was the last season that contracts were entered into the town records, so it is not known whether or not Meneges stayed with Tooker's company.

In 1688, Meneges was employed by a whaling company that included Richard Floyd, Richard Smith, and several other Brookhaven investors. The following list was an account of the goods Meneges received from Floyd for the 1688–89 whaling season:

To 3 pints and 1/2 of rum 0-7-0
To 1 pair of britches 0-6-0

To 1 coat 0-3-0
To 3 quarts of cider 0-1-6
To six quarts of cider 0-4-0
To 1 pair of stockings 0-4-0
To a lined large coat 1-15-0
To 1 pound of tobacco 0-1-0
To cash 0-1-6
To 4 quarts of cider 0-2-0
To 3 gills (1 gill = 5 oz.) of rum
To 5 gills of rum 0-2-6
To 1 peck of corn 0-2-0
To 1 coat 1-0-0
To 9 gills of rum 0-4-6
To 1/2 bushel of corn 0-2-0
To 4 gills of rum 0-2-0
To 3 gills of rum 0-1-6
To 2 gills of rum 0-1-0
To 2 gills of rum 0-1-0
To 6 gills of rum 0-3-0

Meneges's list reflects a pattern of consumption consistent with that of the other Indians in the ledger. Apparently, this entry was a running account of items taken over a period of time, perhaps a whaling season. Unfortunately, the list does not indicate the time intervals at which the gills of rum were taken. The two-gill portions (ten ounces) may have been a daily allotment, a little more than the half pint (eight ounces) daily rum ration in the British Navy (Rorabaugh 1979, 7–8; Mancall 1995, 14). The pattern of alcohol consumption indicated in the account books suggests that alcohol was used to manipulate the whalers and other Indian laborers (RFAC 1: 2).

Meneges may have worked for Floyd for several years, but there is only one other entry for him: charges for a half pound of powder with no date. Two years later he served as the interpreter for a negotiation in 1690 between an Unkechaug named John Mahue and William Tangier Smith of St. George Manor for a tract of land on Mastic (SGMA File AF10). Meneges is identified on the deed as "Tom Ye Interpreter." Over the next three years Meneges was involved in four more transactions with Smith for Unkechaug lands on the Atlantic shore that would become a part of his manorial estate (Strong 2011, 84–89). When Smith's patent was granted in 1697, the manor covered nearly eighty thousand acres, approximately half of Brookhaven Town.

Meneges's story undermines the simplistic stereotypes about Indians and alcohol by providing a more nuanced understanding on a personal level. The raucous behavior in the Robinsons' home has to be put in the larger perspective of his life story. Richard Woodhull and the whaling company owners did not judge Meneges on that incident nor did his kinsmen, who continued to rely on his language skills and his abilities as a representative in their negotiations with the English. Conrad Weiser, Pennsylvania's emissary to the Iroquois, told of an Indian named Andrew Montour, who would binge drink on occasion but was good natured and reliable when sober. Meneges's involvement with alcohol when he worked for Richard Floyd actually reflects badly on the English because it reveals the insidious role that the deadly medicine played in the control and manipulation of Indian labor (Mancall 1995, 27–28).

Grave Goods: Old and New

The demand for European goods did not mean that the Indians had abandoned their traditions and values along with their skins and stone tools. Amid the many changes in material culture during the decades following the arrival of the Europeans, deeply held aboriginal beliefs and practices remained. The new European goods, for example, were often incorporated into the ancient practice of honoring the dead with material gifts. One of the universal characteristics of prehistoric burials is the presence of materials believed to be useful in the spirit world after death. Although the materials had changed along with definitions of "basic necessities," this practice continued into the seventeenth century.

Excavations of postcontact burials located at the end of Long Island's southern fork—at Burial Point, near Montauk; Three Mile Harbor; and Pantigo Hill, near the village of East Hampton—provide insights into this tradition. Two other similar sites were found in southern Rhode Island at West Ferry on Conanicut Island, near Newport, and at Burr Hill, near the town of South Warren (Saville 1977; Simmons 1970; Gibson 1980; Latham 1978a, 1978b; Strong 1993). The Pantigo burials reflect the cultural transitions experienced by the whalers and their communities. In one case, there is evidence of a direct connection linking a Montaukett whaler named Wobetom (a.k.a. Awabetum, Awabetom, Awaupetun) with a burial in a seventeenth-century Indian cemetery. In 1917, Foster Saville, under the sponsorship of the National Museum of the American Indian and the Heye Foundation, excavated fifty-eight burials at the Pantigo Hill site (Saville 1977, 16). One of the graves may have been the burial place of Wobetom, who hunted whales for companies headed by the Reverend Thomas James in 1675, John Wheeler in 1681, and John Miller Jr. in 1684 (RTEH 1: 381–82; RTEH 2: 98–99, 152–53). Wobetom had also worked as a cattle keeper for John Mulford in 1670 (RTEH 1: 330). A globular green glass bottle with a short neck inscribed with the name "Wobetom" was

Figure 26 Green glass bottle inscribed with the name Wobetom, from the Montaukett burial site, Pantigo, East Hampton, N.Y. Courtesy of the National Museum of the American Indian, Smithsonian Institute, Washington, D.C.

found in the grave (fig. 26). Unfortunately, the burial was in an area that had been badly disturbed, making it impossible to determine any further details. Twenty of the other graves, however, brought to light a wealth of information about postcontact funerary practices and beliefs.

In the nineteenth century, an excavation for a canal connecting a mill to a pond in Queens County revealed a precontact burial containing several Indian graves. It was not excavated by professionals but by a local historian, Henry Onderdonck, who believed that it was an early eighteenth-century interment. Near the head of each individual, a glass bottle still containing liquid and what was described as a tomahawk were found (Onderdonck [1822] 1923, 106). In an act that reflected nineteenth-century attitudes toward Indians, one of the bottles was opened and sampled. The rum was judged to be of good flavor and about a century old. Unfortunately, no other details were recorded. Not surprisingly, the report focused on the two grave objects that underscored the conventional stereotypes about Indians.

A small burial site with the graves of three adults, two males and a young female, excavated in 1917 at Three Mile Harbor, a short distance from Pantigo and some of the burials at West Ferry and Burr Hill, revealed a similar pattern of cultural accommodation (Latham 1978a, 6; 1978b, 19–20). The traditional practice of wrapping the deceased in a burial shroud of animal skins or matting continued, but with trade blankets and European-made textiles used instead. At Pantigo twenty-one of the individuals appeared to have been wrapped in "trade blankets, other textiles, bark or animal skins" (Saville 1977, 18, 26). Several burials at Burr Hill and West Ferry in Rhode Island were also covered with textiles (Simmons 1970, 63; Gibson 1980, 17–21).

Another more dramatic expression of this pattern was found at Montauk and at a site in Rhode Island. In Montauk an adult male Montaukett was buried in what appears to have been a wooden coffin constructed with nails. The goods in the coffin included textiles and shoe buttons. In a second such burial located nearby, a female in her twenties was dressed or wrapped in a red textile cloak or dress and interred in a mahogany coffin (Strong 1993, 609). The woman, evidently of high status, may have been Wyandanch's daughter Quashawam, or his widow, Wuch-i-kit-taw-but. She wore beads and a string of copper bells, and the remains of a small dog lay near her head. The presence of dog sacrifices in female graves was not uncommon in precontact burials; the dog's role may have been to accompany the deceased into the spirit world (Strong 1985).

A high-status female burial excavated in Rhode Island in the 1920s was believed to be the grave of Weunquash, a Narragansett sunksquaw (Chapin 1927, 18–32). This woman had been buried in a hollowed-out log coffin along with a five-gallon iron kettle filled with smaller pots, kettles, and skillets, and a large brass pot full of spoons and bottles. The deceased wore a silk robe and cap, leather moccasins with copper soles, a decorative metal chain, a wampum belt with a silver ornament, a necklace, and silver sleeve buttons. Beside her were a mortar and pestle, two coins, a set of Dutch spoons, some thimbles, several Dutch pipes, and a bottle of brandy.

Susan Gibson, archaeologist at the Haffenreffer Museum, concluded that the data from these seventeenth-century sites reflect a continuation of a traditional burial complex incorporating new goods rather than a rejection of ancient customs (Gibson 1980, 13). Archaeologist Constance Crosby expanded on this theme in her study of the burials at the New England sites in her attempt to understand the ritual aspects invested in the European-manufactured grave goods (Crosby 1988). Crosby concluded that the incorporation of these goods revealed the "growing importance and autonomy of individuals, often at the expense of group interests." The Indians, she said, were selecting European items and investing them with a form of spiritual power. This power, referred to by many Indians as *Manitou*, might appear in any form (Salisbury 1982, 39). The effectiveness of an iron plough in preparing a field, a gun for hunting, and a harpoon for whaling were seen as manifestations of Manitou. Crosby argued that by investing these items with such meaning the Indians created bridges of understanding that served to link "two disparate cultures and worldviews and in the process transform themselves and their ideology" (Crosby 1988, 202).

The universal desire for material goods and the increasing amount of European products now available placed a considerable strain on traditional values and customs. The adoption of European goods, however, did not undermine basic traditional values. As these goods became widely available they were often incorporated into Native ceremonies and belief systems, such as burial rites and status markers. Native people lived, as ethnohistorian Kathleen Bragdon has noted, "in a world filled with objects they did not create, clothed in garments that evolved in another social context"; yet, as she concludes, they took their own path to becoming modern Americans (Bragdon 1996, 234).

The persistence of traditional values during this time of change can be seen in Governor Lovelace's 1675 ordinance restricting the distribution of alcohol to the Indians. In a separate clause he prohibited "Powwowing in or near the towns," on the grounds that it was an "outward form of devil worship" and "contrary to the laws established in these his Royal Highnesses territories and dominions." Lovelace was restating a provision in the initial body of legislation called Duke's Laws, set forth by Governor Nicolls after the English seized New Netherland. The clause prohibited powwows, ordering that "no Indian whatsoever shall be at any time be suffered to Powwow or perform outward worship to the devil in any town in this government" (Lincoln 1894, 1: 42). It is noteworthy that the Indians maintained many of their traditional ceremonies and belief systems while they were in the process of adjusting to the English market economy and adopting European manufactured goods.

6

Debt Peonage and Indentured Servitude

Entering the Global Marketplace

At the same time that Indians were being absorbed into the local English economy, that economy itself was going through significant changes. Long Island farmers continued exporting agricultural products to the West Indies in exchange for sugar and rum, but this exchange was dwarfed by whale oil trade with Europe. Now, for the first time, the Long Island farming families could afford such luxury goods as mahogany furniture, fine linen, pewter ware, and porcelain.

David Goddard, in his analysis of similar transformations in the history of Southampton, agrees with T. H. Breen, adding that the winter whale oil production enabled the small whaling companies to enter the European commodity trade (Goddard 2011, 15). "Without exports," wrote Breen, "they could not participate in this enticing consumer market." In a larger sense, as William Cronon noted in *Changes in the Land*, both Indian and English cultural communities were becoming part of a single world, a global community (Cronon 1983, 14–15). Ironically, it was these material desires that drew the Indians deeper into the local English market system and ensnared them in a web of debt.

Origins of the Contract System, 1670–1672

The contracts are an invaluable source of historical and anthropological data. They list the names of the leading investors, the terms agreed to with the Indians, the dates and duration of the contract, the names of most of the Indians, and the signatures or marks of the witnesses. Unfortunately, most of them give only one or two of the investors' names, followed by the phrase "and associates." Although the contracts provide important insights for scholars today, the local historian William Pelletreau, who in 1873 discovered the original Southampton Town records rolled into coils and stored in cloth bags, did not consider them significant enough to include the full text in the published records. Pelletreau, reflecting the biases of his time, ignored or abstracted many whaling contracts, publishing only the names of the English investors. In many instances he decided arbitrarily to make abstracts of documents, noting that "nothing is omitted therein, which sheds light upon the genealogical or historical facts recited in the originals" (RTSH 2, preface). He did not consider the names of the Indian whalers on the abstracted documents to be significant "historical facts" worthy of preservation in the published records.

The contracts obliged the whalers to serve the employers, sometimes addressed as "masters," for the season, which usually ran from December to March. The length of time stipulated in the contracts is not consistent, varying from one season to an indefinite term related to the whaler's indebtedness to the company owners. Many contracts included a clause stipulating that the whaler had to continue whaling for the company "until all debts to the company were resolved." These contracts would soon become a form of debt servitude that might continue for many years because Indians frequently ended each season in debt to the company for the value of goods, particularly alcohol, taken on credit. Company owners could be taken to court if they hired an Indian who had not paid his debts to his employer.

Compounding the debts incurred for the goods taken were the fines imposed for absenteeism. The Indians, unaccustomed to the patterns and obligations expected in the English contract system, often showed up irregularly during the season. Frustration with the limits of their control over Indian labor led many owners to impose bonds and fines. John Cooper was the first to make use of such measures in his 1672 contract. The whalers were fined for every day they were absent during the season. Henry Pierson inserted a clause in his contract with a crew of Shinnecock whalers, stipulating that they had to continue going to sea every season for him "til we have cleared all debts to him whatsoever" (SHTA Book D2: 73). In 1675, Jacob Schellinger went one step further and required his whalers to agree to pay a bond of ten pounds if they failed to meet the obligations of the contract. Their only capital was the promise of their labor in the future. A day laborer in the seventeenth century could earn from two to three schillings a day. At that rate it would take a whaler from two to three months of labor to pay off the bond.

The patterns in the contracts suggest that the system may have developed, in part, as a means of preventing rival company owners from luring away the more competent and reliable hunters. Many of the contracts signed on fewer than the twelve men needed for two whaleboats. In some cases, there were not even enough to launch a single boat, suggesting that the other whalers in the boats had been hired without a written contract.[1] If so, there would have been a considerable number of hunters each season who were, for whatever reason, not under contract to the company owners. Possibly only the best and most experienced whalers were put under contract to secure them for the owner. If so, they would likely include the steersman and the harpooner. Andrew Lipman, noting the arrangement of two names side by side and above the other four on a 1673 whaling contract, postulated that the two names set apart might have belonged to men with these specialized skills (Lipman 2015, 230). Although there are no other contracts with this particular arrangement, it is possible that the harpooner and steersmen might precede the other names on the contracts. Eleven of the ninety-seven surviving contracts list only one whaler, while ten others were individual agreements with a single whaler, suggesting that these men may have had such skills.

Recruiting whalers became a sharply competitive enterprise. To secure the best hunters, the owners began their recruiting for the season earlier and earlier. In some cases, Indians were hired in the spring or earlier, long before the season opened the following November.[2] It became customary for company owners to give each whaler a payment of twenty-five pence in addition to goods on credit as many as six or seven months in advance (NYCD 14: 708). After the goods, or a portion of them, were delivered by a company owner, rival owners might come along in October and offer more goods to those whalers not under contract, leaving an owner without a full crew at the beginning of the season. The whalers were faulted for succumbing to the offers from unscrupulous owners.

The first contract, entered into the records on November 15, 1670, by Josiah Laughton of Southampton, secured the services of two whalers, Towsacom and Philip from Shinnecock, who agreed to hunt whales for three seasons (RTSH 1: 56–57). It appears that Laughton wanted to make sure he had two skilled and reliable men who would form the core of a whaleboat crew. The contract was written as if dictated by Towsacum: "Know all men by these presents that I Towsacom and Philip Indians do and by these presents have bound and engaged our selfs in my own person God permitting life and health unto Josiah Laughton of Southampton and his assignes to go to sea for . . . three complete seasons . . . at Mecox for ye killing and striking of whales and other great fish." The beach at Mecox, an ideal location for launching whaleboats, encloses a tidal pond east of Southampton Village.

Three days later John Howell and Joseph Raynor negotiated a contract with ten Shinnecock Indians led by Paquanung and Poireo (SHTA Liber A2: 85). Both companies must have employed men who were not under contract because Laughton needed four crew members to man a single boat operation and Howell was two men short for a two-boat whale design. It is possible, of course, that Howell sent out two boats manned with a total of ten men who were not under contract.

The contracts, following English legal protocol, were usually signed by at least one Christian witness. The practice presumed that "Christian" was synonymous with "English" and that Indians were vulnerable to manipulations by unscrupulous English entrepreneurs. The absence of a "Christian" witness might make the contract vulnerable to a court challenge. Ironically, no objections were raised if an Englishman recruited a family member to endorse transactions. Surprisingly, in fifteen instances women, who had very limited standing in the colonial courts unless they were single widows or unmarried daughters, served as witnesses.[3]

It was acceptable for Indians to serve as witnesses as long as they were accompanied by at least one English witness. One unusual document bears the endorsement of a Christian woman and a Montaukett Indian. This agreement, negotiated in 1679 between the Reverend Thomas James's company and two Montaukett whalers named Major and Toby, was witnessed by the reverend's eldest daughter, Sarah, and Matompact (a.k.a. Humphrey), a Montaukett (RTEH 2: 77). It would be interesting to know how that came about. The contract is yet another reminder of the family network linking the eastern Long Island elites in a web of economic and political power. The two men, Thomas Dimon and John Stratton, who formed the whaling company with James, were both related to him by marriage. His daughter Mary, one of his ten children, was married to Stratton, and another daughter, Hannah, was the wife of Thomas Dimon's brother, James (Rattray 1953, 562, 283).

The other contracts witnessed by Indians include the Shinnecock contract, two from Brookhaven, one from East Hampton, and one from Southampton. Achedouse, who signed as a witness for a contract between Joseph Tooker and Meneges in 1685; Jacquonung, who endorsed a contract for Andrew Gibb of Brookhaven on March 10, 1681/2; Tauknan, who made his mark on a contract for Joseph Tooker's brother, John; and Poaguamo, one of the witnesses on the Shinnecock contract in 1671, were not whalers (RTBH Book B: 246; SHTA Book D2: 74–75; RTBH Book B: 175). The others, Humphrey (a.k.a. Matomapait) and Scomake, both Montauketts, and Jonaquam, a Shinnecock, had been to sea for at least one season. There is no discernible pattern here. Perhaps these men had been called on as witnesses because of their status in both the Indian and the English communities (RTEH 2: 77; RTEH 1: 430–31; SHTA Liber A2: 90).

Although there had been discussion about the need for legal redress for some time, a question remained about enforcement. A month before Laughton recorded his contract, Francis Lovelace, the colonial governor, had yet to take a position on the matter. John Cooper brought the issue to the governor's attention prior to the 1670–71 whaling season with a complaint against John Topping. He accused Topping of luring away one of his whalers, leaving him without a full crew. Cooper complained to Governor Lovelace that two Indians he had hired left him and went whaling for Topping (Paltsits 1910, 2: 476).

On December 8, 1670, shortly after Laughton entered his contract into the Southampton Town records, Lovelace responded by issuing an order stating that if John Cooper, "who is said to be one of the first that brought Indians to be serviceable in that design . . . , hath already made any agreement with any of the Indians upon this account for any particular season or time precedent to what hath been made with them by others, the first agreement is to stand good and if the Indians so agreed with do refuse to make good their engagement [with Cooper] they are not to be permitted to work with any others . . " (NYCD 14: 646; Paltsits 1910, 2: 460).

Topping objected to the governor's ruling, but the governor did not respond. Instead he passed the matter over to John Mulford and the Commission on Indian Affairs the following February. Mulford let the governor's order stand, thereby endorsing the new precedent and establishing a basic legal protocol for the whaling contract system that remained in place for the next fifteen years (Paltsits 1910, 2: 457). Shortly thereafter the governor made it clear that his ruling applied to Cooper as well. When John Topping's brother Elnathan, charged that John Cooper had hired four Indians who were under a previous contract with him, Governor Lovelace ruled that the Indians were to "remain in the service of the said Elnathan Topping and Benjamin Hand" (Christoph and Christoph 1982, 402).

The incidence of such contract violations is difficult to document because the owners apparently settled the matter most of the time without going to court. A close look at the recorded contracts, however, reveals what certainly appears to be examples of "contract jumping." An Indian named Addam signed on with Jacob Schellinger of East Hampton in the summer of 1675 and then joined Thomas James's crew the following December (RTEH 1: 378–79, 381–83). In 1679, Jeremy Indian signed with Richard Howell in January 1679 and then with Thomas Cooper Jr. a month later (SHTA Liber A2: 122, 123). That same year Scanderbag jumped from a contract signed on March 13 with Richard Shaw of East Hampton to hunt whales for Jacob Schellinger three weeks later (RTEH 2: 78–79, 430–31).

These incidents and perhaps others as well prompted John Topping, somewhat hypocritically, to write Governor Andros on December 6, 1680, complaining,

Diverse of my neighbors of Easthampton have been with me complaining that they are like to be much disappointed and damnified in their business of whaling by the decites and unfaithfulness of the Indians with whom they did contract the last spring for their service in whaling this present season, who notwithstanding said contracts under hand and seal do now betake themselves to the service of other men who do gladly accept them pretending some former engagement by which they intend to hold them. So yet the Indians having received goods of one man in the spring . . . and now again of another to fit them for the sea, leave their masters to quarrel. (NYCD 14: 756–57)

Andros responded to Topping's ordering that contracts engaging Indians already under contract with another company owner "to be void and the Christian soe doing to be proceeded against for damage to the first contractor" (NYCD 14: 757). The contract "jumping," however, continued on occasion throughout the period when the contracts were recorded (1670–85). Only three months after Andros's response, Samuel Mulford of East Hampton complained that fellow townsman John Wheeler had signed on a Montaukett Indian named Witness, who was under contract to him. Mulford, unlike Topping, charged that both Witness and Wheeler were guilty of contract violations (RTEH 2: 100).

The early contracts recorded by Laughton and Howell were based on the colonial barter system wherein goods were exchanged for services. Howell agreed to pay the Indians "what they had done the three years before" and, in addition, an iron pot "as John Cooper gives to his Indians." They were to hunt whales in exchange for coats, shoes, stockings, shot, powder, and a bushel of Indian corn apiece at the end of each season. The total value of the goods offered by Laughton was slightly over twenty-two pounds, based on the prices listed in the Suffolk County estate records (RCSS). Each man therefore earned about seven pounds for a three-month whaling season, a little more than two pounds a month. English day laborers, in comparison, earned three shillings a day. If they worked for twenty-five days a month, they would earn about three pounds for work on shore in safer and in far less arduous conditions. The system worked well for the owners unless the company failed to kill any whales that season, in which case they still had to give the Indians the goods. That would seem fair enough because the whalers had dutifully gone to sea or put in their time on the cold winter beaches watching for signs of the whales. The owners, dissatisfied with having to pay whalers after an unsuccessful season, soon found a way to avoid that obligation.

The interest in shore whaling was increasing sharply. In January 1671, several Brookhaven residents applied to the governor for permission to purchase Indian land on the south shore "to better prosecute the design of whale fishing" (NYCD 14: 649). Four months later the town of Huntington issued its first ordinance related to whaling, ordering that "no foreigner or any other persons of any other town upon this island shall have the liberty to kill whales or any other small fish within the limits of our bounds at the south side . . ." (RTH 1:

179). It was the Southampton investors, however, who took the lead in the whaling business.

John Cooper was quick to follow the precedent set by Howell and Laughton. On March 4, 1671, at the end of the 1670–71 season, he signed the contract with a Shinnecock named Artor, engaging him to hunt whales for the next ten seasons. The agreement (mentioned briefly below and in the previous chapter) was not endorsed by a Christian witness and may not have been enforceable in the courts. It appears that the protocol for these agreements with Indian whalers was still a work in progress.

Two months later John Howell's brother, Arthur, signed a Shinnecock named Akuctattrias to a one-year contract to hunt and flense whales in exchange for one coat in advance and two more coats, a pair of shoes, a pair of stockings, one bushel of corn, a half-pound of powder, and three pounds of shot. Akuctattrias agreed "to engage myself that god permitting me life and health I will in my own person go to sea for Arthur Howell" (SHTA Liber A2: 88). In June Anthony Ludlam reached an agreement with an Indian named Atungquion, who asked for one coat in advance, one coat when the season was half over, and one coat at the end of the season (SHTA Liber A2: 87). Neither Akuctattrias nor Atungquion appears to have been satisfied with his experience, because neither name is found on any other contracts after this.

A Company of Their Own: Challenging the System

The barter arrangements for the first season under the contract system were challenged in the fall of 1671 by a group of Indians who entered an agreement into the Southampton Town archives (SHTA Liber A2: 90). A company of seventeen Shinnecocks and one Montaukett formed their own whaling company. The date on the contract notes the day and month, November 24, but not the year. The previous three pages include entries made by Henry Pierson, the town clerk, in the summer and fall of 1671. It seems likely, therefore, that the contract was entered in that year. The first to sign was Anthony Indian, who may have taken the lead in the undertaking. Another of the Shinnecocks was Artor, who decided to simply ignore his ten-year agreement with Cooper, perhaps because he knew there had been no Christian witnesses. Papasaquin, a Montaukett, may have had kinship connections among the Shinnecocks. He had come from Montauk after a failed attempt at resisting English control over the Montauketts. His story will be told in the next chapter.

The Indians bound themselves "jointly and severally . . . that god permitting life and health we will attend all opportunities to go to sea." They also agreed "to do our best endeavor to save what shall be by god's providence procured or gotten by us upon the penalty of three pence a day [if] any of us shall be negligent either in the going to sea or giving attendance in the cutting out of what fish or fishes be taken" (SHTA Liber A2: 90). They planned to launch their boats from the beach at Sagaponack, an area near the border between Southampton and East Hampton (see map 4).

The reference to God's providence and the legal language of the contract was similar to that found in contracts entered into the records by Howell and Ludlam, suggesting that Anthony probably had some help, perhaps from the three English witnesses who endorsed the contract.[4] The use of English legal structures here may mark the early stages of assimilation wherein the Indians began to make use of these norms in an effort to protect their own interests. In addition to the three Englishmen, two Shinnecock Indians, Jonaquam and Poaguamo, also signed as witnesses. The two names underscore the unusual nature of this contract. Indian witnesses endorsed only five other contracts between 1670 and 1685, and in only one other case were there two Indian witnesses. Poaguamo's name does not appear on any other contract, nor on any of the deeds and indentures during this time. Jonaquam, however, participated in five whale hunts from 1675 to 1683. Jonaquam, along with Lenard and Artor, was listed on a 1698 census of Shinnecock men taken by Matthew Howell (Howell 1887, 42–43).

Another marker of culture change here is the adoption of English names. When Indians became more involved in the English economy as laborers and consumers they often took on an English name at the urging of their employer for his convenience. Four of the seventeen whalers on the contract had adopted English names; Anthony, Artor, Jeremiah, and Lenard. Jonaquam later anglicized his name to John Aquam on a contract in 1675 (SHTA Liber A2: 99–100). This transition undoubtedly also marks a decline in the use of traditional languages.

The English investors, whose families owned the trying stations; the warehouses storing the oil and bone; the access to the markets in New York and Boston; and the support of local political and judicial officials posed insurmountable challenges to the Indian company. Members of the Topping and Howell families, for example, held influential political positions in the local and colonial government. John Howell, who had negotiated a three-year whaling contract in 1670, was appointed justice of the peace for East Riding (present-day Suffolk County) in October 1671 (Christoph and Christoph 1982, 448). The Shinnecock found themselves on the margins of an economic system controlled by their employers.

Governor Lovelace, who relied on the support of these Southampton families, expressed a high opinion of Howell and vested him with the full power and authority to enforce the laws of the colony. Howell had also been appointed to

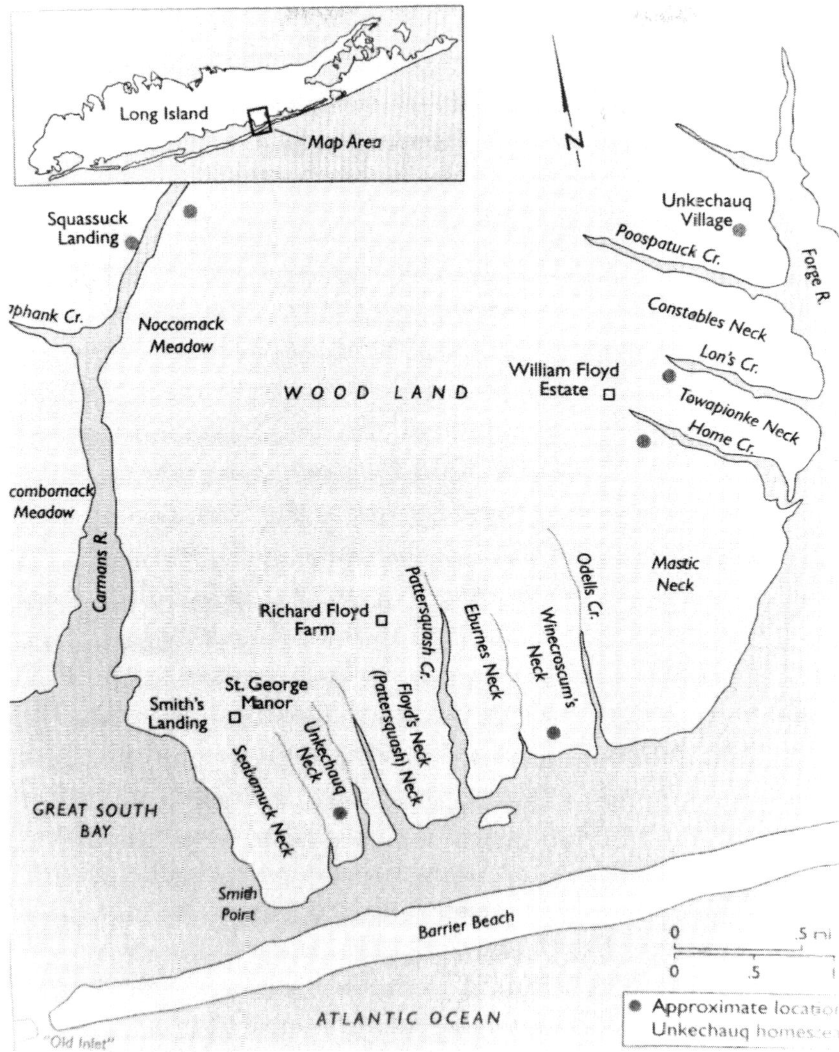

Map 4 Map of Mastic Peninsula, showing the Floyd and Tangier Smith Estates and the approximate locations of the Unkechaug villages.

the Commission on Indian Affairs by the governor. John and Thomas Topping, who negotiated a whaling contract in May 1672, were frequently elected or appointed to serve as magistrates and town overseers. Governor Lovelace's predecessor, Richard Nicolls, had appointed Thomas Topping and John Howell to represent the town of Southampton at the Hempstead conference in 1664, where the legal structure of the new colony was drafted. The two families were closely related by marriage. John Topping's second wife was Deborah Howell, the daughter of John Howell's brother, Edward, who also invested in a whaling operation (Howell 1887, 300–306; SHTA Liber A2: 121). An independent Indian whaling operation had little chance to prevail against these odds.

Not surprisingly, no further mention of the Indians' company appears in the records. Six of the Shinnecocks, recognizing the cards were stacked against them, moved on, joining English companies the following spring. Cowus, Lenard, Quanuton, and Pinis were recruited by John Topping. Jeremiah joined John Laughton's crew, and Sacaspan went to sea for John Cooper (SHTA Liber A2: 93; SBD 36–38). Artor may have returned to John Cooper's employ. Seven of the seventeen members of the company, however, never went whaling, apparently unwilling to work for an English contractor.

A Trucking Coat or Half the Blubber: Southampton Town Ordinance, 1672

The Southampton Town officials, fearing that experienced and reliable Indian whalers might demand more goods, due to their scarcity, approved an ordinance regulating the payments to Indian whalers. The ruling established that "whosoever shall hire an Indian to go a whaling shall not give him for his hire above one trucking cloth coat for each whale he and his company shall kill or half the blubber, without the whale bone" (NYCD 14: 475). The ruling presented the owners with a choice of a direct payment in kind of twelve coats for the men on the two crews or half of the blubber to be divided up among them. The second option removed the obligation to pay for the whalers' time during an unsuccessful season. Both options protected the owners from having to pay competitive wages. The Indians could not bargain with the owners as the Shinnecock whalers had, when they demanded iron pots "as John Cooper gives to his Indians."

The half share of the blubber as payment soon became the standard arrangement, one that was still in effect until the decline of the whaling era in the mid-nineteenth century. The share was usually paid in goods, not cash. In most cases it appears that the investors gave each crew member what amounted to a letter of credit against which he could purchase the items offered by the company owners. Unlike contracts negotiated the previous fall, the new agreements established that Indians would be paid on commission. A good season, such as the one recorded in William Tangier Smith's ledger for 1706–7, could bring in as many as seven whales and produce over two hundred barrels of oil (PSB, Memorandum). The following year, however, none were killed. The Indians, therefore, received nothing for their labor and found themselves in debt because they had received some goods in advance. They also had to pay for the gills of alcohol they had consumed during the season.

The investors kept a record of the total amount of blubber and the market value. The goods received by each Indian whaler were listed by his name along with the market value set by the investor. Prices of the goods would then be deducted from the individual's portion of the half share. Accounts kept by the Tangier Smith family reveal that the Indians ended each season encumbered with a debt against the anticipated share of the following season (see below). They were trapped in an endless cycle of debt. This explains, in part, why only twenty-seven of the 290 Indians who signed contracts between 1670 and 1685 went to sea for more than one or two seasons (see appendix 1).

The lay share agreement did not go into effect immediately. A few weeks after the new regulations were issued, whalers who had joined with the independent Shinnecock company in the fall of 1671 began signing up with English employers, apparently deciding this was the best they could do under the circumstances. Josiah Laughton's brother, John, and James Herrick hired four Indians, including Jeremiah, from the Shinnecock company. Three days later, Captain Thomas Topping and his son, John, hired nine Shinnecocks, three of whom had been with the company: Phineas, Cowes, and Quanuton. These contracts did not spell out the terms of employment, stating only that the Indians would receive "what other Indians hath for the design during this season" (SHTA Liber A2: 93). There was no mention of the "half-share" option in these contracts, but most likely this is what the other Indians were getting.

John Cooper's Contract, June 17, 1672

John Cooper Jr., an astute entrepreneur, negotiated an unusually detailed agreement with eighteen Shinnecocks in the spring following the Indians' attempt to establish their own company. The contract provides important insights into the economic and cultural aspects of shore whaling on Long Island. Cooper did not bring in any copartners to help finance the operation because his family was one of the more prosperous in Southampton. When John Cooper Sr., one of the town founders, died in 1662, he left his son his estate. The young man was familiar with the tools and procedures used in the processing of whale oil and baleen and the logistics involved in shipping these products to market. Cooper also would have had knowledge, if not direct experience, with the equipment and strategies that worked best for killing whales. The characteristics of the North Atlantic right whales were, by now, well known to most residents on eastern Long Island. Cooper, undoubtedly influenced by John Ogden's efforts and his father's business acumen, soon became one of the leading whaling company owners.

In May 1672, matters related to whaling again came before the governor's council. John Cooper complained that the Unkechaugs had carried away the baleen from a whale beached on the shore area he had leased in southern Brookhaven. Cooper was authorized to investigate the matter and "make seizure of such whalebone if it be found" (NYCD 14: 665). No further mention of the matter is made, perhaps because the council was more concerned about the English who harvested the baleen and blubber from the town beaches without paying the colonial tax. Lovelace complained about the "great abuse and neglect" of tax collection by the officers of the eastern Long Island towns (NYCD 14: 664).

Cooper's troubles with the Indians in Brookhaven did not hamper his attempts to recruit Shinnecock whalers a month later. He signed eighteen Indian whalers to a five-year contract, including Sauspan (Sacaspan), who had been a member of the Shinnecock company. The number of whalers indicates that Cooper either intended to send out three boats with six-man crews rather than the two boats described by the seventeenth-century sources or he wanted the other men as reserves.

Cooper's contract, one of the longest and most detailed in the town records, is the first to be explicitly based on the half-share system. The document is divided into six sections, beginning with the basic terms of service. The Indians were to go to sea as his servants for five seasons. During this time, they were to "faithfully and diligently" take all possible opportunity for killing whales, cut out blubber and bone, and secure both out of the tide's way. The next section imposed a fine of five shillings a day for each day they were absent, ten if the whaler was absent when a whale was killed. The five-shilling fine was nearly twice the average daily wage of a laborer on land. The third section spoke to the physical risks inherent in the hunting and flensing operations. Cooper agreed that any whaler injured or disabled during the hunt would not lose his share. The fourth section concerned Cooper's obligations to provide "competent boats" and good oil barrels for each whaler and to "give an honest account unto the Indians of the quantity of the oyle so obtained." The clause also stipulated that the Indians were to cart the blubber to Cooper's home, where it would be tried out and put in barrels.

The fifth clause sets forth in great detail the market costs of the oil and the goods distributed to the Indians for their half share. Cooper was to have all the oil and to "allow the said Indians the full and just value of half the said oyle, it being accounted at forty-five shillings a barrel. . . ." The goods listed in the clause included broadcloth at eighteen shillings a yard, "trucking cloth" britches at five shillings and nine pence a pair, porringers at two shillings and six pence each, spoons at fourteen pence apiece, shot at eight pence a pound, powder at three shillings a pound, and, "when they need it," liquor at six pence a gill. The value of these goods certainly exceeded the limit of one cloth coat set by the Southampton officials, a matter that later may have created some tension between Cooper and the governor.

The last clause appears to be related to Governor Lovelace's endorsement of the town ruling setting the limits for payments to the Indian whalers. "In case our honorable governor or his substitute approve not of the said John Cooper his making such pay as is aforespecified that notwithstanding the said Indians are to perform their covenant as aforesaid. . . ." Even if the governor forced Cooper to reduce his payments in goods, the Indians were still obliged to honor their obligations to hunt whales for Cooper.

The provision protecting injured or disabled whalers strongly suggests that such injuries had occurred in the past and had left some whalers without their share. Cooper's detailed account of the market cost of oil and goods and his promise to provide a full account at the end of the season suggests that this issue had been raised by Indians in the past. Cooper's list of commodity prices also gives scholars a chance to examine a frequently asked question about the level of economic exploitation experienced by the Indian whalers.

Cooper's price of forty-five shillings is a bit higher than prices cited in other sources. In 1707, Governor Cornbury reported that a barrel of oil would bring forty shillings (see previous chapter). Although estate inventories in East Hampton from 1677 to 1682 listed the same price in the final year, there are occasional evaluations ranging from one pound to one pound ten shillings in the records (RCSS 65, 71, 78, 127). Cooper may have anticipated that the market price would be higher, but he was clearly not setting the price in his favor. Much lower figures of twenty, twenty-five, and thirty shillings per barrel were set in agreements between Brookhaven men in 1675 and 1678, but these lower figures may have been for oil of poorer quality (RTBH Book A: 39, 40; RTBH 1924, 61). If the oil, for example, was overcooked, unclean, or contained water, it would bring a lower price on the market.

The prices Cooper set for broadcloth and trucking cloth britches are more difficult to compare because of differences in both the quality and the cost of production as well as the inconsistent use of the most commonly used names for textiles in the seventeenth-century sources. Terms such as broadcloth, duffel, trading cloth, barter cloth, and trucking cloth, for example, were often used interchangeably. Most of these textiles were a kind of coarse, woolen carded flannel first produced in the area of Duffel, located in the province of Antwerp in Belgium, and later in the West Riding area of England. The material was shipped to the colonies in large quantities during the seventeenth century (Ulrich 2001, 55; Becker 2005, 769–70). The cloth for the Indian trade was usually dyed in bright red and blue stripes, colors much preferred by Indians (Ulrich 2001, 55; Montgomery 1984, xv–xvi, 159–60; Becker 2005, 732).

Cooper claimed the broadcloth he offered was "of the sort they usually have of him." He set the price at eighteen shillings a yard, well below the twenty-six shillings per yard listed in the estate of Elias Cook, a Southampton resident who died in 1678 (RCSS 83). The difference in price suggests that Cooper was giving the Indians the coarser grade, but it does not appear that he was cheating them on the price. The five shillings nine pence he charged for the cloth britches was similar to the amount Richard Floyd charged Bumbrest and Indian Tom (Meneges) in 1689. Floyd set the price at six shillings (RFL 1: 24v). The estate inventories list "wearing clothes" without a separate price for britches, making a precise comparison impossible.

The request for britches is significant because it exemplifies a stage in the transition from traditional apparel. The first stage in this process was noted by Daniel Denton, a Long Island resident from Hempstead, writing in 1670. Indians, he said, were replacing animal skin breech wear with broadcloth garments (Denton [1670] 1968, 13). The last stage in the transition was to abandon the breechcloth for European-style britches.

The Indians were adopting new eating utensils as well as new attire. Cooper offered spoons at fourteen pence each and small bowls of pewter, ceramic, or wood, each six inches in diameter, three inches deep, with a flat handle on one side, called porringers. The price Cooper set for porringers, two shillings and six pence, is comparable to the listings in the estate inventories (RCSS 41, 58, 83). The spoons listed in the estate inventories ranged from six to seventeen pence apiece (RCSS 114, 227, 316). It is possible that Cooper purchased the cheaper spoons for the Indian trade.

The prices for powder and shot by weight were not recorded in the Long Island estate records. Some of the town residents made lead shot from their own molds. The estate inventory for John Cooper's brother, Thomas, listed three sets of shot molds probably for different sizes of shot (RCSS 318). John, therefore, could easily obtain quantities of shot at a cost lower than the eight pence per pound he set in the contract. Cooper's price set at eight pence a pound for shot and three shillings a pound for powder are the same as the rates Richard Floyd listed in his account book (RFL 1: 8). They both appear to have inflated their prices. The amount for a pound of powder listed by William Penn in 1682 was a little less than one shilling (Becker 2005). Even though the cost of transporting the powder from Philadelphia to Long Island would certainly have added to the cost, it would not justify the price set by Floyd and Cooper.

Rum, as we have seen, was readily available in large quantities on Long Island. The expansion of whaling operations and the increasing reliance on Indian day laborers on farms prompted many Southampton and East Hampton residents to seek exemptions from the laws prohibiting the sale of alcohol to Indians. In July, shortly after Cooper entered his contract into the town records, Zerobabel Philips, a tavern owner in Southampton, requested and quickly received an exemption from Governor Lovelace (Paltsits 1910, 2: 472–73). Cooper himself, along with John Laughton and John Jennings, did the same the following November. The memorandum to Cooper stated that he could "furnish his Indians with a [five ounce] gill of liquor now and then as occasion shall require, placing it into the account as part payment of their wages" (Paltsits 1910, 2: 475).

It was a lucrative business. Both Floyd and Cooper charged the Indians six pence for a gill of rum that they could purchase for two pence or less. In their estate inventories Joseph Taylor of Southampton listed a barrel of rum at four shillings a gallon and Thomas Jessup left behind a supply of rum valued at three shillings a gallon (Strong and Lamont 2015; RCSS 126, 160). Considering there were thirty-two gills in an English gallon, even if Cooper paid the higher price, he was charging the Indians a highly inflated price of nearly sixteen shillings a gallon. If Cooper went to Philadelphia or New York, he could buy all he wanted for two shillings a gallon (Becker 2005).

The question of exploitation, therefore, centers largely on the prices charged for rum, the arbitrary imposition of fines by the company owners, and the owner's control of available goods. The lay system, based on credit rather than cash, prevented the Indians from purchasing goods on the open market, where they could shop around for the best price. In the case of alcohol, the Indians could not go to another source even if they had cash because the company owners were the only ones exempted from the laws prohibiting the sale or distribution of alcohol to the Indian whalers. The owners had a monopoly of sorts wherein the customers had no choice but to purchase the goods on credit from them, much like the "company store" for coal miners in the nineteenth century. It was a good system for the owners. Their employees became their customers at the end of each season.

Debt Peonage on Saint George Manor: A Case Study, 1695–1721

William Tangier Smith and Richard Floyd relied on the nearby Unkechaug villages along the freshwater streams on the peninsula for their labor supply. These two large estates, which divided the Mastic Peninsula between them, were both engaged in whaling operations, but Smith kept the best records. He had established his whaling operations at the end of the seventeenth century, a decade or more after the last contract was entered into the town records. His lay system for Indian shares, however, varied little from the previous practices.

Colonel William "Tangier" Smith, so named because he had served in the English administration of an outpost on the North African coast until it was abandoned in 1683, came to Long Island, where he purchased large tracts of land from the Setauketts on the north shore and from the Unkechaugs on the Atlantic shore. Three of the Unkechaugs, Ioten (John), Weramps, and Tapshana, who represented their people on five of these land transactions in the 1690s, later served as members of Smith's whaling crew. Smith used these purchases to support his 1693 petition for a manorial estate that included about 160,000 acres in the town of Brookhaven. The Indian deeds, however, were subject to scrutiny by colonial governors. Although Smith had few of the powers associated with manorial estates in England, he gave his estate the rather pretentious title of "The Manor of Saint George." After Smith died in 1705, his wife Martha managed the estate until her death two years later. Her son, William Henry Smith, inherited the property and kept the ledger during the declining years of shore whaling on Long Island.

The Smiths kept a record of estate activities in a leatherbound ledger called the "pigskin book," now located in the Bellport-Brookhaven Historical Society in Bellport, New York. The ledger, about fourteen and a half inches long, nine and a half inches wide, and one and a half inches thick, resembles a modern spreadsheet, showing debits on the left half and credits on the right. The debit pages itemize goods taken by whalers on credit and the credit entries record the market value of the whale oil and baleen harvested that season. The names of thirty-one Indians appear in the ledger. All but six of the Indians on the Smith estate took part in whaling operations at one time or another. Many lived in the Unkechaug village on Poospatuck Creek, a short distance to the east on the Mastic Peninsula. The Indians provided year-round farm and domestic labor for Smith and for his neighbor, Richard Floyd. The two families, prominent in local affairs, occupied most of the land on the Mastic Peninsula.

Unlike John Cooper's 1672 contract, the ledger contains the prices of only a few specific items. An Indian named Wahamehoe was charged ten pounds, ten shillings, and six pence for duffel, corn, and shot, but there is no indication of the price per unit (PSB 27–28). In other instances, the entry only notes that a whaler was charged for unnamed "sundries." A whaler named Pumpsha, for example, was charged ten pounds "to sundries thou received" after the 1703–4 season (PSB 9).

In 1700, Smith granted the Unkechaugs a 175-acre reservation on the Mastic Peninsula. Although the grant appears to be an altruistic act, Smith was actually protecting his manorial estate from hostile scrutiny by New York governor Richard Coote, the Earl of Bellomont, a Whig who believed that the manorial estates created by his predecessors served to establish a local aristocracy. He had vacated several such grants and, in one case, he charged that the land acquisitions from Indians were fraudulent (NYCD 4: 622; Varga 1960, 251). Smith, aware that the boundaries of his purchases from the Unkechaug were poorly defined and vulnerable to challenge, wanted the Unkechaug to confirm his purchases in exchange for a grant of land in perpetuity.[5] He negotiated with a delegation of eleven Unkechaug representatives asking them to confirm all of his prior purchases in exchange for deed in perpetuity (WFEA, FIIS 6606, folder 17). The Unkechaug delegation included four men—John Indian, Weramps, Tapshana, and Wacus—who had a relationship with Smith going back at least a decade.

The men, who depended on Smith for employment and were carrying a yearly burden of debt to him, may well have found themselves at a disadvantage in the negotiations. That was certainly the case over the next three decades as the Smith family pressed the Unkechaug with a series of highly questionable transactions eroding the original grant of 175 acres to a small fifty-acre tract on Poospatuck Creek, where their descendants live today (see below in chapter 8; Strong 2011, 84–92).

The entries in the ledger make it possible to track some of Smith's whalers over a decade or more. Although the names of thirty-one Indians appear in the ledger, only seven of them—Abraham, Cownus, Pumpsha, Sacutaca, Tony, Towntuck, and Weramps—served on Smith's whaling crews for eight or more seasons. The yearly accounts of these men are a window into the debt peonage system. All the Indians in the ledger began their employment under the burden of a debt accumulated in previous years and ended their last season still in debt to the Smith family. The first entry associated with their names recorded a debt "carried over" from the past, and the last entry listed the debts remaining after their last season with Smith, often a decade later. Table 1 lists the first and last entries for the seven whalers mentioned above. Debts are entered in pounds:shillings:pence.

The data in the table below come into sharper focus when we follow the entries for a single individual. Pumpsha's account began in 1695, following the 1694–95 season, and ended in 1718 with a note that he had received "sundrys"

Table 1 Debts recorded for the first and last seasons

Name	Date of first entry	Previous debt carried over	Date of last entry	Debt on last entry
Abraham	1711	1:8:9	1721	10:9:0
Cownus	1696	8:5:0	1707	27:15:0
Pumpsha	1695	25:7:5	1718	49:19:5
Sacutauca	1697	26:14:8	1708	6:6:8
Tony	1704	4:14:3	1721	17:13:3
Towntuck	1697	33:18:0	1706	21:4:3
Weramps	1697	18:8:6	1708	52:0:0

for several years and was in debt for eleven pounds and seven shillings (PSB 9–10). He was involved in whaling for ten seasons during those years, beginning with the 1694–95 season, after which he received a share of oil and bone valued at six pounds, ten shillings. He earned another eight pounds and five shillings the next year. His income of fourteen pounds, fifteen shillings for the two seasons covered a little more than a quarter of the charges that Smith made for the goods Pumpsha took on credit. The entries for December 1697 indicate that he owed a total of twenty-five pounds, seven shillings, and five pence carried forward from an earlier time. He was charged with an additional five pounds, one shilling, and six pence for the following items:

    1 pair of mittens and 1 pair of stockings
    4 1/2 bushel of corn
    4 1/2 pound of powder
    16 1/2 pounds of shot
    4 quarts of cider

The cost of these items does not appear to be inflated, but the debt further accumulated.

Pumpsha may have continued to work on the Smith estate, but he did not go to sea again until the 1703–4 season. With the exception of the 1699–1700 season, Smith's crews brought in an average of about sixty barrels a year over that seven-year period. There is no explanation for Pumpsha's absence from whaling. He may have left Smith's employ, but no mention is made of his working elsewhere. In the fall of 1703 a record number of whales appeared off the Long Island shores, encouraging Smith to nearly double the size of his crew from six in 1702 to ten in 1703.

That season Smith's whalers brought in one hundred and twenty barrels of oil valued at two hundred and forty pounds. It is noteworthy that the London customs records report that only 3,379 gallons of oil (about 120 barrels) were imported from New York that year. Either Smith was the only whaling company operating that year or, as is more likely, few of the Long Island companies were shipping their oil through New York and paying the New York taxes. The year before, for example, the East Hampton trustees' records reported that thirteen whales had been killed from stations at Mecox, Saggaponack, and East Hampton, carted to Northwest [Harbor], and from there sent to Boston and transshipped to London (EHTR 4: 25). The London customs reported that only thirty-eight gallons of oil had come from New York (Reeves, Breiwick, and Mitchell 1999, 25).

The whalers' shares for the 1703–4 season amounted to about forty pounds (PSB 9–10). Pumpsha received three and a half barrels of oil and thirty pounds of baleen valued at eight pounds, ten shillings. He used his share to purchase ten pounds' worth of "sundries" from Smith's inventory. Pumpsha, therefore, started the season as an employee and ended as a customer in debt. The following season, Smith's crews brought in only one yearling whale yielding twenty-eight barrels of oil and about fifty-eight pounds of baleen. No record for the 1704–5 season was entered into the London customs books.

The 1705–6 season was again disappointing as the crew harvested only twenty-four barrels. Apparently there was a sharp decrease in the number of pregnant females heading south to give birth in the warmer southern waters. The same decline in whale catches was recorded for other areas along the Atlantic Coast from New England to Pennsylvania (Reeves, Breiwick, and Mitchell 1999, 24, 26). Pumpsha, who was credited with a total of thirty gallons of oil and seven pounds of baleen for the two seasons, found himself in debt for forty-five pounds and eleven shillings.

In the winter of 1706 the whales returned in much larger numbers. The 1706–7 season was not only one of the best yields in Smith's records but also one of the most productive whaling seasons for the colony. Governor Cornbury reported that four thousand barrels of oil were harvested that season off Long Island shores (NYCD 5: 59). Such fluctuations in whale movement may have been caused by changes in food supplies or shifts in ocean currents (Warren, personal communication, April 24, 2016). The females and their calves came north along the Atlantic beaches south of Mastic in January and February of 1707. Pumpsha and his crew, including Nero, Tony, Toby, Tom Indian Jr., and Quogue, with help from Will Beane, Wamahoe, and Naturamy, killed a yearling whale that yielded twenty-eight barrels on the sixteenth of January and a second that produced twenty-seven more barrels a week later.

The next week Pumpsha's crew helped a company crew from Southampton led by Indian Harry to bring in a "stunt" whale and were given four barrels for their assistance. Three weeks later, on February 22, Richard Floyd's crews joined with Pumpsha to bring in a yearling whale that yielded thirty-six barrels of oil. The oil was divided equally, with eighteen barrels to each company. The whales kept coming. Over the next three weeks, four more were killed, a "school" whale and three yearlings. It was a lucrative season for Widow Smith. When the flensing and trying were completed, 201 barrels of oil were ready for shipping to market. Pumpsha and the other crew members shared a line of credit based on sixty-three barrels of oil, well short of the half-share payment that had been the standard during the period of 1672 to 1685 recorded in the contracts. Pumpsha, Nero, and Tony were each credited with seventeen pounds and four shillings.

Martha Smith, who was in her second year as manager of the manor during this successful season, shared the stereotypes about Indians held by many white people. She suspected the worst motives for any absences from their assigned

Table 2 Value of shares for the 1706–1707 season

Name	Oil	Baleen	Value in pounds	Source
Pumpsha	7 barrels, 8 gals.	54 lbs.	17:04:00	PSB 9–10
Nero	7 barrels, 8 gals.	54 lbs.	17:04:00	PSB 14
Tony	7 barrels, 8 gals.	54 lbs.	17:04:00	PSB 38
Toby	7 barrels, 4 gals.	47 lbs.	16:14:00	PSB 34
Tom Jr.	7 barrels, 3 gals.	49 lbs.	16:12:04	PSB 44
Quogue (Tim)	6 barrels	45 lbs.	14:05:00	PSB 26
Will Beane	5 barrels	43 lbs.	12:18:03	PSB 35
Wamahoe	4 barrels, 13 gals.	24 lbs.	10:00:00	PSB 28
Natutamy	3 barrels, 19 gals.	23 lbs.	8:06:09	PSB 32
TOTAL	53 barrels, 63 gals.	393 lbs.	181:05:09	

tasks. She noted in the ledger that she had fined Wamahow three pounds, six shillings, and six pence and for missing work when he was "hurt in the head by Pumpsha" (PSB 28). There were no details about the incident; it may have been an accident or the result of an altercation between the two whalers. Widow Smith seemed to have little interest in the reason, imposing an exorbitant fine equivalent to nearly a month's wages for a laborer.

In 1708, following the successful season, the whales did not come. Several whalers decided to tend to personal matters elsewhere. Martha Smith, perhaps upset by the failure to obtain yields comparable to the previous year's, entered frequent complaints about this behavior in the ledger. In one instance, she voiced irritation when a whaler named Sacutaca left the estate for ten days in 1708 to be with his wife. Smith noted only that his absence "was a great loss to me" (PSB 30). She had harsher words for Will Beane, who had, she said, "like a base rogue, run away after he had his clothes," apparently a reference to a payment in kind (PSB 36). She paid two men thirty-five shillings to find Will and force him to return. Will, however, resisted her efforts to control his movements. He stayed at the Smith estate, reported Martha Smith, for "but nine weeks and run away to Rockaway." Natutamy, she complained, "left the beach like a villain," feigning sickness, and "never came again."

Dependency, Dispossession, and Survival

Richard White, in his classic analysis of the early contact period between Indians and Europeans, concluded that the dispossession of aboriginal land and the implementation of control over Indian labor led to a pattern of dependency within Indian communities (White 1983, xv–xix). He also noted that the growth of global capitalism affected North American Indian societies: "The collapse of their subsistence systems and their integration into world markets brought increasing reliance on the capitalist core, lack of economic choice, and profound political and social changes within their societies" (White 1983, xix). The Indian whalers, domestic and field laborers, and others who worked for the English became the primary source of goods now deemed necessities by the members of their communities. Although these individuals had to accept the terms established by their employers, they gained influence within their communities. Meanwhile sachems such as Wyandanch and Tobacus who no longer controlled and distributed resources saw their influence and status wane.

Becoming dependent within a global market system, however, did not mean that Indians lost their identity or assimilated into the dominant culture. Many aspects of their traditional world view, such as a cohesive kinship system, seasonal rituals, and concern for and knowledge about the natural environment, remain vital today (Strong 1998). What it did mean, however, was that they found themselves relegated to the political and economic margins of a world that was once theirs alone. The labor contracts had an unintended cultural impact. Unlike the earlier negotiations for land, the agreements involved individual Indians rather than tribal groups. The sachems were marginalized as their followers now established direct relations with the English.

The decline of the sachems' authority upset relationships that had served the English well in the early postcontact period. The English, for example, had manipulated this loosely structured political system by selecting Wyandanch, a friendly, cooperative, Montaukett sachem, and giving him economic and military support to ensure his loyalty and to bolster his status among the Indian communities on Long Island (see above). The whalers, domestics, and day laborers were now the primary sources of European trade goods. The death of Wyandanch and the devastating impact of the smallpox epidemic in the late 1650s left both the Shinnecocks and the Montauketts without leaders who could act as reliable surrogates.

In a rather desperate and blatantly transparent attempt to find acceptable leaders, the English arbitrarily imposed a system of governance with both English and Native American elements. On January 2, 1671, Governor Lovelace issued an ordinance addressed to the Southampton officials, noting that the Shinnecock were "destitute" in terms of leadership and endorsing a man named Quaquashawge as their sachem. It is possible that Quaquashawge had actually been serving in that capacity for some time because there is an entry in the town records for October 9, 1666, wherein the constable called for the town residents "to bring in to the towns men the wampum they are to pay for Qua qua" (RTSH 5: 25). This may be a reference to a tax on town residents to pay Quaquashawge's salary. The governor said the Shinnecock had "nominated and elected" the man, who was "likewise approved by the English to be a fit person amongst them for that purpose by reason of his quiet and peaceable disposition." The Shinnecock were ordered to "take notice and obey him as their chief and sachem." Quaquashawge was to "keep his Indians in peaceable and good order both amongst themselves and also amongst their neighbors" (Paltsits 1910, 2: 461).

Lovelace sent a similar order to East Hampton for a Montaukett sachem "with a blank to put in a name," leaving East Hampton officials free to select a sachem of their choice. Two days later the governor sent a second commission to Southampton to appoint a Shinnecock named Cawbutt to serve as a constable under sachem Quaquashawge. Cawbutt was described as "a person of peaceable character" and given a constable's staff as he had requested (Paltsits 1910, 2: 462). The six-foot staff, emblazoned with the king's arms, was carried by the constable when he opened the meetings of the town court (Varga 2010, 191). Cawbutt must have made quite an impression when he appeared with it in his village. His appointment may also have been influenced by his involvement in whaling. He was hired by John Cooper in June 1672 for the 1672–73 whaling season along with eighteen other Shinnecocks. Cawbutt's status may have played a role in recruiting his fellow tribesmen.

Overlapping Systems of Control: Indentured Servitude and Contract Labor

The ten-year agreement between Artor and John Cooper illustrates the blurred lines between seasonal contracts and indentures. Artor agreed to "do the said Cooper good and faithful service in and about whaling or cutting out of the whale" in exchange for four trading cloth coats each year (SBD 84). The contract was similar to the "long hire" labor agreements used in England and was a variation of the colonial indenture system (Towner 1998, 8). An indenture bound a laborer or a house servant for a period of about three years or, in the case of a young child, from the age of four until maturity (Strong 1997, 276–78; Strong 2011, 179–84). Artor's agreement, however, was seasonal: he was not to live in Cooper's household and be provided with food and clothing. The fact that Artor simply walked away from the contract after a year and signed with the Shinnecock company may explain why company owners sought an arrangement that would entrap the whalers in debt.

Another example of overlapping systems was an indenture in the summer of 1683, wherein Wobetom, a Montaukett whaler, indentured his son, John Indian, to Richard Stratton of East Hampton for a two-year term. Wobetom had hunted whales for Stratton's fellow East Hampton residents, including

Thomas James, John Miller, Jacob Dayton, and John Wheeler. The basic format of the agreement read like an indenture: "The said John Indian doth bind himself a servant unto the said Richard Stratton of East Hampton and with him to serve and dwell after the manner of such an apprentice . . ." for two years (RTEH 2: 123–33). Stratton agreed to provide John with shelter, meat and drink, and, at the end of the term, give him twelve pounds. Unlike the conventional indentures, John, with the permission of Stratton, could go to sea to hunt whales. If he did this he would then receive his half share of the oil and bone in addition to his twelve pounds. The agreement differed from the whaling contracts in that Stratton was obliged to feed and house John during the two-year term.

The indenture system had its origins in preindustrial England, where it served as a major source of hired labor (Galenson 1984, 2–3). Children and young adults from thirteen to twenty-five came to live in their master's household for annual terms. The system was adapted in the seventeenth century, first as a vehicle for bringing immigrants to the Americas and later as a basic structure for the labor market and a solution to the problems caused by the disparity of wealth. The major adaptation was the lengthening of the terms to seven or more years of servitude.

Indentures, unlike the whaling contracts, created a servant class that included whites, Indians, and African Americans (Towner 1998, 3). Most Indian labor, noted Yasuhide Kawashima, was in the form of indentures for various periods of time (Kawashima 1988, 404–6). With the important exception of whaling, Indians were mostly employed as general day laborers with little opportunity for advancement. Whites, unlike Indians and African Americans, had a limited possibility for improving their status if they mastered a trade. Parents in poor English families would often negotiate indentures for their children that called for a cash payment to the parents upon signing the contract and a guarantee that the child would be properly fed and clothed. There would be a payment to the child and often a suit of clothing upon completion of the indenture. In many instances, the child would be taught to read and write and, in some cases, given training in a skilled trade.

Provisions for literacy and skills, however, were seldom included in indentures for Indians (Seybolt 1917, 90–91; Kawashima 1988, 405). The contract contained no stipulation relating to literacy or to marketable skills (RTEH 2: 132–33). In contrast to John Indian's agreement with Stratton, the next entry in the town records is the indenture of an English child bound out by his father, Renock Garrison of East Hampton, to Isaac and Elizabeth Mills of Southampton. The Mills promised to teach Garrison's son, Samuel, to read and write and to instruct the boy in the "art and trade of carpentry" (RTEH 2: 132).

There was one example, however, of an Indian who received training as an apprentice to a carpenter. In 1684, Arthur Furthy, a Brookhaven farmer, signed an indenture with an Unkechaug named Toby for three years, agreeing to teach him the art of carpentry as he worked for his master by day and night, never leaving his residence without permission (RTBH Book B: 191–92). Toby's indenture is unique, the only one in the town records with the promise of a marketable skill. Most were similar to the indenture negotiated by the Reverend Thomas James of East Hampton in February 1678 with a Montaukett named Tom Indian. Tom agreed to obey all of the reverend's "lawfull commands," day and night, in exchange for room, board, clothing, and a new coat each year for three and a half years. There was no mention of literacy or marketable skills (RTEH 1: 411). The indenture was witnessed by Tom's brother, Abel (alias Tomhage), who had gone whaling for Reverend James's company in 1677 and would later sign a contract in 1684, along with Adsoe and Wobetom, to hunt whales for Miller and Dayton (RTEH 2: 152–53). The whaling contracts, unlike these indentures, did not require the employer to pay for daily living expenses. The whalers lived at home and showed up for the hunt when the whales were spotted. This, of course, served the interests of the owners. It would not be long before this would be one of the few differences distinguishing the indenture from contract labor.

The indenture system served to ensure a steady source of labor for the colonists. Whalers had to take jobs such as wood cutting, clearing farm lands, livestock tending, fence building, and maintenance and daily farm labor in order to pay off the debts. A farmer who needed work done could buy an Indian's debt from a whaling company owner, thereby obtaining what amounted to an indentured servant. Whaling debts were only one part of a system that gave the English control over Indian labor. In 1685, for example, Arthur Furthy purchased the debts that two Unkechaug whalers, Bumbrest and Jeremy, owed to Adam Smith and John Thomas. Furthy paid Smith one pound, thirteen shillings, and Thomas six shillings and took over the debt (RTBH Book B: 242–43). Furthy had the men cut six hundred split rails and prepare them for carting in six weeks. He did pay them an advance of six shillings, but when they missed the deadline, Furthy hauled them into court. The judge forced them to cut an extra one hundred rails as a penalty and added six more days of work to pay the court costs (RTBH Book B: 254).

In that same court session, John Tooker Jr., another Brookhaven landowner, sued Bumbrest and an Indian named Kellis, charging them with failing to meet his deadline for the completion of a fence (RTBH Book B: 254). The court ordered them to pay Tooker twenty shillings and added court costs. Bumbrest now found himself back in debt, still trapped in a cycle of debt peonage.[6] In a somewhat similar situation, a Montaukett named Adsoe signed a contract with John Miller and Jacob Dayton in October 1684 for the 1684–85 season. A month later the two men turned over "all title and interest to the bounded Adsoe to Richard Shaw of East Hampton" (RTEH 2: 152–53).

A similar system of English control over Indian labor has been identified in Nantucket by Daniel Vickers, in New England by David Silverman, and in southern New England by Kathleen Bragdon (Vickers 1983, 576–85; Silverman 2001, 622–28; Bragdon 2009, 160–67). "Indebtedness," said Vickers, "had been important in Indian-white relations since the very beginning, but to the shore fishery, it was indispensable." As Vickers observed, the Indians were lured into the credit system because of short-term advantages that resulted in "a type of communal labor control, an informal brand of debt peonage" (Vickers 1983, 574, 577). T. H. Breen concluded that the Montauketts were drawn into a form of economic bondage, a system he described as a "more effective device for controlling Indian labor than liquor or enslavement" (Breen 1989, 174). Breen failed to note, however, that liquor played a major role in the accumulation of those debts.

How Richard Floyd Got His Land

The pattern of debt was often related to the dispossession of Indian land. Richard Floyd's purchase of a tract of Unkechaug land on Mastic in 1684 is one example. The land, located on Pattersquash Creek, a small stream flowing into Moriches Bay, gave him a foothold in Mastic, which he later expanded into a four-thousand-acre estate covering half of the Mastic Peninsula. This area proved a convenient place for a whaleboat launch (Pelletreau 1903, 2: 264).

At the Court of Sessions held in Southampton on March 3, 1682, an Unkechaug named Mahaine (Meheane), who lived on Mastic Peninsula, was fined by the province of East Riding (now Suffolk County) for an unspecified violation. When Mahaine was unable to pay, Tobacus, the Unkechaug sachem, and two of his "chief men," Wauphague (alias Porrig) and Rowepone, met with the East Riding officials and agreed to pay Mahaine's fine by mortgaging a five-hundred-acre tract of Unkechaug land located on Pattersquash Creek (map 5). Tom Francis, Indian, signed as the translator of the document. It is likely that he was the Unkechaug named Meneges (a.k.a. Tom Indian; see previous chapter).

The Unkechaug, unable to come up with the payment, had to forfeit the land to the court. They met with John Youngs, the high sheriff of East Riding, and agreed to "give, grant, bargain and sell . . . unto the said Captain John Youngs his heirs, executors, administrators all the upland being and existing

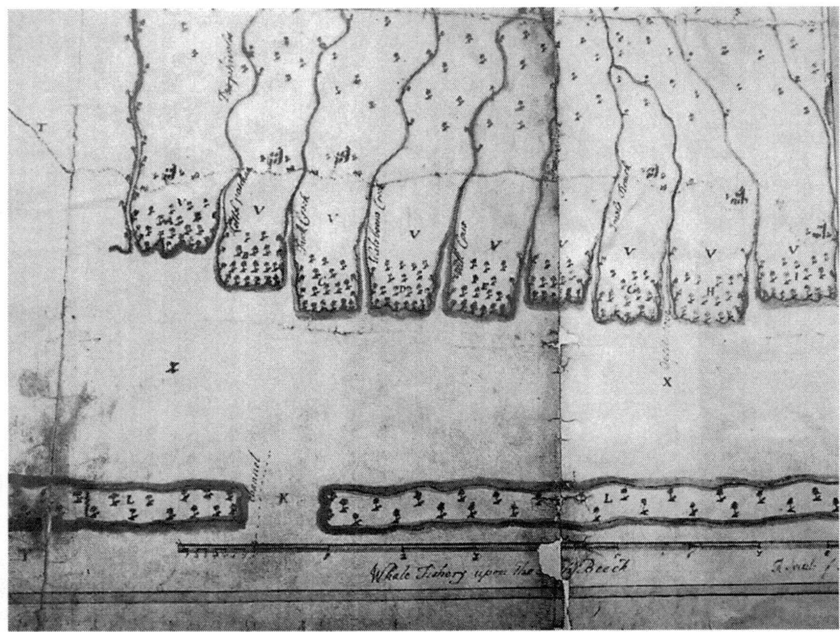

Map 5 Ryder map of western Brookhaven Town (1670) that Robert Ryder, a schoolmaster in Setauket, N.Y., is believed to have drawn.

in Pattersquash" (WFEA FIIS 9665, box 1, folder 17). The tract actually became the property of the court and was used to pay for services rendered to the court by John Jennings, the Southampton town marshal (Pelletreau 1903, 2: 264). In a formal acknowledgment, Jennings stated that "I John Jennings, of Southampton, Marshall, having several fees due me from the county . . . the Worshipful Court of Sessions having given me . . . the land that was fallen unto the Court of Sessions for the default of Mohave [Mahaine] an Indian by his non payment of his fine and court charges . . ." (Pelletreau 1903, 2: 264).

Mahaine, now freed from debt, signed a whaling contract with Joseph Davis of Brookhaven in August for the 1683–84 season. The contract had a clause that put Mahaine at risk for more debt. He had to agree that "if I the said Mahaine shall not attend when there is sea weather, I am contented to pay for every day soe missing tenn shillings and to the true performance of the same I doe here unto sett my hand this 16 day of August 1683" (RTBH Book B: 175). Mahaine may have ended the season in debt once again, because he did not work for Davis again; instead, he signed on with Obadiah Seward, a company owner who did not impose fines on his whalers (RTBH Book B: 197).

In March of 1684, about the time that Mahaine finished his contractual obligation to Davis, Jennings sold the five-hundred-acre tract to Richard Floyd for what amounted to a token fee of nineteen pounds, far below the value of a tract that size. Fourteen acres of meadowland in the estate inventory of Samuel Clark, for example, was assessed at thirty pounds (RCSS 86). The purchase enabled Floyd to expand his estate from his holdings in Setauket on the north shore to the Mastic Peninsula with its fertile southern meadows and its Atlantic barrier beaches. The beaches had served as a launching place for whaling operations for over a decade prior to 1684. A 1670 map by Robert Ryder, a Setauket schoolmaster, of the barrier beach a few miles west of Pattersquash Creek shows Whalebone Creek flowing into the bay directly north of a channel opening to the ocean (map 3). A notation on the map reads, "Whale fishery upon the beach." Another reference to whaling in that area describes a house and a whale watchtower called "Bayley's Stage," established by Stephen Bayley for his whaling company in 1690.[7]

Floyd may actually have been launching whaling crews off the beaches south of Whalebone Creek even before he obtained possession of the tract. It is also possible that he may have had a hand in the 1682 arrangement with the Unkechaug. Certainly he had established a close working relationship with Wauphague by the fall of 1685. In December, prior to the 1685–86 whaling season, Floyd gave a gun to Wauphague with the understanding that he would pay for it with a barrel of whale oil and twenty pounds of baleen at the close of the season (Osborn Shaw Papers, BTH). That amount of oil and baleen came to about two pounds eleven shillings, enough to buy two guns at market prices, according to the estate records for the 1680s (RCSS).

Wauphague continued to play an important role in the dispossession of Unkechaug lands over the next decade. He signed off on eight land transactions alienating or confirming the prior alienation of tribal lands from 1682 to 1694.[8] In most cases, the burden of debt was a factor pressing the decisions by the Indian chief men. It is not too much of an exaggeration to say that the use of Indian indebtedness to obtain land was as successful, and perhaps even more widespread, than the use of alcohol or fraud.

The documents cited in this chapter, spelling out the agreements between the owners and the Indian whalers and bearing the signature of one or two witnesses, provide a window into a period when the Native peoples of Long Island were gradually adjusting to the increasing pressures of an alien way of life. The contracts reflect the problems posed by cultural differences as the Indians and the English sought to pursue a common goal while protecting their own interests. Both parties were working in a fluid political and economic context with no precedents to guide them.

A closer analysis of the labor system that evolved over the last half of the seventeenth century contradicts conventional wisdom and simplistic assertions about English-Native relations. The Indians were not easily manipulated victims of crafty English exploiters, nor were they chronic alcoholics in a disappearing culture. They quickly grasped the basic mechanisms of the English market system and protected their interests as best they could. The power remained in the hands of a literate people with a scientific technology capable of producing guns, metal tools, textiles, and an administrative system that could control the flow and production of these goods. In spite of these disadvantages, the Native peoples played their hands astutely and survived in the face of these odds.

7

Papasaquin's World

Politics, Economics, and Family in Seventeenth-Century Long Island

Introduction

Papasaquin, born at Montauk about the time the English settlers arrived, saw his world change dramatically in his lifetime. His story broadens our understanding of the period by drawing on documents related to land transactions, court records, indentures, and other activities. When his involvement with English whaling companies from 1677 to 1684 is placed in the larger historical context, it provides a number of significant cultural insights into the process of accommodation and acculturation following the imposition of an alien political, economic, and social system. Papasaquin, for example, was among several prominent Native American leaders who went to sea for English employers. Their names can be found on land transactions and other documents related to diplomatic negotiations with the English. Ten of these men were specifically identified on the whaling contracts as sachems. The contracts, therefore, reveal only one part of their life stories. A closer look at the experiences of men such as Papasaquin and Meneges also belie the stereotypes that often portray Native peoples as easily manipulated innocents or as befuddled alcoholics.

Papasaquin developed a relationship with six elite families in East Hampton and Southampton over the years: the Schellingers, Wheelers, Coopers, Conklings, Osborns, and Rogers. He and Meneges, who had established close contacts with Brookhaven officials, recognized and undoubtedly took advantage of their association with the wealthy and influential members of the local elites, but there was an obvious price to be paid. Their economic dependency on the English compromised their attempts to defend their sovereignty and retain their land.

Papasaquin first appears in the records a decade after the English settlement was established at East Hampton. He was probably born in the early 1640s, a decade before a group of settlers "hived out" of Southampton and put down their roots in the meadows and bays west of the Montaukett villages. As a young man, Papasaquin became involved in three failed challenges to English domination. In his middle years, he took up whaling, negotiating contracts with English company owners. Once his whaling days were over, he turned his attention to family matters, indenturing his son and daughter to wealthy whaling company owners. At the turn of the century, when he was in his late fifties, he again became involved with tribal affairs. Although resigned to the hard fact of English domination, he and the Montaukett sachems skillfully played the colonial authorities from Manhattan against the East Hampton town officials in a maneuver to gain the best deal possible for their lands. His story illustrates the multidimensional life of the Indians who hunted whales during the half century following the arrival of the English on Long Island.

The Niantic Alliance

In the decades prior to his birth, Papasaquin's people had looked to the Pequots, one of the dominant tribes in southern New England, for trade and military protection. In exchange, the Montauketts paid them wampum tributes and tended their corn fields on Long Island. The dramatic defeat of their protectors by the English troops under the leadership of John Mason, John Underhill, and Lion Gardiner in the Pequot War (1636–37) convinced Wyandanch, the Montaukett sachem, to form a tributary relationship with the victors (Cave 1996; Salisbury 1982; Strong 1997, 154–62).

The steady expansion of the English settlement at East Hampton and the death of Wyandanch in 1659, however, led Papasaquin and others in his age set to question their relationship with the English. He was personally involved in three confrontations: the Niantic alliance, the formation of the Shinnecock whaling company, and the dispossession of Montaukett lands, all of which resulted in or demonstrated an assertion of English power. These experiences led Papasaquin and others of his generation to develop strategies enabling them to protect their interests as much as possible in a world that was no longer their own. They came to recognize that English governance was not monolithic. The colonial authorities in New York, for example, could be played not only against those in Rhode Island but also against the East Hampton officials. Papasaquin and many other whalers also realized that internal tensions among the elite families and company owners in East Hampton provided some leverage in the contract negotiations.

The balance of power among the major tribes in southern New England and Long Island was disrupted by the decisive Pequot defeat. The English now became the dominant power in the region, setting in motion a struggle among the tribes to establish a new political order. Ninigret, the Niantic sachem whose villages were in southern Rhode Island, made several attempts to bring the Montauketts into a tributary relationship under his authority. The first came in the late spring of 1638, when Ninigret approached several of the Montaukett elders with gifts and offers of protection. "The English are liars," said Ninigret. "They will take your wampum and give you nothing" (Strong 1997, 159; WP 4: 43–44). When Wyandanch rejected these overtures, preferring a tributary alliance with the English, Ninigret burned some wigwams and humiliated the Montaukett sachem by stripping him in public.

After Wyandanch fled in disgrace, some of the Montauketts accepted Ninigret's proposition, giving him thirty fathoms of wampum and a bow and quiver of arrows as a symbol of their tributary relationship. The English, fearing that the Niantics would gain control over the Montaukett lands, blocked Ninigret's efforts by patrolling the sound and providing the Montauketts with powder and shot and, in one instance, giving them refuge close to the village of East Hampton. Ninigret, however, never completely abandoned his efforts to bring the Montauketts under his control. He continued sending war parties against the Montauketts over the next three decades (Strong 1996, 2013).

Ninigret's resolve in the face of pressure from the English undoubtedly resonated with many of the Montauketts. After the death of Wyandanch in 1659, the Montauketts experienced difficult times. Their alliance with the English following the Pequot War had produced unanticipated consequences. In 1662, the East Hampton officials pressured the Montauketts to give them a 4,200-acre tract of land that extended the town boundaries eastward as a "gift in appreciation" for protecting them from Ninigret (RCSS 183–86). Papasaquin and a faction of Montauketts saw this as a betrayal, prompting them to reassess Ninigret as a potential ally rather than as a nemesis.

The undercurrents of anti-English feelings among the Montauketts surfaced in the spring of 1668, when a Montaukett named Nangenutch was convicted of attempted rape on the person of Mary Miller, an East Hampton resident.[1] Nangenutch was imprisoned in Manhattan, awaiting deportation to the Caribbean, where he would be sold into slavery. The money from the sale was to defray the costs of the trial. Four Montauketts defied the English by going to New York City and breaking Nangenutch out of the prison (Christoph and Christoph 1982, 200–201). Governor Lovelace demanded the return of Nangenutch, but the Montauketts refused to comply. The governor's action caused a rift in the Montaukett community. Sachem Poniutute, Wyandanch's grandson, and Pauquatoun, who had been Wyandanch's counsellor, remained loyal to the English.[2] Manecopungun (a.k.a. Pawgatun), another of Wyandanch's counsellors, had mixed feelings about the situation, but Papasaquin and his followers saw an opportunity to challenge English authority.

In June, Governor Lovelace wrote to John Mulford, a member of the Commission on Indian Affairs, advising him to "proceed vigorously in their acting" and arrest Nangenutch (Paltsits 1910, 1: 32–33). Rather than risk an open confrontation with the Montauketts, Mulford and two other prominent East Hampton men, the Reverend Thomas James and Jeremiah Conkling, purchased the Montaukett debt and began negotiations with Moshup for a tract of land where the present-day village of Montauk is located. The tract included beach land where James and Gardiner had purchased drift whale rights in 1658 (see chapter 3). Papasaquin and several influential Montauketts, including Missuckquat, Nompum, Naueyauwant, and Akomis, opposed any concession to the English. In desperation they sought an alliance with Ninigret. Manecopungun, who accompanied Papasaquin on his mission of diplomacy to Ninigret, later had a change of heart and informed Mulford of the negotiations with Ninigret. Mulford immediately contacted the Rhode Island governor, Benedict Arnold, warning him of a potential conspiracy.

Ninigret, seeing an opportunity to achieve a goal he had pursued for three decades, invited the Montauketts to send representatives to his annual "Great Dance" in the summer of 1669. This celebration was held, said Ninigret, "from the time after the weeding of our corn to such time as we do eat of it." This was probably the traditional green corn ceremony, usually held sometime in July. The Montauketts responded, sending Papasaquin and three other men to the gathering with an offer to accept a tributary status under Ninigret's Niantics. They brought with them a gift of twenty fathoms of wampum and a gun once owned by Wyandanch as a symbol of their tributary status (RCRI 2: 271). The gesture, of course, recalled the terms demanded by Ninigret in 1638 (fig. 27). The gun had displaced the bow and arrow as a symbol of military power, reflecting the growing dependence on European goods in Native American communities.

Governor Arnold, fearing that Ninigret's Great Dance was the cover for a conspiracy against the English settlements in New England and Long Island, called Ninigret to appear before his council in July and explain his intentions. The sachem denied both Manecopungun's accusation and the rumor about a conspiracy (RCRI 2: 270). Manecopungun, he said, did not speak for the Montaukett: he "is forsaken of all his kindred, and is in a very sad condition, laying his hand over his face." The other Montauketts, continued Ninigret, "say to him, it is justly befallen him for the lies he hath made, and for disturbing the country" (RCRI 2: 271). Ninigret argued that his new alliance with the Montaukett posed no threat to the English, as it was a matter between Indian nations. The governor accepted this explanation but warned Ninigret that the Montaukett must give him the wampum tribute freely. He could not take it by force.

East Hampton town officials, fearing that Ninigret might oppose their plans to obtain the remaining Montaukett lands, were thrown into a panic by the news of this new alliance. Even though their patent in 1666 from Governor

Figure 27 Papasaquin handing Wyandanch's gun to Ninigret, signifying that the Montauketts were now Niantic tributaries. Drawing by David B. Martine.

Nicolls prohibited the Montauketts from selling their lands to agents outside of East Hampton, they feared the clause might not be enforceable. Led by the Reverend Thomas James and John Mulford, the town officials demanded the Montauketts turn over their guns and renounce their alliance with the Niantics. When Papasaquin and other prominent Montauketts refused to comply, the English threatened to take away their corn fields as well as their guns. The standoff continued until members of Wyandanch's family and men who had served as Wyandanch's closest advisors convinced a majority of the tribe that opposition to the English was futile (RCRI 2: 285).

In November 1669, Sachem Poniutute and his supporters reached an agreement with New York governor Francis Lovelace, disclaiming "any such vassalage" to Ninigret and pledging to give him no more wampum as tribute. They further acknowledged that Lovelace was "our Chiefest Sachem" (NYCD 14: 627). The agreement was signed at East Hampton and witnessed by John Mulford and the Reverend Thomas James. Papasaquin, Nopum, Missaquant, and Naveyawont did not sign the document. A year later, Sachem Poniutute, who had now taken the name "Moshup"; Pauquatoun; and Sunksquaw

Wuchkitaubit gave up a tract of land where the village of Montauk is located today (RCSS 168–69). For Papasaquin this must have been a particularly painful turn of events and perhaps spurred his decision to move east to Shinnecock, where he joined a group of independent-minded Indians attempting to form their own whaling company.

The Whaling Years

In the fall of 1671, when Papasaquin learned that a group of sixteen Shinnecock were challenging the practice of paying whalers with trade goods, he joined them. It is possible that he had family connections at Shinnecock, but it was also an action consistent with his independent spirit. The Indians, as noted in the previous chapter, formed their own company but were unable to implement a whale design of their own. Although the failure of the company was not as dramatic as the collapse of the Montaukett resistance three years earlier, it was a forceful reminder of English dominance. Papasaquin's activities during the next three whaling seasons are not documented, but he may have signed on with one of the Southampton whaling companies along with several of the other whalers. Another possible explanation for his absence was that he was wary of involvement with the English after his experience at Montauk and the disappointment at Shinnecock.

Papasaquin would certainly not have been encouraged by the tensions within the whaling industry over the next two seasons. He may have been apprehensive, for example, of the lay system imposed in the spring of 1672. The following month the Unkechaug seized a drift whale claimed by John Cooper, and the next year Tobacus, the Unkechaug sachem, and his followers confronted a Brookhaven whaling company, demanding payment of one barrel of oil from every whale taken by the company as well as reimbursement for the firewood used in trying out the blubber. The Brookhaven residents, outraged by the audacity of the Unkechaug, called on Lovelace to take action (NYCD 14: 678). In an ordinance issued on April 19, 1673, the governor ordered the Indians, "whether sachems or others," to cease all unlawful actions, "molestation or hindrance unto any of the persons or company employed in the [whaling] design and allow them to take firewood necessary for their trying operation." It was one of the governor's last actions before the Dutch invaded New York in the summer.

What must have gone through Papasaquin's mind as he witnessed the suppression of the Unkechaugs' attempt to assert control over their beaches, followed only a few months later by the defeat of the English and the imposition of Dutch rule? Perhaps he even had some sympathy for Governor Lovelace. The governor was blamed for the humiliating loss and recalled to London, where he was imprisoned in the tower for a few months before dying the following spring.

The foreign occupation, while not burdensome, complicated plans for whaling operations. The eastern towns were concerned about the possibility that the Dutch would favor their own whaling operations over English companies. The countries had a long history of contentious rivalry over whaling in the North Atlantic. The towns, led by John Cooper and other whaling company owners, attempted to make their own peace with the Dutch. They pledged that if the Dutch agreed to guarantee freedom of religion, free trade, property rights, free elections, jurisdiction of local courts, taxation by consent, equal rights with Dutch citizens, and the right to procure "warps, irons, or any other necessities, for the comfortable carrying on of the whale design," they would hand over their flags and constables' staffs to the Dutch (NYCD 2: 583–84). It is noteworthy that whaling concerns were placed on the same list as such important rights as voting and taxation.

Surprisingly, the Dutch agreed to all the provisions except for the clause regarding whaling equipment. That article, said the Dutch, "cannot, in this juncture of time be allowed." The town of Southampton reluctantly relinquished the flag and the constable's staff in September but refused to acknowledge Dutch sovereignty until their whaling rights were fully guaranteed. They addressed a letter to the Dutch governor general, Anthony Clove, stating that they would not acknowledge Dutch authority. Clove responded the next month by sending a ship to Southold, hoping to intimidate the east enders without the use of force (NYCD 2: 648–49). The strategy was an embarrassing failure. A hostile crowd from East Hampton and Southampton, urged on by John Cooper, confronted the Dutch, who read a statement demanding the towns swear an oath of allegiance to them. Receiving no response, the Dutch returned to their ship and left.

The Anglo-Dutch War gradually wound down as the English Parliament became increasingly reluctant to grant King Charles more funds. In February 1674, the Treaty of Westminster ended the conflict and the Long Island whaling operations were soon revived. Edmund Andros, the new governor, arrived in New York in November and began the restoration of English governance. The following spring three Southampton and two East Hampton whaling companies began signing up whaling crews. One of the men they recruited was Papasaquin. In March 1675 the first East Hampton company was formed by Reverend Thomas James, Richard Stratton, Thomas Dimon, and Thomas Chatfield, all prominent members of East Hampton elite families (RTEH 2: 373–74).

The contract drawn up by the East Hampton company states that the agreement is between the Englishmen "on one part and Moshup, 'Sachem of the Montaukett' Papasaquin, Anthony, Scummauge, Unquonommo, Uncommouit, Jeffry, Wompaquat, Humphrey, Apunsha, Ben Indian, Quaun, John Indian, and Harry, alias Wossooio, Joseph and the rest of their associates belonging to Meantaukut the other partie, 18 in all." The position of former adversaries at the top of the list may indicate the perception that they were the leaders of the whaling crews. Reverend James, who knew both men well, may have presumed that with their leadership skills, the two would bring success to the hunt. The contract, however, was never completed. The names of the investors and all but three of the Indians were set forth, but no terms or signatures were recorded.

One explanation for the sudden aborting of the negotiations was the emergence of an old conflict between members of the East Hampton elites. Five years earlier, William Edwards, one of the town founders who came to East Hampton from Southampton around 1650, had sued Thomas Dimon, accusing him of "detaining" four of his "skins," probably beaver or deer, and demanding that Dimon pay for the use of his fence (RTEH 1: 326–27). When Dimon failed to appear in court to answer the summons, he was charged with court costs and fined ten shillings. Whether or not Dimon harbored a grudge against Edwards can only be a matter of conjecture, but on March 22, 1675, two weeks after the uncompleted document was entered into the town record, Dimon, on behalf of the company, sued Edwards, demanding that Edwards satisfy a debt to the company of thirty shillings and a gallon of rum (RTEH 1: 375–76). Why these petty suits involving members of elite families went to court under these circumstances is an interesting question. The company members may have been concerned about any erosion of the corporate funds prior to the whaling season. If so, the incident suggests the fragility of the loosely structured whaling companies.

At the same court, Jacob Schellinger and his stepson, James Loper, who were competing with Reverend James for whalers, also had to delay the organization of their whale design to settle a conflict over the allocation of lay shares from the previous season. The two men filed a suit against John Comes, accusing him of stealing whale blubber and baleen that belonged to Loper (RTEH 1: 375–77). Comes claimed that the whale products were his share from the 1673–74 season. He was entitled, he said, to a sixth share of the company half share because he had provided one of the boats for the design. This testimony is one of the few references to the specific distribution of the profits from the company half share.[3] Three months later, the court ruled, after having "seriously weighed and considered the case according to the evidence given . . . [and] having great debate about this case," that John Comes should have one-half of a sixth share. The case delayed the organization of Schellinger and Loper's whale design for the 1675–76 season.

A month later, more serious matters disrupted the English settlements in New England and on Long Island. Word came from across the sound that King Philip had launched attacks on several villages near Plymouth and were soon joined by the Nipmucks (Leach 1958, 30–41). The Long Island Indian communities were immediately under suspicion. Papasaquin may have been singled out immediately by James and the East Hampton officials because of his involvement with Ninigret nearly a decade earlier. Although Ninigret had never given much support to Philip, it was known that Papasaquin and Philip's representative, Cocumscusett, had both attended Ninigret's Great Dance in the summer of 1669. The English had been suspicious at the time, questioning Ninigret about the presence of Philip's man and the purpose of the gathering (RCRI 2: 269–74). Ninigret, however, dismissed the speculations at the time and never supported Philip's war efforts.

War hysteria spread across Long Island in July, prompting Governor Andros to order the town constables to sequester the Indians' guns until peace was restored in New England and prohibit Indians from leaving their villages. The loss of their guns prior to the fall hunting season alarmed the Indians, raising fears about the winter food supply. In September, however, the governor inflamed English fears. He ordered the towns to fortify a place where they could "secure their wives and children" in case of an attack (NYCD 14: 697–98). Rumors of impending attacks throughout the fall upset preparations for the 1675–76 season. The governor charged that the Montauketts and the Manhansetts had given aid to the Narragansett and could not be trusted (NYCD 14: 697). Wary English eyes turned to Papasaquin and those other Montauketts who had been identified as members of the "Ninigret faction." The governor, however, did not distinguish between the Ninigret faction and the rest of the Montauketts. When Andros, moved by the Indians' concerns about the winter hunt, returned the guns to the other Long Island tribes, he exempted all the Montauketts and the Shinnecocks from the order. Their guns were to remain sequestered. The right to seize and sequester the guns was yet another reminder that the English were the final authority over Montaukett and Shinnecock affairs.

In October, Moshup, recognizing this reality, followed the example set by Tobacus, the Unkechaug sachem who had sent Meneges to make an appeal to the governor. Moshup approached Reverend James and asked for his support in drafting a similar appeal to the governor. James, who saw his own advantage here, agreed and added a note on the back of the letter stating that in "the lines upon the other side I wrote upon the desire of the sachem and his men . . ." (NYCD 14: 699–700). Moshup assured the governor that the Montauketts were trustworthy. "My father and grandfather," he said, "have stood always loyal to the English." He acknowledged that they had had "some correspondancy with Ninigret" but were "ever loyal subjects to the king and the duke of York and to your honor and to all authority under you." The letter was endorsed by Manecopungun and three other counsellors "in the name and with the consent of the rest of the Indians at Montaukett." Manecopungun had taken a second name, "Gentleman," perhaps because of his age and his role as a diplomat in tribal relations with the English. Moshup's reference to the Ninigret affair brought attention to Papasaquin and his supporters and may explain why he was not hired by any company for the 1675–76 season. There was no response from the governor as the opening of the hunting season approached.

The settlement with Comes did not end problems for Schellinger and Loper. The governor's order restricting the movement of Indians prevented East Hampton investors from signing on Manhansett whalers from nearby Shelter Island. Unable to fill two boats for the 1675–76 season with the Montauketts, Schellinger and Loper ignored the order and hired four Manhansetts (RTEH 1: 378–79). This move was particularly troublesome because the governor had cited them as untrustworthy. Schellinger, nevertheless, hired them and paid them a twenty-five-shilling advance in accordance with the prevailing practice. The presence of the Manhansetts on Schellinger's crew immediately drew the attention of James and his company investors. On November 5, 1675, the town constables and overseers ordered that, in compliance with the governor's ordinance, they prohibit any man from the town from employing "any strange Indian either to go to sea a whaling or work upon the shore . . ." unless they had an exemption from the town officials (RTEH 1: 380–81). Thomas Baker, speaking for the town, told Schellinger that they would not grant this exemption to them. It was the town's duty to uphold the governor's order. The Manhansetts, he warned, could not serve on his crew.

Schellinger, in desperation, petitioned Andros, protesting the action taken by the town and charging them with conspiring against him in a blatant conflict of interest. Without the four Manhansetts, wrote Schellinger, he could not launch his two boats and the season would be lost. Competing whaling companies, he said, wanted not only to sabotage his season but to recruit from his eight remaining Montaukett whalers, who were now available. According to Schellinger, the town officials "under pretense of zeal in fulfilling your honor's order yet it is more than apparent that they endeavor to break your petitioners company in that manner that so they themselves may have opportunity out of the other eight East Hampton Indians to supply their own wants." To underscore the injustice, Schellinger added, "One of the overseers, being of the company that would so hinder your petitioners" (NYCD 14: 708–9). The names of the officials for that year are not recorded, but three of James's company—Dayton, Chatfield, and Stratton—frequently held these town positions. Thomas Baker, the official who spoke for the town in this matter, was married to Ralph Dayton's daughter.

Governor Andros, aware that the whaling season began later that month, responded. Having either changed his opinion of the Manhansetts or, more likely, recognizing the blatant self interest in James's motives, he now declared the Manhansetts to be "of civil deportment" and not likely to give aid and comfort to King Philip. He then approved the appeal from Schellinger and Loper, saving their season (NYCD 14: 707). The governor may also have been thinking of James Loper's connection to two very prominent and influential Long Island families, the Howells of Southampton and the Gardiners of East Hampton. Loper was married to Arthur Howell's daughter, Elizabeth, who was Lion Gardiner's granddaughter. The episode reveals the high level of stakes in the whaling industry as well as the lengths to which the rivals might go to gain a competitive edge in what had become a very profitable endeavor. James, unable to gain access to any of Schellinger's men, moved hastily in December to complete the contract for his company.

James, moving quickly, made significant changes to his roster of company investors, replacing John Stratton with his brother, Richard, and, perhaps to resolve the conflict between Edwards and Dimon, dropped Dimon and added Will Edwards and his sons, John and Thomas, along with Robert Dayton, John Hoppin, John and Ben Osborn, and Richard Shaw (RTEH 1: 381–83). A company of twelve investors seems most unusual, although in many contracts the names of all the investors are not listed. Possibly, James wanted to attract members of such prominent families as the Daytons, Shaws, and Osborns to face off against the competition from newcomers such as Schellinger and Loper. Moshup, Papasaquin, and the rest of the whalers listed in the uncompleted March entry did not sign with James. The data in the records is insufficient to explain why the Montauketts failed to sign on, but it is possible that, perhaps other than Moshup, the men may have been among Papasaquin's supporters when he had negotiated with Ninigret.

Following the death of King Philip in August 1676 and the restitution of the Montauk and Shinnecock guns, tensions were eased somewhat, but there were only three contracts recorded for the 1676–77 season. In 1677, Papasaquin returned to Shinnecock, where he signed on with John Cooper of Southampton for the 1677–78 season. Although they had all been paid an advance, probably the customary twenty-five shillings, they apparently assumed that Cooper's death freed them to sign on with another company owner. Cooper's wife, Sarah, however, thought differently. She decided to break into what was then a man's world and run her husband's company herself.

In November, at the beginning of the season, Sarah Cooper complained to Governor Andros that the eight whalers had been solicited by "others of the

English" (NYS.MSS 26: 153, 157). In my husband's absence, wrote Cooper, "this at present lies hard on me because the boats and craft which by my husband [was] prepared for the whale design" cannot be employed without Indian whalers. She asked Andros to issue an order requiring the Indians to work for her. Three weeks later, hearing no response, widow Cooper appealed again, but once more heard nothing.

Once again Andros was caught in a difficult position, obliged to balance the competing demands of prominent Long Island families. The reason for Andros's hesitation was undoubtedly related to actions taken by members of three influential Southampton families. Richard Howell and Joseph Fordham, who had hired Artor, one of Cooper's Indians, went to the Court of Sessions for East Riding (present-day Suffolk County) a week later and had Artor appear before Constable Joseph Raynor. His testimony, barely legible, was written on the backs of the January and March contracts by Henry Pierson, the clerk of sessions. Artor stated that he had signed "the present engagement" to go to sea for Howell (SHTA Liber A2, 113; RTSH 2: 68). The same day, Richard Howell's brother, John; Benjamin Davis; and Joseph Fordham brought in Jeffrey, who swore that he had signed in good faith with Howell, Davis, and Fordham (SHTA Liber A2, 114). Andros may have been reluctant to take action against members of the powerful Howell, Raynor, and Fordham families because of events the previous fall, when he had pressed the eastern Long Island towns to negotiate new patents in an effort to raise colonial revenues and limit local autonomy.

When Southampton officials resisted his demands for a new patent, Andros forced them to comply by threatening to seize the town lands (Ritchie 1977, 105). After an uneasy standoff the town reluctantly capitulated. The governor was unlikely, therefore, to take any action in support of Sarah Cooper that might stir up more trouble with the Howells and Fordhams or question the authority of Constable Raynor. Furthermore, animosity existed between Sarah Cooper's late husband and Raynor and Richard Howell dating back to 1663, when John Cooper sued them over the rights to a beached whale (RTSH 2: 27). Howell did not hesitate to sign on Omaagunseis (Omagonsha), one of the men named by Sarah Cooper for his 1678–79 season (SHTA Liber A2: 122). These occasional family squabbles, however, seldom disrupted the network linking whaling entrepreneurs and political officials in the eastern Long Island towns.

Papasaquin does not appear in the records again until the spring of 1679 when he signed on with Jacob Schellinger for the 1679–80 season. Loper, who has been credited by historians with initiating shore whaling on Long Island, is not mentioned in the contract. Perhaps he was meant to be included in the reference to "Schellinger and partners," but he was apparently no longer a prominent member of the company (RTEH 2: 78–79). This once again raises a question about his legendary role in shore whaling. There are other reasons to suspect that Schellinger may not have wanted his assistance. Loper, a contentious sort, had, in addition to his suit against Comes, sued Renock Garrison over a debt of three pounds, Cornelius Williams over blubber valued at one pound, and Isaac Moline over five whaleboat oars. In another court action, Loper threatened the jurors when a judgment went against him. The court fined him for his intemperate behavior (RTEH 1: 284, 344, 416, 389).

More troubling perhaps to Schellinger were indications that Loper had difficulty relating to Indians. In August of 1679, Toby, a Montaukett, complained that Loper had beaten him in a public encounter. Although the court found both parties at fault "in striking one another and so breaking the King's peace," such behavior did not bode well for the operation of an enterprise dependent on Indian whalers (RTEH 1: 423–24). Toby had signed a contract with Thomas James and company three months earlier and would later sign agreements with John Wheeler in 1680 and Benjamin Conkling in 1681 (RTEH 2: 77, 86–87, 96–97). A month later Loper brought suit against a Montaukett whaler named Quasique, charging him with an unpaid debt. Quasique was charged with "nonappearance" and fined for the court costs (RTEH 1: 424). No further mention of the matter appears in the records.

Loper's actions would have endangered the company's relations with Weomps and Scanderbag, whom Schellinger had signed up in April 1679 for the 1679–80 season. Both men had hunted with Quasique on James's crew in 1675 (RTEH 2: 78–79). The two men joined Papasaquin and five others to hunt for Schellinger's company. Schellinger required a ten-pound bond that would have to be paid if a contracted whaler failed to show up at the beginning of the season and other "such fines as is usual for whalemen." The whalers, however, were not obliged to pay the fines or the bonds for the men who "ran away" or were absent on occasion as was the case in some contracts. Schellinger may have decided that such clauses were not enforceable. Papasaquin and Weomps, however, did not stay with Schellinger for the next season.

In January 1680, the two men, along with Toby, signed on with John Wheeler, an influential East Hampton resident who would later represent the town in negotiations that led to the creation of Suffolk County in 1683 (Rattray 1953, 126). The conditions set forth in the contract were similar to many others except for a clause promising that Wheeler would "trust the Indians one barrel of oil and eight pounds of whale bone." This may have been an advance payment. If so, it was worth much more than the usual twenty-five shillings paid by Schellinger. This may have attracted the three Montauketts to hunt whales for Wheeler (RTEH 2: 86–87).

The next season brought many more opportunities for whalers as the number of companies plying the waters off eastern Long Island doubled. Papasaquin and his associates took advantage of the favorable circumstances and left

Wheeler to consider another employer. Sixty-eight Indians signed contracts for the 1681–82 season, but, as noted in chapter 6, the number of whalers may have been much larger. The contracts indicate that four of the companies planned to send out two boats, while the other eight relied on a single six-man whaleboat. Of course, some of the latter companies, whose crew members were not all under contract, may also have sent out two boats, relying on one or two experienced whalers to serve as a core for each crew.

Wheeler now faced a great deal of competition for experienced whalers. He managed to sign up two men on March 14, and four more ten days later. One of the four, however, was a Montaukett who had been given the name "Witness" by the English. On April 1, Samuel Mulford of East Hampton, who had organized what was to be his first and only company, entered a complaint against Wheeler, charging that Witness had signed a prior contract with him (RTEH 2: 100). The controversy was apparently resolved without further involvement from colonial authorities. Mulford probably got his man. His brother, John, one of the town founders, was an important figure in the political life of the colony, and Samuel himself was the town clerk at the time. Samuel would later carry a protest against the tax on whale oil to the parliament in London (Savitt 1970).

After considering the available options, Papasaquin and his two companions joined with Simon and Jeffrey and signed on with Benjamin Conkling for the 1681–82 season. Conkling, the son of Ananias, one of East Hampton's founding fathers, was an influential resident who had served as justice of the peace and held other official posts. The contract clauses included a ten-pound bond, but again there was no mention of fines. The agreement did include one very unusual clause requiring English boats to "attend the said design" (RTEH 2: 95–96). This is the first mention of Englishmen in separate boats accompanying the Indian crews. It is not clear from the text whether the English boats and crews were to engage in the hunt or provide some other service, such as rescuing a whaler thrown overboard or helping to tow the dead whale back to shore.

Papasaquin returned to Southampton at the end of February 1682, perhaps influenced by Ponguamo, who had been a member of the Shinnecock company with him in 1671. It is also possible that he had a kinship connection at Shinnecock. The two men signed on with Matthew Howell, whose grandfather, Edward Howell, was one the town founders. Although the whaling season usually continued into March, the competition for whalers for the 1682–83 season apparently prompted the companies to begin recruiting very early. Four other Southampton companies also began recruiting in January and February of 1682, and Andrew Gibbs signed on ten Unkechaug whalers the following March.[4] Papasaquin, perhaps taking advantage of the demand for whalers, asked Howell to provide his crew with two "good new" cedar "and all other necessary conveniences for carrying on of this design" (SHTA Liber A2: 74–75).

Howell likely granted their request because, in addition to their whaling skills, they were both prominent men in tribal affairs. Ponguamo was identified as a sachem when he hunted whales for Matthew's father the next year (SHTA Book D2: 168). Howell must have been aware that good relations with such men could ease tensions between the two communities that might emerge in the future. Both whalers, for example, were involved in the negotiations with the English over the dispossession of Shinnecock and Montaukett lands in 1703.

Obadiah Rogers, a Southampton company owner, in an unusual move late in the spring of 1682, approached Papasaquin and Seguana, who had served with him on Matthew Howell's crew, and signed them along with two other Shinnecocks, Wahumbaho and Papamacwuot, to a contract for the 1683–84 season a full year in advance (SHTA Book D2: 84). He agreed to find them a good boat, oars, warps, and irons. His contract, witnessed by his father, Obadiah Sr., and John Simon, was at risk given the fierce competition for whalers again that season. The ten companies that launched whaling operations that year put 120 whalers under contract. The competition undermined Rogers's careful advanced planning. It was not surprising, given the length of time between the signing and the opening of the season, that Rogers lost most of his crew.

John Jessup Jr., a Southampton company owner, lured Papasaquin and Sequana away from Rogers and signed them up in April 1683 (SHTA Book D2: 117–18). Wahumbaho also jumped from Rogers, signing with Joseph Raynor Jessup's and Raynor's actions reveal that, although the contract system imposed limitations on the freedoms of the whalers, the owners' willingness to ignore their own regulations provided windows of opportunity. Jessup's contract was also witnessed by family members: his uncle, Thomas Jessup, and another relative, Jonathan Howell. The network of family connections did not always work in a predictable pattern. Both Obadiah Rogers and John Jessup were related to the Howells. Obadiah was married to Sarah, the daughter of Edward Howell Jr.

Papasaquin, who was now probably in his late forties, may have retired from whaling in the spring of 1684. The following fall he turned to matters pertaining to his immediate family. His name does not appear on any of the agreements made during the last two years in which the contract system was in place.

"To serve faithfully and obediently": Papasaquin Indentures His Children, Quausuk and Margot

Papasaquin apparently had established a trusting relationship with Jacob Schellinger, perhaps because Schellinger was not a part of the East Hampton old family elites with whom he had so often been at odds. The whaling contracts, deeds, and indentures suggest that more informal social interactions took place between the two cultures than has been appreciated in the historical accounts. Papasaquin and his wife approached Schellinger in the fall of 1685 and negotiated an indenture for his seven-year-old son, Quausuk. This was one of several such arrangements made by parents of Indians and poor whites in the town records for eastern Long Island. The system, described in chapter 6, was widely used in the seventeenth century by English families without the means to provide food, clothing, and an elemental education for their children. For Indian children, however, the emphasis in the contract was on obedience to the master and safeguarding of the master's property.

Papasaquin and his wife were to deliver Quausuk to Schellinger in 1688, when he reached the age of ten, whereupon they would receive a payment of twenty-five shillings (RTEH 2: 173–75). Quausuk was expected to serve Schellinger for ten years "faithfully and obediently in whatsoever he shall be set about . . . and not to absent himself at any time out of his master's service without his master's leave." Papasaquin was obliged to pay for any damage caused by his son. Schellinger promised to feed and clothe Quausuk and to pay him ten pounds "good current money" at the end of his indenture.

Two years after Quausuk finished his indenture, Papasaquin and his wife indentured their daughter, Margot, to Daniel Osborn of East Hampton. Osborn, the grandson of an East Hampton town founder, paid the parents three pounds in advance. Margot was to remain with Osborn for seven years and receive "meat and lodging with what all is necessary" (EHLPC (X) WB 126). Margot's indenture contract is brief and far less specific than Quausuk's. The difference in the agreements may be related to gender. The decision by Papasaquin and his wife to give their daughter an English name suggests his antagonism toward the English may have mellowed.

Papasaquin and the Final Dispossession of Montaukett Lands, 1683–1703

In May 1683, John Osborn purchased a neck of land called Wattuquasset, located south of Fort Pond near the present-day village of Montauk (RCSS 134). He negotiated with a Montaukett leader identified only as the "young sachem," probably Moshup's successor, and two elders, Manecopungun (a.k.a. Gentleman) and Sasakataka, who had been Wyandanch's chief advisors prior to his death in 1659. The Montaukett leadership had changed little following the restoration of Wyandanch family control in 1669. Under the protocol established by Governor Lovelace in 1670, the town of East Hampton and the governor had to approve the sachem and his primary counsellor or "constable," as the English called him (see chapter 6). This mechanism for monitoring and influencing Indian communities through alliance sachems, established by the English during the early postcontact period, had gradually been displaced thanks to social and economic changes in the relations between the English and Native American communities. These forces were evident on eastern Long Island by the time Osborn sought approval for his purchase. The English found that having close relations with a cooperative sachem was no longer vital. Over the years, the English developed a variety of relationships with the Montaukett men, women, and children, often on a daily basis.

The three Montauketts who came to meet with Osborn were accompanied by twenty-two others, eleven of whom were whalers with economic connections to the English. Three of the men, Jambassu (Iambassu), Wobetom, and Scanderbag, had hunted whales in the 1675–76 season for a company whose investors included John and his brother, Benjamin (RTEH 1: 381–82). One of the others, Cowanuck (a.k.a. Dick), had signed whaling contracts with Richard Shaw (1679) and John Wheeler (1681). The Osborn family, who had been involved with whaling for the previous two decades, was well represented here. John's purchase was witnessed by his brothers, Benjamin and Thomas. In contrast to the early postcontact treaty negotiations, in which the only personal contacts had been between the leaders of the two communities, now most of the men who accompanied the Montaukett leaders had long established familiarity with individual Englishmen. Most of these relationships involved some form of labor-based exchange.

The economic links between the Montaukett whalers and the English investors undoubtedly strengthened Osborn's hand in the negotiations. A closer look at three major land transactions during the last two decades of the seventeenth century reveals that a significant number of the Indians who endorsed the dispossession agreements were whalers or worked for the English in other capacities, such as mending fences, harvesting crops, tending cattle, or as domestics. Their increasing involvement in the English economic system undoubtedly put them at a disadvantage in the land transactions.

Osborn's acquisition of the land at Montauk was viewed by the English in East Hampton as the beginning of the process of land alienation that would inevitably absorb the remaining Montaukett lands. These plans, however, were threatened when Thomas Dongan, who replaced Governor Andros in the fall of 1683, demanded that the Long Island towns negotiate new patents. The governor sought to increase the control of the colonial administration over the fiercely independent eastern Long Island towns and facilitate the collection of taxes. Dongan also had a well-deserved reputation for taking every opportunity to expand his personal estate (Ritchie 1977, 180–90). The governor's view of the town officials was equally negative. He knew that the town residents had gained control of Indian lands through many questionable land transactions and that they were eager to get their hands on the rest.

The original East Hampton patent in 1666, as noted above, established the town boundaries as running from Southampton on the west to Fort Pond on the east, where the Montaukett lands began. The lands east of Fort Pond, extending to the end of the island, remained in the possession of the Montauketts with the proviso that they could not sell them to any purchaser other than an East Hampton resident. Osborn, therefore, had exercised East Hampton's exclusive right of purchase. The town residents, however, were understandably nervous about the fate of that proviso in a new patent.

The patent process, calling for exorbitant fees, was to be completed by April 1684 (Ritchie 1977, 187). When East Hampton stalled well past the April deadline, Dongan threatened to call in and examine all the town's Indian deeds. This threat unsettled the town officials, who were concerned about the possibility that Dongan might question the legitimacy of the title to their town lands and/or remove the proviso that guaranteed East Hampton exclusive purchase rights. In hopes of protecting themselves from either possibility, town representatives were dispatched to obtain a confirmation of all the previous land transactions signed by the Montauketts. The town residents feared that some of those deeds might be challenged and, perhaps, even voided by the governor.

On September 30, 1684, the East Hampton selectmen met with the two Montaukett sachems, identified as Aquaas (Aquosh) and Sasakataka, Wyandanch's chief counsellor (RCSS 169–71). Aquaas was probably the man identified as "the young sachem" the year before. The two Montauketts were joined by their chief counsellor, Manecopungun, and eleven tribal representatives. The selectmen presented a document confirming the original town purchase in 1648, which did not include the Montaukett lands at Montauk, and the 1655 leasing arrangements for grazing land at Montauk (RCSS 170–71). These agreements were the same as those endorsed by Governor Nicolls in 1665, shortly after the establishment of the colony of New York. The town officials added a clause promising to pay the Montauketts four pounds "in good pay" every year in perpetuity if they would build and maintain a fence at the south end of Fort Pond, near John Osborn's tract, to prevent their livestock from wandering into the ocean.

Manecopungun, who had briefly been an ally of Papasaquin before turning against him in the dispute over the aborted alliance with Ninigret in 1667, joined with the two sachems and the other Montauketts in supporting the proposals put forth by the selectmen. Papasaquin, who had just finished the 1683–84 season with John Jessup's company, did not attend the meeting. Eight of the eleven Montauketts who endorsed the agreement—Checkano,

Ungowan (Ungomunt), Ben, Harry, Obadiah, Cowanuck, and Wobetom and his son, John Indian—had been employed previously by East Hampton company owners including John and Benjamin Osborn, Thomas James, John Wheeler, John and Richard Stratton, and Jacob Dayton (RTEH 2: 132–33). Five of the whalers—Cowanuck, Checkano, Ben, Obadiah, and Wobetom—had supported John Osborn's purchase. Fearing Governor Dongan might consider the transaction suspect, the selectmen brought Aquaas, Sasakataka, Obadiah, and Checkano to Southampton, where they were asked to testify before John Howell, the Suffolk County clerk, that the agreement was "their act and deed." The action taken by the officials underscores, yet again, the level of distrust between the governor and the local town officials.

The overseers were confident they would get the confirmation they wanted because, in addition to the economic connection between the whalers and the owners, the sachems themselves had received payments from the town. The town records make references to payments made to "ye great sachem" and to "ye young sachem," probably Sasakataka and Aquaas, on a list of town expenditures for the spring of 1684. Only the year is recorded, but the entries in the ledger are between March and April. Both men were paid two pounds, and Ben (alias Toj), who had hunted whales for Thomas James in the 1677–78 season, was given two pounds of sugar and a knife valued at three shillings (RTEH 2: 143). These payments were likely for services related to the negotiations. Payments to "the young sachem" continued the next year when he received twenty shillings, four pounds of sugar, a dozen pipes, and two yards of duffel cloth (RTEH 2: 159–60).

The town did get the confirmation from the Montauketts, but their fears about the vulnerability of the exclusive purchase clause for the Montauk lands east of the town were realized two years later, in April 1686, when John Delaval, a wealthy New York merchant, joined with a group of New York entrepreneurs and petitioned the Colonial Council for the right to purchase the Montauk lands (CELP 2: 39).[5] The petition failed, but the effect of the move served Dongan's purpose. East Hampton responded quickly to the threat. They sent Samuel Mulford and John Wheeler to New York with instructions to buy a patent.

The town paid the governor two hundred pounds to secure a new patent that confirmed the purchases of the town lands from the Montauketts and again guaranteed the town's exclusive right of purchase for the remaining Indian lands (RTEH 2: 194–203). The patent, ratified by the governor on December 9, 1686, named twelve men as the trustees of the freeholders, six of whom had employed Indian whalers in their whaling designs and three who had close family members in the companies.[6] Brookhaven and Southampton, under similar pressure, followed suit later that same month.

East Hampton now moved quickly to take advantage of the terms in the patent. Town officials met with sachems Aquaas, who now called himself Wyandanch (the second) after his great grandfather (see fn. 2), and Sasakataka in the summer of 1687 and drafted a document ostensibly dictated by the two men: "We Wiandance and Sacakotahou, sachems of Meantauk with ye consent of the Montaukett Indians . . . have for a valuable sum of money in hand received to ye value of one hundred pounds do alienate bargain and sell . . . our tract of land at Montauk bounded by part of the Fort Pond and Fort Pond Bay . . . to the utmost extent of the island from sea to sea . . ." (RTEH 2: 213–14). An addendum gave the Montauketts the right to continue living and planting on the land for a token payment of an ear of corn upon demand. They were now tenants on their ancient lands (Smith 1926a, 48–49).

Seven of the nineteen Montauketts who endorsed the sale were whalers. All of them, except for a Montaukett named Shine, had endorsed one or both of the previous land transactions. Papasaquin, who had returned to Montauk in 1685, did not come forward to join the others in support of the agreement. Although he intended to entrust his son Quausuk to Schellinger the following year, he may have still resisted this final alienation of Montaukett lands. His wariness toward the English was soon shared by others at Montauk, including Wyandanch and Sasakataka. The English, ignoring their promises concerning Montaukett planting grounds, let their livestock wander onto the corn fields at Montauk. Another source of contention involved the payments that, according to the agreement, had been "in hand received." This was untrue: the Montauketts had not received the money; instead they had accepted a payment schedule of two pounds a year for fifty years.

In June 1701, Sasakataka and Wyandanch (the third) protested to the town selectmen because the English sheep were destroying their meadows. The Montauketts also complained that the town had not kept up with the agreed-on schedule of payments. East Hampton, confident that their new patent protected their exclusive purchase rights, paid more attention to the question of sheep. They appointed a committee of eight men to meet with the Montauketts. Five of the committee members—Josiah Hobart, the current justice of the peace; Samuel Mulford; John Wheeler; Benjamin Osborn; and Thomas Chatfield, the town clerk—had invested in whaling operations.

When the committeemen met with the Montauketts on June 30, they promised to pay for the damage done by the sheep but did not address the complaint about the payments (RTEH 3: 7). However, had they known what actions the Colonial Council would take during the early months of the following year, they might have heeded those complaints. Between February and May, the council issued licenses to wealthy Manhattan entrepreneurs, giving them the authority to purchase Indian lands in Westchester, Ulster, and Suffolk counties (NYCCM 8: 164, 165). Two of the men with an interest in acquiring tracts of land in Suffolk County were John Bridges, the newly appointed justice of the Supreme Court, and Rip Van Dam, judge of the Court of Chancery and member of the governor's council. In the inner circle of the Cornbury administration, these men were powerful adversaries for officials from a town on eastern Long Island.

The East Hampton freeholders, however, were so sure of their control over the Montauk lands that they began buying and selling shares in Montauk (RTEH 3: 21). In the fall of 1701, for example, Cornelius Miller sold one-third part of a tenth share in Montauk to John Conklin for twenty-four pounds "in hand paid." Their confident air may have further antagonized the Montauketts, escalating the tensions between the two communities. Over the next months, as the tensions intensified, the committee reported that the Montauketts were "obstinate and averse to agreement" (RTEH 3: 36–37). Very likely Papasaquin was among those "difficult" Montauketts.

In May 1702, the town officials, in frustration, issued a threatening pronouncement giving the committee the power "to do or act in the said affair with the town's whole power and authority, both offensive and defensive . . ." (RTEH 3: 35–36). The Montauketts were not intimidated because they were soon to take an action somewhat similar to their formation of an alliance with Ninigret three decades earlier. Their opportunity came the following September, when Rip Van Dam, who had recently been appointed to the chancery court, and John Bridges, who was now a justice of the New York Supreme Court, used their power and influence to obtain a license from the Colonial Council permitting them to purchase the Montaukett lands out from under the East Hampton residents in spite of the 1687 deed and the exclusive purchase clause in the patent (NYCCM 9: 173). Although the details of their challenge to the East Hampton deed were not recorded in the Legislative Journal of the council for the ninth assembly meeting in Jamaica, very likely the failure of East Hampton Town to make the payments was seized as a reason to nullify the deed (JLCC 1: 176–89).

Bridges and Van Dam sent word to Thomas Longworth, the Suffolk County clerk, to invite Wyandanch and his chief counselor, Sasakataka, and some tribal representatives to Jamaica, where Governor Cornbury and his council were in session, and have them listen to their offer in the presence of the governor. The sachems opened the meeting by presenting Governor Cornbury with a "small present," probably a string of wampum as was the custom for any serious negotiation. Then they listened to Longworth present the offer from Bridges and Van Dam (Pelletreau 1903, 2: 372–73). The larger message was clear: the offer carried the endorsement of the colonial government. The Montauketts accepted the terms believing they now had a powerful ally in any conflict with East Hampton.

According to historian J. Franklin Jameson, Longworth used "trickery and strong waters" (Jameson 1883, 236). Jameson, however, provides no evidence to support this conclusion. His interpretation reflects a common stereotype about Indians and alcohol. Wyandanch and Sasakataka, who knew from their own experience how the colonial administration worked, realized that even if their agreement with Van Dam and Bridges fell through, it gave them leverage to protect their interests and, at the very least, force the resumption of the yearly payments from the town. The Montauketts must have been pleased to have such a satisfying bargaining chip to use against their old adversary. Papasaquin, who may have been one of the Montauketts accompanying the sachems, would have appreciated the strategy.

When word of this reached East Hampton, the town committee sent Samuel Mulford to begin negotiations with the Montauketts, asking them to void their agreement with Van Dam and Bridges. On September 30, 1702, Mulford approached Ungomunt, who had endorsed the 1684 and 1687 confirmations and paid him two pounds for his testimony in support of East Hampton. Ungomunt stated that he had indeed endorsed the 1687 purchase and added that he had received a payment "from the hand of Captain Samuel Mulford" (BHSL grandmother's book). Samuel turned to members of his family for witnesses. Thomas Dibble, who had recently married Samuel's niece, Rebecca, and Isaac Mulford, his eighteen-year-old nephew, signed the document. It is noteworthy here that Mulford enlisted the aid of a Montaukett who had worked for him. Clearly, he hoped that Ungomunt's economic ties and his personal relationship with him would make him more willing to cooperate.

Over the next month Mulford continued to pressure Wyandanch, Sasakataka, and other influential Montauketts. There are no surviving documents similar to Ungomunt's testimony, but Mulford undoubtedly employed the same tactics with the two sachems and twenty-two other Montauketts, inducing them to testify on November 12, 1702, that the 1687 deed was a valid agreement that superseded Van Dam's purchase (Pelletreau 1903, 2: 373). The Colonial Council, however, ignored this testimony and imposed measures on the East Hampton proprietors that cost them time and money, undoubtedly giving the Montauketts some satisfaction.

On December 31, 1702, the council ordered Thomas Cardale, the surveyor-general, and Thomas Longworth to survey the Suffolk lands purchased by Van Dam and Bridges (NYCCM 9: 178). When the two men went to Montauk, they were confronted by an angry party from East Hampton demanding to see the papers that authorized them to conduct the survey of lands protected by the exclusive purchase clause in their patent (NYCCM 8: 166; RTEH 3: 33). The town residents' demands were dismissed, apparently viewed as a mere annoyance by the council.

The following spring Mulford and the town officials met with Sasakataka and Wyandanch and thirty Montaukett representatives in East Hampton, requesting a more formal confirmation of the 1687 purchase (Smith 1926a, 49–51). Papasaquin, whose daughter was now living in Daniel Osborn's household, was confronted once again by a difficult decision, as were a majority of Montauketts who also had economic and social ties with the English in East Hampton.

Thirteen of the Montauketts who attended the meeting had been employed in the past by company owners to hunt whales, seven of these men had endorsed one or both of the previous agreements, and many others worked as domestics or day laborers or had family members indentured to the English. Jeffry, who hunted whales for Benjamin Conkling in 1681–82 and later tended cattle for the town, was indentured to Richard Shaw of East Hampton in 1687 for a term of seven years. Tom Indian served as an indentured servant in the household of Thomas James from 1678 to 1681. And Obadiah had been hired in 1670 to tend English cattle at Montauk for ten shillings a week. All of these men were among those invited by the English (RTEH 1: 330, 411; RTEH 2: 145–46, 212). The whalers in the following table had all been employed by whaling companies in the past. Their employers, with the exception of John

Table 3 Whalers who endorsed the 1703 Confirmation and their employers

Name	Date	English company owner	Source
Ben Witness	April 1, 1681	Samuel Mulford	RTEH 2: 99–100
Ben (a.k.a. Towis)	December 27, 1677	Thomas James	RTEH 1: 407–9
Jeffry	March 5, 1681	Benjamin Conkling	RTEH 2: 95–96
John Indian, son of Wobetom	August 12, 1683	Richard Stratton	RTEH 2: 213–14
Natt (a.k.a. Jumpas)	December 27, 1677	Thomas James	RTEH 1: 407–9
Obadiah	June 26, 1682	John Cooper	SHTA Book D2: 94
Papasaquin	March 5, 1682	Benjamin Conkling	RTEH 2: 95–96
Shine	February 16, 1683	John Kirle	RTEH 2: 119
Ungomunt	April 1, 1681	Samuel Mulford	RTEH 2: 99–100
Unquanamuck	March 24, 1681	John Wheeler	RTEH 2: 98–99
Wobeton	October 28, 1684	John Miller	RTEH 2: 152–53
Weomp	March 5, 1681	Benjamin Conkling	RTEH 2: 95–96
Wyandanch (Moshup)	December 27, 1677	Thomas James	RTEH 1: 407–9

Kirle, were all members of wealthy and influential East Hampton families. These economic ties to the English undoubtedly put the Montauketts at a disadvantage in the negotiations.

Papasaquin likely had mixed feelings about the meeting. As a young man, he had taken a strong position against attempts by the English to obtain the Montaukett lands, but he had since worked for English whaling companies and had placed his children in the care of English families. His decision to attend the meeting was undoubtedly influenced by these life experiences. The agreement reached at the meeting affirmed the 1687 purchase and established a payment schedule that drew on the interest accruing from the purchase price of one hundred pounds (Smith 1926a, 49–54).[7] This arrangement guaranteed payments in perpetuity as opposed to one lump sum that would quickly be spent. Although the Montauketts finally gave in to the pressure from East Hampton, the settlement was still a better deal than had been in place before. It is not possible to know with any degree of certainty if the Montauketts were planning at the outset to use Van Dam as a stalking horse for their interests. Perhaps the Montauketts were employing the same strategy that they used when they threatened to form an alliance with Ninigret three decades earlier. The 1703 compromise settlement held until the early twentieth century, when the Montauketts were finally evicted from Montauk following a lengthy court battle (see Strong 2001, 107–55).[8]

8

Leaving the Shore

The End of an Era

Ironically, the unusually successful 1706–7 whaling season, bringing in four thousand barrels of oil from over one hundred whales, marked the beginning of the decline of the shore whale design along the North Atlantic coast. The season was followed by a disappointing drop to six hundred barrels in 1707–8. Governor Cornbury, in his July 1708 report to the Commissioners for Trade and Plantations, explained that the sudden change was understandable because whaling was an uncertain business. "Some years they have more fish than others," he stated, implying there was nothing he could do about a natural phenomenon over which he had no control (NYCD 5: 59).

Decline and Denial

There were many on the colonial council who did not agree with Governor Cornbury. Convinced that the Indian whalers were being distracted by the lure of demon rum, which led to absenteeism and a subsequent drop in whale oil production, they drafted a legislative act reflecting their stereotypical views of both Indians and lower-class white settlers. According to the "Act for the Encouragement of Whaling," passed on September 18, 1708, the whalers were selling or pawning the goods given to them by the company investors prior to the opening of the season in November and buying rum. The problem, from the lofty view of the council members, was exacerbated by the "lower sort" of Englishmen who drank along with the Indians, often inviting them into their own homes. The bouts of drinking, they assumed, frequently resulted in arrests and fines for disturbing the peace, which also prevented the Indians from showing up for the hunt. The reference to such social interaction between Indians and the English, if accurate, suggests that there may have been closer relations between the cultures than has been noted by social historians.

To address this perceived problem, the council ordered that any person who sued, arrested, molested, or detained an Indian who was hired to hunt whales from November to April each year was subject to a fine (LCNY 610–11). The act spelled this out in detail, implicating anyone who bought, or accepted on pawn, goods from a whaler prior to the hunt, or who should suffer any such Indian to be drinking in or about their houses when they should be at sea . . . or carry or cause to be carried any drink to them whereby such Indians are made incapable of doing their labor and duty in and about their master's service between the first day of November and the fifteenth day of April following.

The act further held that anyone, "he, she, or they, so offending, besides restoring to such master such clothing gun or other necessities, shall forfeit and pay to the master of such Indian or Indians the sum of thirty shillings." The reference to "she" as well as "he" and "they" suggests that English women too might have been involved in the purchase of the goods, in the liquor trade, and perhaps also in the festivities. The wording also suggests that the practice was widespread. The law was to continue in force for the next seven years.

The first four seasons following the enactment of the ordinance did not bring the desired results. Estimates based on the London customs records of oil imports from New York indicate that there were only seven whale catches in 1708, eight in 1709, and seven in each of the following years (appendix 5). In 1711, one of the few years when we have a detailed record of Long Island whaling activities, Daniel Sayre of Southampton sent a letter to George Clark, the colonial secretary in New York, listing the names of eastern Long Island companies and the number of barrels of oil each company harvested that season (NYS.MSS 54: 188).[1] Nine companies reported shipping a total of only 304 barrels to London, about half the number shipped in 1708.

Table 4 1710–11 whaling season

Names of Investors	Number of Barrels
John Gardiner's Company of eighteen men	36
Capt. Theophylus, Elisha, and Lemeul Howell	22
Hezekiah Howell, Samuel Johnes, and John Cooper	48
John Mitchell, Thomas Stanford, Benjamin and Thomas Howell	7
Samuel Mulford	48
Isaac Raynor and Daniel, Edward, and Jonathan Howell	24
Thomas Stephens, James Cooper, Henry Pierson, and Ichabod Sayre	6
Capt. Josiah Topping, Theodore Pierson, and Stephen and Hezekiah Howell	84
Richard Smith (justice of the peace), Israel Howell, and Moses Culver	29
Total	**304**

Although the law had no effect on the productivity of the whaling operations, making it quite clear that the whalers could not be blamed for the continuing decline in whale catches, the council renewed the law in 1712 for another four years (LCNY 1: 887). There were no catches in 1713 and only four the following year. The year 1715, however, was relatively high-yielding, bringing in eleven whales, but was followed by a drop to four in 1716. Still, the council clung to their perception that the Indians were at fault as they renewed the law for another four years. The next year only two whales were killed, but the last three years of the law, however, did see a sharp increase. In 1718, the best of those years, fifteen whales were killed, still far short of the catches in 1707 (Reeves, Breiwick, and Mitchell 1999, 29).

The decline in whale oil continued as did the discussions and debates about the causes. Some argued that the whales wounded and lost by less-skilled whalers frightened other whales from the seasonal migration paths. In a report to the Commissioners of Trade in London, Governor Robert Hunter dismissed this as a distraction offered by eastern Long Island whaling companies to divert attention from their covert practice of sending their oil to Boston in order to avoid the New York customs agents (NYCD 5: 498). There was some truth in this. Samuel Mulford complained that his two sons, Timothy and Matthew, and Richard Floyd had been arrested in 1712 by Governor Hunter for failing to pay the taxes on their oil and baleen (NYCD 3: 372). None of these explanations, however, considered the possibility that whale hunting was gradually reducing the critical mass of the North Atlantic right whale population.

Shore Whaling in the Mid-Eighteenth Century

The involvement of Native Americans continued even as the number of whales killed in the waters off Long Island slowly decreased. In 1720, for example, Jambush, a Shinnecock, was bound out by his father Raif and his mother, who is not named, to Joseph Halsey, the Southampton blacksmith, for four years or four whaling seasons. Jambush would be paid a half share of the oil and bone "according to custom." The oil was valued at one pound and twelve shillings per barrel and the baleen at two shillings per pound (SHSA Rogers File).

Halsey's mother was a Howell, making him a third-generation descendant of the two most prominent founding families in Southampton. He was, however, the first Halsey to take up whaling. Joseph later sold the remainder of Jambush's indenture to his brother, Jonah. Although the agreement is called an indenture, the terms are similar to those in the seventeenth-century whaling contracts, underscoring the blurred lines between indentures and the whaling contracts discussed in chapter six. Jambush's parents endorsed the agreement as was required in an indenture, but the young man was not provided with food, clothing, and lodging, nor was he promised to receive a payment at the end of four years.

Unkechaug Whalers: 1720–1732

Richard Floyd's journals and indentures indicate that he hunted whales continuously from 1684 to 1746. During the decade covered in RFL 2 the names of nine Unkechaug men appear: Harry Indian, Jacob Indian, James, Nimrod, Philip, Thom Washam (Warishon), Surroot, Lewey, Philip, and Will (a.k.a. Umpatrina). These men, as was the case with Tangier Smith's Indian employees, probably were engaged in various agricultural duties as well as whaling. Floyd's method of payment, however, is difficult to determine from the scattered entries in the ledger. Some are brief and do not appear to be related to whaling. Jacob Indian, for example, was charged with small amounts of powder and rum and a yard of cloth that appear to have been taken at the same time. Jacob was probably too old for the arduous demands of whaling. He would have been at least twenty years old when he signed the agreement with Tangier Smith in 1700 granting the Unkechaugs their 150-acre reservation (see chapter 6). In his forties during the ledger years, he likely worked at less strenuous tasks around the farm.

Floyd and Smith did not have to recruit whalers each season, nor did they have to compete with other owners, because they had a year-round arrangement with the neighboring Unkechaug villagers. On at least two occasions the two families joined together on a whaling enterprise. In 1718, Floyd paid William Henry Smith, Tangier's son, eighteen pounds and nineteen shillings for his share of the profits (Osborn Shaw Papers, BTH). Two decades later, Richard Floyd delivered a sum of eight pounds to Smith, which satisfied a debt owed by a whaler named Indian Jack "on account of whaling" (Osborn Shaw Papers, BTH). Entries for James, Philip, Surroot, and Thom Washam are similar in form to the whaling accounts in the St. George estate records. They are all dated in the spring, suggesting a relationship to the previous whaling season. Floyd, however, did not enter an estimated monetary value of the goods. Washam's account on April 5, 1720, followed a fairly successful season for those years. The London records indicated that an estimated fourteen whales were killed off Long Island (Reeves, Breiwick, and Mitchell 1999, 29). Washam ended the season in debt for twelve quarts of cider, fourteen (pecks?) of corn, six quarts of rum, a new homespun shirt, and a yard of blue pennystone (Peniston) cloth (RFL 2: 5). Brightly colored blue and red coarse woolen cloth from the small village of Peniston in Yorkshire had become an essential item in the eighteenth-century Indian trade (Willmot 2005, 205). By then, textiles had replaced wampum as the "source and mother of the fur trade." Success in the fur trade now depended on a steady stock of the material. Floyd had it readily available for the Unkechaugs working on his farm.

After Washam paid off his debt, Floyd made a large X through the account and drew a line underneath the entry. He returned to the book two years later, at the close of the 1721–22 season, and made entries for three men: Philip, James, and Surroot Indian (RFL 2: 4v, 5). The season had been disappointing. Only eight barrels of oil were shipped to London following the 1720–21 season, when eleven whales produced five hundred barrels. Surroot's account raises some puzzling questions. The items taken by Surroot far exceed those received by Washam and the other whalers. The list fills the bottom half of the page and continues on all of the next page. Surroot received, in small measured portions, a pound and a half of powder, five pounds of shot, pork, seven and a half pecks of corn meal, leather for shoes, two quarts of molasses, four gallons of rum, pennystone cloth, lining cloth, a shirt, stockings, and a Dutch blanket (RFL 2: 5–5v). There is no indication of a time frame for the receipt of the items, but the measured portions indicate that they were not dispensed all at once. The rum, for example, was parceled out in ten individual units, usually one or two quarts at a time.

Surroot likely had a special relationship with Floyd, perhaps because of his skills as a whaler or his status in the Unkechaug community. His name appears on seven pages in the ledger, whereas the names of James, Washam, and Jacob are each entered twice and the others' names just once each. Surroot's accounts document his receipt of a disproportionate amount of goods, particularly rum.[2] He was allotted a total of ten gallons in contrast to a gallon or less for each of the others. Surroot may have distributed the goods and the rum to meet family obligations and enhance his status, just as the alliance sachems had a century earlier. Floyd would have found it useful to have such a liaison with the Unkechaug workers. On May 1, a few days after Floyd entered Surroot's account, he recorded a smaller list of items for James and Philip. James received rum, molasses, leather for shoes, a yard of pennystone cloth, and a "fine shirt," and Philip received a nearly identical set of goods (RFL 2: 4v).

The uncertainty of the whale design was evidenced sharply by the seasonal catches from 1721 to 1726. In 1723, ten thousand gallons were harvested from about eight whales recorded for the Long Island area. That year Surroot was advanced a gallon and three quarts of rum, a Dutch blanket, sugar, bread, and meal (RFL 2: 14). The next season, however, brought in only five hundred and sixty gallons, about sixteen barrels, perhaps from North Atlantic pilot fish (*G. melas melas*). Surroot's account for that season had five separate entries for rum and four listings for corn, suggesting that the items were given out over a period of time as was the practice for whalers during the hunting season. Surroot also received a Dutch shirt and a knife (RFL 2: 7).

There are no entries listing goods advanced to Indian whalers for 1724–25 and 1725–26. James Indian has an entry for April 30, 1727, that lists two quarts of molasses, a half a bit's (small-denomination coins based on the Spanish *reales*) worth of pipes, three quarts of cider, two more quarts of molasses, four gills of powder, two gills of shot, and twelve pots of cider (RFL 2: 4). There is no data in the London customs record for that season, and the numbers for the next five years never exceeded one whale catch per year. The entry for James is the last one in the ledger related to Indian whalers.

Three of Floyd's whalers—James, Philip, and Will—became involved in a land transaction while they were working for Floyd. In 1730, Richard Floyd's brother, Nicoll, approached William Henry Smith, the son of Tangier Smith, who had died in 1705, asking permission to purchase a hundred-acre tract from the area that his father had granted in perpetuity to the Unkechaugs (map 4). William Henry had no objection, ignoring the specific language in the 1700 grant (Strong 2011, 115–16). Nicoll then sought out Sachem Wacus, who had hunted whales for Tangier Smith in 1697 and had led the Unkechaug representatives in their negotiations with Tangier Smith in 1700. He was joined by his son, Richard, and thirteen other Unkechaugs, most of whom were probably well known to the Smith and Floyd families. In addition to the three Floyd whalers, there were three other Unkechaugs—Weramps, Robin (Reuben), and Awanose—all of whom had hunted whales for English companies. The Unkechaug delegation, therefore, included a majority of whalers and a sachem's son. Nicoll offered them twenty Dutch blankets, four barrels of cider, and three pounds in "current money of New York" (WFEA, FIIS 6928). Not surprisingly, the Unkechaugs, most of whom were dependent on the Smiths or Floyds for their livelihood, accepted the offer reducing their reservation to seventy-five acres. By the end of the century, only fifty acres remained.

The Last Days: 1732–1750

In 1732, Francis Pelletreau of Southampton wrote to Stephen Delancy, a New York merchant, giving him an account of whales taken in the 1731–32 season by companies in Southampton and East Hampton.[3] Three adult whales and eight yearlings had been killed, six had landed, and five were still floating toward shore. This is the second reference to a practical alternative to towing the huge carcasses to shore. The six whales alone yielded about 220 barrels of oil and 1500 pounds of baleen, "good for the London market." Pelletreau estimated that the remaining five whales would yield about 150 more barrels of oil and 1,000 more pounds of baleen, if they could successfully be landed. The 370 barrels of oil would bring over 700 pounds, and the 2,500 pounds of baleen would have been worth about 350 pounds sterling. Even though the total number of whales was small when compared to the sixty or more whales taken yearly during the peak years in the 1680s, the total value of the oil and baleen, slightly over 1,000 pounds sterling, was a significant amount of new capital for the local economy, enough to purchase over twenty farmsteads on eastern Long Island.

The last two seasons on the London customs books, 1732–33 and 1733–34, reported a total of only five whales. It is possible that the 1732–33 season would have been more productive had it not been for a smallpox epidemic that swept through Brookhaven Town in the spring of 1732. The town, assuming the disease was spread by Indian servants and African American slaves, issued an ordinance restricting their movement and prohibiting the sale or distribution of alcohol to them by their employers or owners (RTBH Book C: 149). These restrictions may have interfered with the preparations for the whaling season.

Smith, Floyd, and some farmers with access to the Atlantic barrier beaches continued to hunt whales on a random basis. In December 1742, Reverend Azariah Horton, the missionary who preached to Indians from 1740 to 1744, noted that some Montauketts moved their wigwams to an area on Napaegue "in order to attend the whaling design, in which they are engaged with some of the inhabitants of East Hampton" (Horton 1993, 200). Two of the last surviving shore whaling indentures on record were recorded by Richard Floyd in 1746. Rueben Indian, probably the son of the Reuben who signed the 1730 deed, bound himself to go whaling for Floyd for the following three seasons, and Indian Ned Laine agreed to "go a whaling" for one season.[4] Reuben would receive four pounds "in cash" for each season, but there is no mention of payment in Laine's agreement and no mention of a lay share, fines, or bonds in either of the contracts.

A decade later Rueben was among the Unkechaugs who negotiated a transaction with the town of Brookhaven in 1755 for the oyster-rich underwater bay lands lying west of the Carman River, where the small community of Bluepoint is now located (Strong 2011, 119–20). The underwater tract, the last of the ancient Unkechaug lands to be alienated, became one of the world's richest sources of oysters called "bluepoints." The Unkechaug received five pounds sterling for the tract. Brookhaven was represented by Richard Floyd, Rueben's former employer. Most of the eleven Unkechaugs who signed the deed were on the Floyd payroll at the time.

In the early spring of the year in which Reuben and Ned Laine signed their whaling indentures, James, Surroot, and Nimrod, who must have been in their early forties, left the Floyd farm and joined the colonial militia fighting in King George's War (1746–47), a precursor to the French and Indian War. Military service, for some Indians, may have replaced whaling as an opportunity to earn status and obtain English goods. The English and French saw the immediate advantages offered by recruits with hunting skills and the ability to survive on limited supplies in unchartered territory. In June 1746, Governor George Clinton called for troops to assemble in Albany in response to an attack on Saratoga by the French and their Indian allies (NYCD 6: 318). James Fanning of Smithtown raised a troop of one hundred men from Suffolk County that included several Indian recruits (Strong 2011, 134–36). The company spent a hard winter in Albany awaiting orders to march against the French in Canada. The state assembly, influenced by merchants in Albany who had lucrative trade relations with the French, declined to provide funds for the attack and sent Fanning's company back home (NYCD 6: 316–17, 337, 341).

Although the muster rolls provide some important information about individual Indians during this period, they must be approached cautiously and within the context of related primary sources. Fanning's roll included an addendum listing thirty-eight names under the heading "Indians and Negroes" (NYSH 1: 624). Several familiar names—Nimrod, Surroot, and Mahaine— mentioned in the Floyd records appear on Fanning's addendum. There is also a recruit identified as James Floyd, Indian, who was probably the James Indian in the Floyd ledger. He may have taken the Floyd name when he signed on with Fanning.

The adoption of English family names by Indian and African Americans was not uncommon during this period. Thomas Howell, another name on the Indian roll, had taken the name of a Southampton founding father. Others added an English first name to their traditional name. The roll listed a Nimrod and a Ned Nimrod, probably father and son, and four others apparently related to Mahaine, the Unkechaug whose debt enabled Floyd's purchase of the Pattersquash. The men were identified as Charles, Sam, Sam Jr., and Tom Mahaine (NYSH 1: 624–25). Two others, Jacob and Stephen Surroot, were likely the children of Surroot Indian.

A decade later the conflict between England and France resumed, engulfing most of eastern North America. The family names of some whalers again appear in the muster rolls. The incentives for military service were enhanced by a bounty system offered to recruits in 1760. Those volunteers who signed up received a cash bounty of fifteen pounds, one blanket, one pair of buckskin breeches, two shirts, two pairs of stockings, a hat, and one shilling and three pence a day for the duration of their one-year enlistment (CNYHS 524). Unlike the goods taken from the whaling companies, this advance came debt-free. Anticipating that some men might take the bounty and run, the clerks, "muster masters," charged with keeping the records, wrote down the ages and physical description of the recruits that would be useful in tracking them down.

Jacob Surroot, a veteran of the aborted Albany campaign, described as a forty-two-year-old Indian, five feet five inches "with remarkable white spots on his body," enlisted in a militia company from Brookhaven, led by Thomas Brewster, in 1759. Several men in their forties and fifties were listed on the rolls, suggesting that, even with the bounty, it was difficult to attract volunteers (NYSH 1: 945–53). For Indians, however, the bounty was a much better deal than they could get in any other employment. The following year James Surroot, age thirty-seven, perhaps Jacob's younger brother, signed up with Captain Jonathan Baker's company (NYSH 2: 573).

Reuben Indian, who had been paid four pounds to hunt whales for Richard Floyd in 1746, undoubtedly had no trouble deciding to join the militia. In 1761, at the age of forty-eight, he signed up with the Suffolk County company under the command of Captain Daniel Griffin (NYSH 2: 656). Another elderly whaler, Harry Indian, who had worked for Floyd and Smith in the 1720s, also joined the militia. Harry, along with Reuben, Nimrod, and Will (Umpaquas), signed the 1755 transaction mentioned above, granting Brookhaven the rights to fish and take oysters from the waters south of Bluepoint (RTBH Hutchinson, 177–79). Harry, described as a fifty-year-old "homely Indian," was recruited by Captain Stephen Sayre of Brookhaven in 1759 (NYSH 1: 950–53). How such a description would be helpful in locating Harry is open to question. Harry may have signed up the following year with Captain Jonathan Baker. The muster master here identified Harry as a forty-nine-year-old Indian with no comment about his looks. Either this is a younger, better-looking Harry or, perhaps, a comment on the imprecise descriptions entered by muster masters (NYSH 2: 572).

A decade after the peace settlement ending the conflict with France in 1763, many Long Island Indians followed Samson Occom, the Mohegan Indian missionary, to join the Brotherton community on land granted to them by the Oneida in central New York State. The descendants of Unkechaug whalers, Weramps, Wacus, and Dick (Cowanuck), for example, are listed on the Brotherton rolls (Venables 1993, 526). Others, however, remained home and would continue hunting whales far from the familiar shores of their native Long Island.

Leaving the Shore: New Wine in Old Bottles

The success of the shore whale design led to the near extinction of the North Atlantic right whale by the mid-eighteenth century. Randall Reeves initiated an extensive study of right whale demographics from 1650 to 1918, when the last killing of a right whale by commercial hunters was recorded (Reeves, Smith, and Johnson 2007, 39–74). Relying on his research on the London customs records of oil imports from 1697 to 1734 and on scattered reports of whale catches in the colonial records (as noted in a previous chapter), Reeves concluded that the peak years were 1670 to 1750.

Faced with the loss of their ancient lands and the rapidly declining whale population, the Indians adapted once more to a changing world around them. Their hunting and navigating skills were still in demand, but in a very different universe. The large whaling vessels were sent around the world in search of sperm and humpback whales. The small "catcher" boats that the Indians had learned to maneuver with such skill and courage were put on board along with all the equipment. The same hunting strategies were used, but now the whale was towed back to the mother ship, flensed, and stored away in barrels for the trip back to the trying stations on shore.

On these early hunting expeditions, no one had yet resolved how to safely operate try pots and furnaces aboard ship. As a result, voyages were constrained by the need to reach a trying station before the blubber went rancid. In 1761, Nathan Fordham and James Foster were given permission to build a wharf and a trying station in Sag Harbor. Small ships, such as the *Good Luck* owned by Joseph Conkling, hunted whales in the Atlantic and brought in blubber to be tried out here. Sometime in the later decades of the eighteenth century, the problem of shipboard processing was solved and the whole shore whaling design, from killing the whale to trying out its blubber and storing the oil, could be carried out aboard ship, enabling far larger expeditions to the deep waters of distant seas. The first ship from Sag Harbor carrying the furnaces and try pots on board went out in 1784.[5] The ship named *Hope*, owned by David Gardiner, undoubtedly had some Montaukett crew members on board (Adams 1918, 233).

Some aspects of the whale design did not change. The ships, the equipment, the whale oil, and the market system all belonged to the whites. In the early years of the deep-water whaling operations, some of the descendants of the seventeenth-century investors became ship captains, shipowners, or agents negotiating contracts for the Indian whalers. Stephen Howell, for example, owned three ships, the *Nancy*, the *Minerva*, and the *Betsy*. William Herrick, a Southampton merchant who arranged contracts for whalers in 1803, could trace his family line back to seventeenth-century investors. His ancestors, William and James Herrick, had invested in whaling companies from 1672 to 1682.

Herrick and Uriah Rogers, another Southampton merchant who was also descended from whaling company investors, were well placed to recruit whalers because of a political system imposed on the Shinnecock by the English at the end of the eighteenth century. This system, modeled after the Southampton Town government, was designed to bring order to what had become a chaotic scramble for access to reservation lands by local farmers, who sought out individual Shinnecocks and offered them cash for the use of grazing and planting grounds. This practice frequently led to conflicts among Shinnecock families who claimed proprietorship rights over the desired tracts. Their claims, of course, were not based on written records but rather on tribal tradition. Farmers often exacerbated the problem by approaching Shinnecocks with an offer to lease a tract already under contract to another farmer. Once again, as had been the case with the scramble for Indian whalers, unwritten Native traditions created problems for the English system of property law based on written records and legal codes.

The solution reached in 1792 was similar in some ways to the contract system in the seventeenth century. The town and tribe agreed to establish an English-style political structure wherein the leases would be approved by three elected tribal trustees in a yearly meeting at town hall. The meetings were supervised by the town clerk and witnessed by the justice of the peace and one or two town residents. The primary agenda each year was the election of three trustees by the male members of the tribe and the allocation of leases. The traditional system, which gave women a major role in issues relating to planting grounds, was ignored by the English, who imposed their own male-dominant structure on the Shinnecocks. Herrick and Rogers were in a position to influence tribal affairs and recruit whalers because of their official positions in the town government. Herrick was the town clerk and Rogers served as the justice of the peace. This put them in a good position not only to negotiate whaling contracts but also to influence the decisions about leasing reservation lands.

The two men developed a working relationship with David Jacob, who served as a trustee from 1792 to 1794, when the new tribal government was being implemented. William Herrick, who took down the minutes, recorded these transactions, and certified the results of the yearly elections, must have played a significant role in the process. David also served on the committee established to allocate portions of reservation land to individual Shinnecocks, who could, if they so desired, lease out this land to local farmers. Herrick monitored the meeting and Uriah Rogers, as justice of the peace, served as a witness.

One of the first problems the trustees had to deal with was directly related to whaling. A farmer falsely claimed that he had leased a tract from a Shinnecock whaler before he went off to sea. The absent whaler, of course, was unable to speak on his own behalf. To prevent such abuses, the trustees ruled on April 2 1793, that "no person or persons on pretense of having hired land of Indians whom are gone to sea . . . shall challenge or improve lands . . ." (Papageorge 1983, 143). The following year, another entry notes that "whereas there are a number of Indians gone in the whaling business . . . ," land would be reserved for them when they returned home. These entries are significant because they indicate that Shinnecock whalers had been engaged in deep-water whaling for some time.

During David's tenure, the trustees were generous in the leasing of tribal lands. Zebulon Jessup, the first farmer to take advantage of the leasing arrangement, was granted twenty-one acre lots. Other recipients included Joseph Marshall, who received three lots; Uriah Rogers, who got twenty-two lots; and William Herrick, who took two acres (Papageorge 1983, 143–53). The practice of leasing out reservation lands to white farmers continued into the 1960s, when it was discovered that the pesticides liberally applied to the crops, particularly potatoes, was poisoning the ground water.

Whaling Agents for the New Era: 1803–1805

Three documents, all drawn up by Rogers and Herrick and, fortunately, preserved in the Southampton Historical Society collections, provide a window into the early years of the deep-water whaling era. In 1803, the two men negotiated contracts with two Shinnecock whalers, James Courageous and Hugh Jacob. Courageous gave them power of attorney, authorizing them to "appear in my behalf, and to call on Captain Wier Swaine, late of the ship *Toby*, with whom I have lately made a voyage and have returned laden with a cargo of whale oil . . . and in my name to receive the net proceeds of my share of said cargo" (SHSA Rogers File 1803). It appears that Courageous did not trust the captain nor the shipowners to give him his fair share of the profits. His suspicions were undoubtedly based on experiences he heard about from other Shinnecock whalers. He turned to Herrick and Rogers for help, probably because he had met them at the tribal meetings.

The second document, negotiated by Hugh Jacob that same year, was somewhat similar to the ones signed by Reuben Indian and Ned Laine in 1746. Jacob was obliged "to go to sea for them in the customary way as has been practiced by those who have been in the habit of fitting out Indians on whaling voyages." Jacob bound himself for a two-year term "or longer if necessary to pay a debt from him to them." Herrick and Rogers agreed to outfit the Shinnecock whaler from time to time. Unlike an indenture, however, this contract did not require any payment at the end. Instead, Jacob might well end up in debt just as his ancestors often had in the seventeenth century. He shipped out of Sag Harbor on either the *Abigail*, the *Nancy*, or the *Minerva*, the only three departures listed for that year (Adams 1918, 315–16). Two of these three ships were owned by Stephen Howell.

The third document was negotiated by David Jacob when he decided to go to sea two years later. David Jacob turned to the men with whom he had worked so closely on tribal affairs, Herrick and Rogers, signing with them in July and shipping out on either the *Minerva* or the *Abigail*. His contract differed very little from the one Hugh Jacob signed two years earlier (SHSA Rogers File 1805).

Conclusion

The whale design brought with it dramatic cultural changes to the Native people on Long Island. The English commodified the sacred whale, the communal lands, and the traditional custom of gift exchange. Land alienation on Long Island, beginning with the English arrival, was nearly complete by the end of the seventeenth century. The loss of their traditional hunting, gathering, and planting grounds gave the Native people little choice but to enter the English economy as laborers on the margins of the dominant colonial society. The whaling documents over three centuries reveal the detailed inner workings of the lay system, which brought a steady flow of material goods into the Indian villages, including, unfortunately, large quantities of alcohol and a form of debt peonage. Debt continued to be a major mechanism not only for controlling Indian labor but also for advancing the process of assimilation.

Although such patterns of economic dependency emerged, there were also important aspects of traditional culture that survived, including religious concepts, family and kinship systems, and a close relationship with the natural environment. The Unkechaug Nation is recognized by the state of New York, the Shinnecock Nation is federally recognized, and a bill granting state recognition to the Montauketts is before the New York legislature as this book goes to press

Appendix 1

Examples of Whaling Contracts

First Whaling Contract on Record, Nov. 15, 1670

Towsacum and Philip Indian agree to hunt whales for Josiah Laughton of Southampton and his associates. The text was recorded as if the Indians were dictating it to the Southampton Town clerk. The two Christian witnesses were Josiah's brother, John, and Christopher Leaming, of Sag Harbor.

Know all men by these presents that I Towsacum & Philip doe by theses presents have bound and engaged ourselves in my own person God permitting life and health unto Josiah Laughton of Southampton, and to his associates to goe to sea for him or them for the full end & term of three compleat seasons from ye day of this date hereof to bee fully ended, at Mecox, for ye killing and striking of whales and other great fish. And that in the said term or time wee will attend all opportunities to goe to sea for ye promoting of ye said design, for and in consideration hereof hee the said Josiah Laughton or his assignes doe engage to us the said Towsacum & Philip that for every season they will give unto us, three Indian coats, one pair of shoes or a buck neck[1] to make them, one pair of stockings, three pounds of shot, half a pound of powder, and a bushel of Indian corn,[2] and wee doe further engage to help cut out and save all such fish as shall be by the company taken. In witness whereof wee have hereunto set our hands this 15 day of November 1670.

The mark of
Towsacum
Philp Indian
His mark

---

1. A "buck neck" may be related to shoemaking, but the meaning is not clear.

2. The estimated cost of these items per season for each man, based on prices of goods in estate inventories comes to three pounds, thirteen shillings, and seven pence. The total cost (rough and rounded off) for three seasons would be about twenty-eight pounds, fifteen shillings, and six pence. One whale yielding thirty-five barrels of oil (two pounds per barrel) would bring the owners seventy pounds.

Witness
Christopher Leaming
John Laughton
A true copy by me
Henry Pierson

Source: RTSH 2: 56–57.

Shinnecock Contract, Nov. 21, c. 1671

This contract is unique. There is no other contract wherein the Indians organized their own company. The language, however, suggests that the English, perhaps the ones that signed as witnesses, were providing some assistance.

Know all men by those persons that wee the underwritten being joined in a company for this ensuing season to go to sea for the killing and procuring of whales and other great fish doe by these presents bind ourselves jointly and severally in our own persons that god permitting life and health wee will attend all opportunities to go to sea for the procurement of those promises and to cut out and doe our best endeavor to save what shall be by god's providence procured or gotten by us upon the penalty of three [pence?] per day that any of us shall bee negligent either from those going to sea or giving attendance in the cutting out of what fish or fishes [be] taken in witness whereof wee have here unto set to our hands this 24th day on November. In memorandum the place appointed to go to sea at Saggobonick [see map 4].

Signed in the presence of   Anthony Indian
Benjamin Smith   Phineag Indian
Jonathan Morehouse   Jachaneg Indian
Jonaquam Indian   Pochecor Indian
His mark   Lenard Indian
Poaguano Indian   Cowas Indian
His mark   Pockanera Indian
Clem Salmon   Papasaquin Indian
                            Jerimia Indian
                            Artor Indian
                            Pongoma Indian
                            Manusmy Indian
                            Sucaspan Indian
                            Sasaquad Indian
                            Amoachee Indian

Quanuton Indian
Nansaquid Indian

Source: SHTA Liber A2: 90.

John Cooper Jr.'s Contract, June 17, 1672

This contract is the only one that includes a list of trade goods and the costs of the items. It is also the last one before the half-share payment protocol was imposed.

Firstly

These presents witness a contract or covenant between John Cooper of South-ampton in New York shire on Long Island of the one part and the Indians hereunto subscribed of the other part. Made this 17th day of June ano. Dom. 1672, as followeth: [——] said Indians are to go (as servants) to sea fir him, the said John Cooper or his assignes, on whaling the whole season the full time and term of five years next ensuing the date hereof: each season of every five years the next five years to begin 16th November and to end the 16th of April during all and every of the said seasons, life and health permitting, they are faithfully and diligently to take all opportunity possible for killing whales and cutting out both blubber and bone and secure both out of the tides way.

Secondly

It is agreed upon between the parties that if any of the said Indians shall be at any time absent themselves from or neglect their duty as aforesaid hee that so negleth shall pay five shillings for each day and if a whale bee killed by ye rest, then ten shillings the one half of each to bee the company, and ye other half to the said John Cooper.

Thirdly

The said Indians mutually agree together, with the consent of him the said John Cooper, that if any of them shall at any time within the said term of seasons come to be hurt or wounded in the said design, whereby such person or persons shall be disabled from their duty aforesaid, that then notwithstand-ing hee or they so hurt, shall not lose his or their share of profit, or any part thereof, but have equal with the rest each person so hurt paying five shillings in good pay for every whale that shall bee gotten whereof 2 shillings, 6 pence is to bee to the rest of the company and the other 2 shillings, 6 pence to him the said John Cooper.

Fourthly

Hee the said John Cooper is to find the Indians competent boats and craft for the design all said seasons and also to provide for each Indian seamen good oyle barrels each season and to cart to his home or to his house all the blubber that shall at any time be gotten. And there to try it out: and at the end of each whale season to give an honest account unto the said Indians of the quantity of the oyle soe obtained.

Fifthly

He the said John Cooper or his assigne is to have all the said oyle that shall be produced as aforesaid. And to allow the said Indians the full and just value of half the said oyle, is being to be accounted at forty-five shillings a barrel out of which is to bee discounted or abated five shillings for the barrel and half for carting the blubber, whatsoever or shall not bee brought by them unto the plains adjacent to the town: the remainder to make up the said half value, hee the said John Cooper is to pay unto the Indians respectively in broadcloth (of the sort they usually have of him) at eighteen shillings a yard by the list: trucking cloth britches at five shillings, nine pence, per pair and porringers at 2 shillings 6 pence per piece. And if they need it, each boat's crew 3 gills of liquor, 6 pence per gill: spoons at 14 pence a piece, shot at 8 pence, powder at 3 shillings or in other goods answerable in price thereunto (And whatsoever shall become due from any of the said Indians for neglect of their duty as aforesaid is to be discounted or abated out of their proportion of oyle) or if paid in money then the oyle be accounted at twenty [?] shillings per barrel abating therefrom five shillings for each cask.

Lastly

It is agreed upon and concluded by ye said parties, that in case our honorable governor or his substitute approve not of the said John Cooper his making such pay as is aforespecified that yet notwithstanding ye said Indians are to perform their covenant as aforesaid, and hee the said John Cooper is to satisfy (ns?) pay unto the said Indians as his [honor?] or his substitute shall appoint or prescribe or else to pay them as formerly hee used to do: In witness whererof the parties have mutually hereunto sett their hands.

John Cooper
Amagausha, Tauckaumnia, Tagian,
Cohenade, Toutow, Argogoneg, Harry,
Quaquahaugh, Watuagguack, Sauspan,
Mantaman, Wauby.

In the presence of us witnesses,
John Howell, Samuel Mulford

Written on the back
Know all men whom it may concern that wee the underwritten Doe Bind ourselves to John Cooper as fully and firmly in every particular as the other Indians on the other side subscribed have and doe binde themselves jointly and severally in every particular doe we in our persons doe jointly and severally binde ourselves: In witness hereof wee have hereunto set our hands this 17th of June 1672.

Caubut, Pagarement, Webonuck,
Perhant, Jepery, Suncuttums.
In the presence of us
Samuel Mulford, Walter Mellven
A true copy by Henry Pierson
Clerk of the Sessions.

Source: SBD 36–38.

Papasaquin's Contract with Jacob Schellinger, April 7, 1679

Papasaquin's contract with Jacob Schellinger of East Hampton, April 7, 1679. The Montaukett whaler's name (seal) is the first one beneath the text, suggesting that he may have been the leader of the whaleboat crew. The contract is written as if it were dictated by the whalers. They agree to be ready at the appointed place when the whales appear in November. Although the whalers here were burdened with a ten pound bond, they were not obliged to pay fines or bond for crew members who "ran away," a stipulation often imposed by company owners.

Know all men by these presents yt wee the under written have and by these presents doe engage ourselves in our own persons yt god permitting life and health wee will bee readie at or before ye fifteenth of November next to goe to sea to kill whales and doe our faithful endeavor to obtain all profit lawfull to be gotten upon ye Designe of Whaling for Jacob Schellinger of Easthampton and partners and yt wee will be comfortable to goe in such boats and places as our owns shall appoint us to and to such fines as is usual for whalemen in case of killing and cutting and saving and to continue in ye aforenamed their employment from season to season soe long as wee shall bee indebted unto our said owners or employers upon their fitting us for this design we each of us bind ourselves in ye sum of ten pounds sterling for him yt shall fail in not performing according to the engagement to ye aforementioned owners for and in consideration whereof ye aforesaid owners by these presents doe bind and engage themselves in ye said sum to provide boates and Craft and all necessaries for ye Carrying on ye aforesaid designe: and to allow unto us ye under written the halfe of all profit that wee shall obtain with their said boates and Craft during this engagement and to Cart ye same six miles East and West to ye saving of the same to ye true and faithful performance hereof wee everie one of us bind ourselves our heirs executors administrators and assignes in witness whereof wee have hereto set our hands and fixed our seales this seventh day of April anno 1679.

Papasaquin his mark
Signed sealed and delivered

In presence of	John Eacoms His mark
	(Jonaquam?)
Thomas Chatfield	Skanderbags his mark
His mark	Weompes his mark
John J. Parsons	Jeorgkee his mark
His mark	George his mark
	Unquonomcmat his mark

Source: RTEH 2: 78–79.

Contract Between Papasaquin and Benjamin Conkling, March 5, 1681

This contract between Benjamin Conkling and a crew led by Papasaquin for the 1681–82 season is the first of only two contracts suggesting that Englishmen may have joined whaling crews. Papasaquin and the other crew members stipulated that "the English with their boats goe to sea and attend the said designe." The other contract was negotiated by Thomas Cooper for the 1679–80 season, who was not very enthusiastic about joining the hunt. "I the said Thomas Cooper do engage to go to sea with them, lameness and sickness excepted." Whether he actually went or not is not recorded. Weomp, the whaler who was the only crew member on both contracts, may have been the one urging English involvement.

These presents witneseth [that] we the subscribed doe oblige ourselves each man for himselfe to goe upon a whaling design for Benjamin Conkling or his assignes the next whaling season which will bee in the year 1681 upon halfe share as is usual between the English and the Indians that is to say the said Conkling or his assignes to find all boats and other whaling craft necessary and wee the subscribed are to attend duely in season all season soe long as the English with their boats goe to sea and attend the said designe: and soe what oyle and bone is made upon the designe we are to share it at equal halves only wee to show what charge is usual and necessary for cask and trying and other things upon the terms that the late company of Indians called Mr. James' Indians went to sea upon: it is also agreed and we hereby oblige ourselves each one for himselfe unto the said Conkling or his assignes, that in case at the end of the said voyage wee or any of us shall bee in debted unto the said Conkiling or his assignes, then we doe oblige ourselves to goe to sea for him againe the season that shall follow upon the same terms and soe from year to year until wee shall have wholly payd what wee are indebted to him: and for sure performance of all and every article and particular one the abovesaid agreement wee the subscribed doe each of us for himselfe bind our selves in penalty some of ten pounds currant pay of the merchant, to bee forfeited unto the said Conkling or his asignes by every or any of us that shall not fulfill and keep all the abovesaid articles of agreement: Witness our hands and seals this 5th of March 1680–1.

The mark of Papasoquon
The Mark of Weump
The Mark of Tobe
The Mark of Simon Indian
The Mark of Jephery Indian
Signed Sealed and delivered
In ye presents of   A True Record by mee
Aaron Burnat   Samuel Mulford
Jeremiah Conkling Jr.   Recorder

Source: RTEH 2: 95–96.

Appendix 2

Whaling Contracts by Season

The 1670–1685 Whaling Seasons

The table below brings into sharper focus the impact of the whale design on Native Americans and English communities as well as on the whale population. The demographics reflected in the table indicate that a significant number of the Indian male population was engaged in whaling. Based on a conversion rate of twelve whalers for each company, there were at least one hundred and eighty Indians hunting whales for fifteen companies during the 1681–82 season. Matthew Howell in his census of Shinnecocks reported that he found fifty-two men over the age of fifteen living at Shinnecock (Howell 1887, 42–43). Howell did note, however, that "the heathen were so scattered to and fro . . ." that he may have underestimated their numbers. Even so, it is quite probable that most Indian families had a member involved with some aspect of the whale design.

The prominent English families on eastern Long Island are also well represented in the table. The names on the contracts include members of founding families who dominated the political and economic life of the eastern Long Island towns: the Howell, Cooper, Topping, Raynor, and Rogers families in Southampton; the James, Schellinger, Mulford, Stratton, and Conkling families in East Hampton; the Gibb, Tooker, and Biggs families of Brookhaven; and the Higbe and Mowbray families of Huntington.

Whaling Contracts, 1670–1685

Dates	Investors	Sources
1670–71 Two companies 24 Indian whalers	Josiah Laughton, John Howell	SHTA Liber A2: 85–86
1671–72 Five companies 60 Indian whalers	Josiah Laughton, John and Arthur Howell, Cooper, and Ludlam	SBD 84; SHTA Liber A2: 87, 90

(continued)

Appendix 2 table (*continued*)

Dates	Investors	Sources
1972–73 Six companies 72 Indian whalers	John Laughton, John Howell, Cooper, Herrick, Topping	SHTA Liber A2: 93; SBD 36–38
1973–74 Two contracts, 24 whalers Dutch occupation September 1673–October 1674	Herrick, Cooper	SHTA Liber A2: 73
1674–75 One company	Cooper's five-year contract was in its third year	SBD 36–38
1675–76 Four companies 48 Indian whalers King Philip's War, June 1675–August 1676	Richard Howell, Cooper, James, Schellinger	SHTA Liber A2: 99–100; RTEH 1: 407–9, 378–79
1676–77 Three companies 24 Indian whalers	Cooper, James (existing contracts), R. Howell	Existing contracts (see above) SHTA Liber A2: 113
1677–78 Three companies 36 Indian whalers	Davis, James (existing contract) Hobert (January 1678)	SHTA Liber A2: 114; RTEH 1: 407–9; SHTA Liber A2: 119
1678–79 Nine companies, five begin in January 108 Indian whalers	Howell and James (existing contracts), Hobert, Herrick, E. Howell, R. Howell, Sayre, Rose	SHTA Liber A2: 72, 82, 119, 121, 122, 124
1679–80 Six companies 72 Indian whalers	T. Cooper, Shaw, James, Schellinger, Jessup, Fordham	SHTA Liber A2: 122, 123, 133; RTEH 2: 77–79
1680–81 Six companies 72 Indian whalers	Wheeler, Hildreth, Jessup, Biggs, Raynor	RTEH 2: 86–87; SHTA Liber A2: 126, 135, 136; RTBH Book B: 358–59; SHTA Book D2: 49

(*continued*)

Appendix 2 table (*continued*)

Dates	Investors	Sources
1681–82 Fifteen companies 180 Indian whalers	Stratton, Throp, Conkling, Wheeler, Higbe, Fordham, Pierson, T. Cooper, Raynor, Jessup, J. Howell	RTEH 2: 94, 95–96, 96–97, 98–99, 100, 101; RTBH Book B: 62–63; RTH 1: 295–96; SHTA Book D2: 52, 53, 71, 72, 73
1682–83 Eleven companies 132 Indian whalers	Jessup, I. Raynor, M. Howell, J. Cooper, Gibb, Tooker, Pierson, Rogers, Herrick, Barnes, T. Cooper	SHTA Book D2: 71–72, 73, 74–75, 84, 86–87, 93, 94, 103, 107; RTBH Book B: 105, 107, 110
1683–84 Ten companies 120 Indian whalers	Hand, Kirle, Kedy, J. Raynor, Jessup, Dayton, Marshall, Stratton, Davis, Jenners	SHTA Book D2: 112, 117–18, 119, 127; RTEH 2: 119, 120, 213; RTBH Book B: 156, 169–70, 175
1684–85 Seven companies 84 Indian whalers	Raynor, J. Howell, S. Seward, A. Dayton, Muncey, O. Seward, Miller	SHTA Book D2: 168, 172; RTBH Book B: 197; RTEH 2: 152
1685–86 Four companies 48 Indian whalers	Hildreth, Floyd, Thompson, Tooker	SHTA Book D2: 187; *Long Island Forum* 20, no. 5 (1957): 89–92; RTBH Book B: 241–42, 246

The 1686–1687 Whaling Season

The report of the 1686–87 season is one of only two that provides the names of owners, the location of their operations, and the number of barrels they processed. This data was used as a basis for map 3. The estimates of whale catches are based on the conversion rate of thirty-six barrels per whale developed by Randall Reeves in 1986 (Reeves and Mitchell 1986, 202; Reeves, Breiwick, and Mitchell 1999, 27).

The 1686–1687 Whaling Season

Investor	Location	Barrels	Whales
John Cooke	Mecocks	72	1+
James Cooper	Quaquanantuck	144	4
Shamgar Hand	Saggaponack	300	8
Abraham Howell	Wickapogue	36	1
John Jessup	Ketchapanack	96	2+
Joseph Moore	Mecocks	120	3+
Robert Norris	Saggaponack	108	3
Lt. Henry Pierson	Saggaponack	276	7+
Joseph Pierson	Pines	240	6+
John Post	Pines	228	6
Isaac Raynor	Wickapogue	48	1+
Francis Sayre	Town beach	132	3+
Thomas Stephens	Quaquanantuck	264	7
James Topping	Saggaponack	84	3+

TOTAL FOR SEASON 2,148 barrels. Market value at ca. 4,300 pounds sterling. A twenty-acre farm with buildings could be purchased for approximately seventy pounds. Robert Fordham, the wealthiest man in Southampton, left an estate valued at 2,349 pounds sterling. Lion Gardiner (938), A. Howell (887), T. Topping (703).

Source: Pelletreau 1903, 2: 495–96.

Appendix 3

St. George Manor

Whale Catches, 1694–1721

The following table is taken from the entries in Pigskin Book kept by the William Tangier Smith family.

St. George Manor Whale Catches, 1694–1721

Season	Barrels	Whales
1694–95	32	1+
1695–96	48	1+
1696–97	64	2
1697–98	28	1
1698–99	36	1
1699–1700	156	4
1700–1701	84	2+
1701–2	76	2
1702–3	84	2+
1703–4	120	3
1704–5	32	1
1705–6	32	1
1706–7	200 (see table below)	
1707–21	Scattered entries for gallons of oil (no barrels)	

Source: Pigskin Book, Bellport Historical Society, Bellport, N.Y.

Ledger Book, 1706–1707 Season

Date	Description	Barrels
January 16, 1707	A "guit" whale	28
January 24	1 yearling whale	27
February 4	1 stunt whale	4
February 22	1 yearling whale	36
February 24	1 "scoule" whale	35
March 13	1 yearling whale	30
March 17	1 yearling whale	27
March 17	1 yearling whale	14
Total 201 barrels		

NOTE: Whaling contracts beginning in late December, January, or February: January 28, 1677; December 27, 1677; January 30, 1678; January 7, 1679; January 22, 1679; January 23, 1679 (three contracts); January 9, 1680; January 6, 1681; January 18, 1681; December 28, 1681; January 7, 1682; January 16, 1682; February 25, 1682; February 29, 1682; January 9, 1683; February 16, 1683; NONE in 1684–85 or 1685–86.
Source: PSB 48.

Appendix 4

Estimates of Shore Whale Catches, 1697–1734

New England and Long Island compared. These estimates are also based on a conversion rate of thirty-six barrels per whale.

Year	New England	Long Island	Total
1697	23	27	5
1698	25	−1	25
1699	25	1+	26
1700	76	14+	87
1701	65	13+	86
1702	87	−1	87+
1703	47	10	57
1704	39	3+	42+
1705 no data	—	—	—
1706	2	−1	2+
1707	95	29	124
1708	109	9	118
1709	47	10	57
1710	72	9	81
1711	64	8+	72+
1712 no data	—	—	—
1713	50	−1	50+
1714	83	5	88
1715	140	14	154
1716	125	5+	130+
1717	85	2+	87+
1718	107	19	126
1719	96	14	110
1720	130	18	148
1721	174	15	189
1722	109	1+	110+
1723	142	9+	151+

(continued)

Appendix 4 table (*continued*)

Year	New England	Long Island	Total
1724	147	−1	147+
1725	128	2	130
1726	128	7+	135+
1727 no data	—	—	—
1728	187	1+	188+
1729	122	1	123
1730	186	1	187
1731	130	0	130
1732	169	2	171
1733	168	4	172
1734	248	3	251

Source: Randall, Breiwick, and Mitchell 1999, 24.

Appendix 5

Names of Indian Whalers and English Investors on the Whaling Contracts, 1670–1685

This database is taken from the whaling contracts entered into the Southampton, East Hampton, Huntington, and Brookhaven town records from 1670 to 1685. Most of the contracts list only the name of the principle owner, while some enter a second or third name. The exception is the company headed by the Reverend Thomas James of East Hampton wherein all the investors are listed. Here only the first two are entered.

Name	Date	English Investor	Source
Abel (Tomhage)	December 27, 1677	Thomas James, John Stratton Sr.	RTEH 1: 407–9
****	October 28, 1684	John Miller	RTEH 2: 152–53
Abraham	September 4, 1718	William Smith	PSB: 46–47
****	December 26, 1716	William Smith	PSB: 45
Acquaquonack	April 10, 1683	Joseph Raynor	SHTA Book D2: 119
Addam	July 4, 1675[1]	Jacob Schellinger	RTEH 1: 378–79
****	December 2, 1675	Thomas James, William Edwards	RTEH 1: 381–82
Adso	October 28, 1684	John Miller, Jacob Dayton	RTEH 2: 152–53
Agut	April 10, 1683	Illegible	SHTA Book D2: 119
****	April 30, 1683	John Jessup Jr.	SHTA Book D2: 117–18
Ahichoo	May 5, 1681	John Howell, Joseph Raynor	SHTA Book D2: 52
****	December 28, 1681	Joseph Raynor	SHTA Book D2: 71
****	March 8, 1682/3	Robert Keidy	RTEH 2: 120
Akuctattrias	May 31, 1671	Arthur Howell	SHTA Liber A2: 88
Amagausha (Amagunsot)	June 17, 1672	John Cooper	SBD: 36–38
****	March 17, 1680	Richard Howell	SHTA Liber A2: 136
****	December 3, 1681	Henry Pierson	SHTA Book D2: 73
Amoachee	November 21, c. 1671	None	SHTA Liber A2: 90
Anatahut	January 23, 1678/79	John Rose	SHTA Liber A2: 123
Andrew	No date	William Smith	PSB: 33
****	April 19, 1684	John Howell	SHTA Book D2: 168
Anthony (see Wunnanaugema below)	November 14, c. 1671	None	SHTA Liber A2: 90
Apunsha[2]	March 9, 1674/5	Thomas James	RTEH 1: 373–74
Arqogoneg	June 17, 1672	John Cooper	SBD: 36–38
Artor	March 4, 1670/1	John Cooper	SBD: 77
****	November 24, c. 1671	None	SHTA Liber A2: 90

****	April 7, 1675	Richard Howell, Joseph Raynor	SHTA Liber A2: 99–100
****	January 28, 1676/77[3]	Richard Howell, Joseph Fordham	SHTA Liber A2: 113
****	January 7, 1678/9	Edward Howell	SHTA Liber A2: 121
****	December 10, 1679	Joseph Fordham	SHTA Liber A2: 133
****	February 29, 1681/2	James Cooper	SHTA Book D2: 103
****	June 26, 1682[4]	James Cooper (same season as above)	SHTA Book D2: 94
Askut (Agut)	May 21, 1672	James Herrick, John Laughton	SHTA Liber A2: 93
****	April 19, 1679	John Jessup	SHTA Liber A2: 122
****	March 29, 1680	John Jessup	SHTA Liber A2: 136
****	April 10, 1683	Joseph Raynor	SHTA Book D2: 119
****	April 30, 1683	John Jessup	SHTA Book D2: 117–18
Atungquion	June 26, 16?1	Anthony Ludlam	SHTA Liber A2: 87
Awaubeton (see Wobetom)			
Awonsis	May 29, 1672	Thomas Topping, John Topping	SHTA Liber A2: 93
****	May 20, 1673	James Herrick	RTSH 2: 246–47
****	March 26, 1677	Capt. Howell	SHTA Liber A2: 114
****	March 17, 1680	Richard Howell	SHTA A2: 135
****	December 3, 1681	Henry Pierson	SHTA Book D2: 71
****	June 14, 1682	James Hildreth	SHTA Book D2: 87–88
****	June 4, 1685	James Hildreth	SHTA Book D2: 187
Awagnos	June 3, 1682	William Herrick	SHTA Book D2: 86
Awaubaubasheag	December 2, 1675	Thomas James, William Edwards	RTEH 1: 381–82
Ayoty (John Indian)	March 10, 1682	Andrew Gibb	RTBH Book B: 105
****	January 18, 1681	John Thorpe	RTBH Book B: 62–63
****	May 20, 1673	James Herrick	RTSH 2: 246–47
****	January 23, 1678/9	John Rose	SHTA Liber A2: 124

(continued)

Appendix 5 table (*continued*)

Name	Date	English Investor	Source
****	May 8, 1682	Joseph Pierson	RTSH 5: 199
****	December 20, 1697	William Smith	PSB: 21–22
Beanes, Will	1704/5–1707/8	William Smith	PSB: 35–36
Bombrest (a.k.a. Wawassaquohague)	1688	Richard Floyd	RFL 1: 7v–8
****	1689	Richard Floyd	RFL 1: 25
Capunch	April 10, 1683	Joseph Raynor	SHTA Book D2: 119
Caubut (Cobitt, Cawbut)	June 17, 1672	John Cooper	SBD: 36–38
****	March 26, 1677	John Howell, Benjamin Davis, Joseph Fordham	SHTA Liber A2: 114
Checkano[5]	July 4, 1675	James Schellinger, James Loper	RTEH 1: 378–79
Chise, Chice (Sachem)	January 30, 1678	Josiah Hobert, James Herrick, John Cooper[6]	Liber A2: 119
****	March 1, 1682	John Jessup	SHTA Book D2: 72
Chesen[7]	March 29, 1682	Andrew Gibb	RTBH Book B: 105
Conjamyis	December 20, 1697	William Smith	PSB: 21–22
Cohenade	June 17, 1672	John Cooper	SBD: 36–38
****	January 28, 1677	Richard Howell, Joseph Fordham	SHTA Liber A2: 113
****	April 19, 1679	John Jessup	SHTA Liber A2: 122
****	February 29, 1682	James Cooper	SHTA Book D2: 103
****	June 26, 1682	James Cooper	SHTA Book D2: 94
Cones	May 24 (29), 1672	Thomas Topping, John Topping	SHTA Liber A2: 93
Copye, Copyo	March 10, 1682	Andrew Gibbs	SHTA Book D2: 75
Coponsh	June 3, 1682	William Herrick	SHTA Book D2: 86
Coush (Cough)	May 20, 1673	James Herrick	RTSH 2: 246–47
****	March 26, 1677	Captain Howell, Benjamin Davis	SHTA Liber A2: 114
Cuttawas, Cuttwas	January 23, 1679	John Rose	SHTA Liber A2: 124

****	June 26, 1682	James Cooper	SHTA Liber A2: 94
Cowanuck (Dick)	March 13, 1679	Richard Shaw	RTEH 1: 430–31
****	March 14, 1681	John Wheeler	RTEH 2: 96–97
Cownus	December 20, 1697	William Smith	PSB: 17
****	December 23, 1715	William Smith	PSB: 45
Cowus	November 24, c. 1671	None	SHTA Liber A2: 90
Dirk	January 30, 1678	Hobart, Herrick	SHTA Liber A2: 119
Fox	May 5, 1681	John Howell, Joseph Raynor	SHTA Book D2: 52
Francis	January 30, 1678	Josiah Hobert	SHTA Liber A2: 119
Gackapes	April 7, 1675	Richard Howell, Joseph Raynor	SHTA Liber A2: 99–100
Garret	April 28, 1675	Richard Howell	SHTA Liber A2: 100
****	January 28, 1677	Richard Howell, Joseph Fordham	SHTA Liber A2: 113
Gateeus	No Date	William Smith	PSB: 35
Georg	May 15, 1681	Thomas Higbe	RTH 1: 295–96
George (Sauan)	December 27, 1677	Thomas James	RTEH 1: 407–9
****	April 7, 1677	Jacob Schellinger	RTEH 2: 78–79
Gover	March 10, 1682	Andrew Gibb	SHTA Book D2: 74–75
Goodger	March 19, 1682	Andrew Gibb	RTBH Book B: 105
****	September 8, 1683	John Jenners	RTBH Book B: 169–70
Gie (Sachem)	September 8, 1683	John Jenners	RTBH Book B: 169–70
Hanas Cut	May 15, 1681	Thomas Higbe	RTH 1: 295–96
Harry[8]	June 17, 1672	John Cooper	SBD: 36–38
****	January 28, 1677	Richard Howell, Joseph Fordham	SHTA Liber A2: 113
****	January 30, 1678	John Hobert, James Herrick	SHTA Liber A2: 119
Harry (a.k.a. Woossooio)	March 9, 1675	Thomas James, John Stratton	RTEH 1: 373–74
Harry (a.k.a. Queguahide)	January 6, 1681 for 81–82 season	John Stratton	RTEH 2: 94

(continued)

Appendix 5 table (*continued*)

Name	Date	English Investor	Source
****	March 18, 1681 for 81–82 season[9]	John Stratton Sr. and John Stratton Jr.	RTEH 2: 97
****	February 16, 1683	John Kirle	RTEH 2: 119
Hoboneck	July 4, 1675	Jacob Schellinger	RTEH 1: 378–78
Hopewell	May 21, 1672	James Herrick, John Laughton	SHTA Liber A2: 93
Humphrey	March 9, 1675	Thomas James, John Stratton	RTEH 1: 373–74
****	March 31, 1679	Thomas James, Thomas Chatfield	RTEH 2: 77
Jachancy (Jackachimi)	November 24, c. 1671	None	SHTA Liber A2: 90
****	December 11, 1670	John Howell, Joseph Raynor	SHTA Liber A2: 85
****	May 24 (29), 1672	Thomas Topping, John Topping	SHTA Liber A2: 93
Jack	May 5, 1681	John Howell, Joseph Raynor	SHTA Book D2: 52
Jacob Indian	March 10, 1682	Andrew Gibb	SHTA Book D2: 75
***	August 7, 1684	Samuel Seward	RTBH Book B: 197
Jafet Indian (Japhet)	February 19, 1679	Thomas Cooper Jr.	SHTA Liber A2: 123
****	May 28, 1683	Ralf Dayton	RTBH Book B: 156
Jambasha	December 2, 1675	Thomas James, William Edwards	RTEH 1: 381–82
****	March 13, 1679	Richard Shaw	RTEH 1: 430–31
****	April 1, 1681	Samuel Mulford	RTEH 2: 99–100
Jambotack	July 4, 1675	Jacob Schellinger	RTEH 1: 378–79
James Indian	December 1698	William Smith	PSB: 39–40
Japhetnod	March 13, 1679	Richard Shaw	RTEH 1: 430–31
Jasot	February 19, 1679	Thomas Cooper Jr.	SHTA Liber A2: 123
Jeorgekee	April 7, 1679	Jacob Schellinger	RTEH 2: 78–79
Jeffrey	June 17, 1672	John Cooper Jr.	SBD: 36–38

****	March 26, 1677[10]	John Topping, Benjamin Davis, Joseph Fordham	SHTA Liber A2: 114
****	April 19, 1679	John Jessup	SHTA Liber A2: 122
****	September 28, 1681	Joseph Fordham	SHTA Book D2: 72
****	December 3, 1681	Henry Pierson	SHTA Book D2: 73
****	September 8, 1683	John Jenners	RTBH Book B: 169–70
Jeffrey (a.k.a. Ombomuck)	March 9, 1675	Thomas James, John Stratton	RTEH 1: 373–74
****	December 27, 1677	Thomas James, John Stratton	RTEH 1: 408–9
****	March 5, 1681	Benjamin Conkling	RTEH 2: 95–96
Jerimia	November 24, c. 1671	None	SHTA Liber A2: 90
****	May 21, 1672	James Herrick	SHTA Liber A2: 93
****	January 28, 1676/7	Richard Howell	SHTA Liber A2: 113
****	January 22, 1679[11]	Edward Howell	SHTA Liber A2: 122
****	February 19, 1679	Thomas Cooper	SHTA Liber A2: 123
****	December 27, 1680	Isaac Raynor	SHTA Book D2: 49
****	June 26, 1682	Thomas Cooper	SHTA Book D2: 94
****	March 5, 1684	John Raynor	SHTA Book D2: 172
****	August 7, 1684	Samuel Muncey	RTBH Book B: 197
John (Unkechaug)	December 20, 1697	William Smith	PSB: 21–22
John Eacoms	April 7, 1679	Jacob Schellinger	RTEH 2: 78–79
John Man[12] (Shinnecock)	May 20, 1673	James Herrick	RTSH 2: 246–47
****	January 28, 1677	Richard Howell, Joseph Fordham	SHTA Liber A2: 113
****	May 8, 1678	James Herrick	RTSH 2: 55
****	January 23, 1679	John Rose	SHTA Liber A2: 124
****	May 8, 1682	Joseph Pierson	SHTA Book D2: 84
John Indian (Montaukett)	March 9, 1675	Thomas James, John Stratton	RTEH 1: 373–74
****	December 27, 1677	Thomas James, Will Edwards	RTEH 1: 381–83
John (Unkechaug)	January 18, 1681	John Throp	RTBH Book B: 62–63

(continued)

Appendix 5 table (*continued*)

Name	Date	English Investor	Source
John alias Ayoty (Unkechaug)	March 10, 1682	Andrew Gibb	SHTA Book D2: 74–75
John, son of Wobetom (Montaukett)	August 12, 1683	Richard Stratton	RTEH 2: 132–33
John Passin	December 11, 1670	John Howell, Joseph Raynor	SHTA Liber A2: 85
Jonaquam	November 24, c. 1671	None	SHTA Liber A2: 90
****	April 7, 1675	Richard Howell and Joseph Raynor	SHTA Liber A2: 99–100
****	April 19, 1679	John Jessup	SHTA Liber A2: 122
****	March 29, 1680	John Jessup	SHTA Liber A2: 136
****	May 5, 1681	John Howell, Joseph Raynor	SHTA Book D2: 52
****	January 7, 1682	Thomas Jessup	SHTA Book D2: 72
****	June 18, 1683	Joseph Marshall, Richard Howell	SHTA Book D2: 127
Johanaquaham	May 18, 1681	John Jessup Jr.	SHTA CTD 2: 75
Johnpassin	December 11, 1670	John Howell	SHTA Liber 2A: 85
Jounbuck	November 1708	William Smith	PSB: 23–24
John Reuemo	May 15, 1681	Thomas Higbe	RTH 1: 295–96
Johnsonsam	June 3, 1682	William Herrick	SHTA Book D2: 86–87
Joseph	March 9, 1675	Thomas James, John Stratton	RTEH 1: 373–74
****	July 10, 1682	Matthew Howell, Thomas Cooper	SHTA Book D2: 93
Judas	April 7, 1675	Richard Howell, Joseph Raynor	SHTA Liber A2: 99–100
****	January 30, 1678	Josiah Hobert, James Herrick	SHTA Liber A2: 119
****	May 8, 1678[13]	James Herrick	RTSH 2: 55
Jumpaus (Nat)	December 27, 1677	Thomas James, John Stratton	RTEH 1: 407–9
Keassowouk	December 2, 1675	Thomas James, William Edwards	RTEH 1: 381–82
Kellis	1697–1708	William Smith	PSB: 11–12

Lenard	November 24, c. 1671	None	SHTA Liber A2: 90
****	May 29, 1672	Captain Topping	SHTA Liber A2: 93
****	December 27, 1680	Isaac Raynor	SHTA Book D2: 49
****	June 14, 1682	James Hildreth	SHTA Book D2: 87–88
Linaus (Fox)	December 18, 1697	William Smith	PSB: 3–4
Livewell	July 4, 1675	Jacob Schellinger	RTEH 1: 378–79
****	March 13, 1679	Richard Shaw, Goodman Garlick	RTEH 1: 430–31
****	March 14, 1681	John Wheeler	RTEH 2: 96–97
Machat Hart	May 15, 1681	Thomas Higbe	RTH 1: 295–96
Mahaine	August 16, 1683	Joseph Davis	RTBH Book B: 175
****	August 7, 1684	Obadiah Seward	RTBH Book B: 197
Major	March 31, 1679	Thomas James, Thomas Chatfield	RTEH 2: 77
Mamanum (Sachem)	March 2, 1675	Richard Howell	SHTA Liber A2: 99
****	March 26, 1677	Richard Howell	SHTA Liber A2: 114
****	September 28, 1681	Joseph Fordham	SHTA Book D2: 72
Maneeg (Will)[14]	December 27, 1677	Thomas James	RTEH 1: 408
Manusmy	November 24, c. 1671	None	SHTA Liber A2: 90
Mareene	January 30, 1678	Josiah Hobert, James Herrick	SHTA Liber A2: 119
Mashungansag	December 19, 1681	Thomas Cooper, Samuel Barnes	SHTA Book D2: 77
Mascombom	March 26, 1677	John Howell, Benjamin Davis, Joseph Fordham	SHTA Liber A2: 114
Matanuks	March 5, 1684	John Raynor	SHTA Book D2: 172
Matompact	March 31, 1679	Thomas James, Thomas Chatfield	RTEH 2: 77
Matuagguack	June 17, 1672	John Cooper	SBD: 36–38
Mautaman	June 17, 1672	John Cooper	SBD: 36–38
Mechgraes	July 4, 1675	Jacob Schellinger	RTEH 1: 378–79
Meelchebo	June 3, 1682	William Herrick	SHTA Book D2: 86–87
Menan	February 16, 1683	John Kirle	RTEH 2: 119

(continued)

Name	Date	English Investor	Source
Meneges (Tom)	December 27, 1680	Isaac Raynor	SHTA Book D2: 71
****	December 3, 1681	Henry Pierson	SHTA Book D2: 73
****	September 8, 1683	John Jenners	RTBH Book B: 169
****	c. November 1685	Joseph Tooker	RTBH Book B: 246
Miller	March 10, 1682	Andrew Gibbs	SHTA Book D2: 75
Moshup (Sachem)	March 9, 1675	Thomas James, James Stratton	RTEH 1: 373–74
****	December 27, 1677	Thomas James, John Stratton	RTEH 1: 407–9
Muddoah	April 1, 1681	Samuel Mulford	RTEH 2: 99–100
Muhauah	April 10, 1683	Joseph Raynor	SHTA Book D2: 119
Muttabaune	December 2, 1675	Thomas James, William Edward	RTEH 1: 381–82
Nagamen	January 28, 1676/77	Richard Howell	SHTA Liber A2: 113
Nahancuttoro	May 15, 1681	Thomas Higbe	RTH 1: 295–96
Nansaquid	December 11, 1670	John Howell, Joseph Raynor	SHTA Liber A2: 85
****	November 24, c. 1671	None	SHTA Liber A2: 90
Nanaimo	June 4, 1685	John Hildreth, Jeremiah Jagger	SHTA Book D2: 187
Nattume	December 26, 1716	William Smith	PSB: 45
Natacomoge	March 26, 1677	John Howell, Benjamin Davis, Joseph Fordham	SHTA Liber A2: 114
Natutamy	1704–9	Martha Smith	PB: 31–32
Noodr	January 28, 1677	Richard Howell, Joseph Fordham	SHTA Liber A2: 113
Nero	1704–8	William Smith	PSB: 13–14
Nultwhos (Hid)	December 20, 1697	William Smith	PSB: 19–20
Nunsogoda	December 11, 1670	John Howell, Joseph Raynor, Richard Howell	SHTA Liber A2: 85
Obadiah	December 3, 1681	Henry Pierson	SHTA Book D2: 73
****	June 14, 1682	James Hildreth	SHTA Book D2: 87–88

****	June 26, 1682[15]	James Cooper	SHTA Book D2: 94
Occogonik	June 3, 1682	William Herrick	SHTA Book D2: 86–87
Omagonsha (see fn. 10)	January 22, 1679	Richard Howell	SHTA Liber A2: 122
Ompacnoe	January 7, 1682	Thomas Jessup	SHTA Book D2: 72
Ouncocochaug	January 30, 1678	Josiah Hobert	SHTA Liber A2: 119
Owanamako	June 14, 1682	Samuel Barnes	SHTA Book D2: 107–8
Pabocowit	March 16, 1677	John Howell, Benjamin Davis, Joseph Fordham	SHTA Liber A2: 114
Pabomocon	May 29, 1672	Thomas Topping, John Topping	SHTA Liber A2: 93
****	May 20, 1673	James Herrick	RTSH 2: 246–47
Padacoto	January 23, 1679	John Rose	SHTA Liber A2: 124
Padyquia	May 5, 1681	John Howell, Joseph Raynor	SHTA Book D2: 52
Pagarement	June 17, 1672	John Cooper	SBD: 36–38
Panasham	June 14, 1682	Samuel Barnes	SHTA Book D2: 107–8
Pagonungut			
Papamacruot	May 30, 1682	Obadiah Rogers	SHTA Book D2: 84
Paparagun	January 7, 1679	Edward Howell	SHTA Liber A2: 121
Papasaquin	November 24, c. 1671	None	SHTA Liber A2: 90
****	April 7, 1679	Jacob Schellinger	RTEH 2: 78–79
****	January 9, 1679/80	John Wheeler	RTEH 2: 86–87
****	March 5, 1681	Benjamin Conklin	RTEH 2: 95–96
****	February 25, 1681/2	Mathew Howell	SHTA Book D2: 74
****	May 30, 1682	Obadiah Rogers	SHTA Book D2: 84
	1683–84 season		
****	April 30, 1683	John Jessup Jr.	SHTA Book D2: 117–18
Paquanungualt	December 11, 1670	John Howell, Joseph Raynor	SHTA Liber A2: 85
Paraquam	February 19, 1679	Thomas Cooper	SHTA Liber A2: 123
Patlqua	March 10, 1682	Andrew Gibbs	SHTA Liber A2: 75

(continued)

Appendix 5 table (*continued*)

Name	Date	English Investor	Source
Patumbum	June 14, 1682	Samuel Barnes	SHTA Book D2: 107–8
Pauwasik	December 2, 1675	Thomas James, Will Edwards	RTEH 1: 381–82
Pawbawmacout	May 20, 1673	James Herrick	RTSH 2: 246–47
Pemeson	July 4, 1675	Jacob Schellinger	RTEH 1: 378–79
Pesance	December 3, 1681	Henry Pierson	SHTA Book D2: 73
Peserhaut	June 17, 1672	John Cooper	SBD: 36–38
Pesserham	January 23, 1679	James Herrick	Liber A2: 124
Perroal	May 15, 1681	Thomas Higbe	RTH 1: 295–96
Peter	January 30, 1678	Josiah Herbert, James Herrick	SHTA Liber A2: 119
Petowunk	May 15, 1681	Thomas Higbe	RTH 1: 295–96
Philip	November 15, 1670	Josiah Laughton	RTSH 2: 56–57
Phineas (Pinis)	November 24, c. 1671	None	SHTA Liber A2: 90
****	May 29, 1672	Captain Topping	SHTA Liber A2: 93
****	May 20, 1673	James Herrick	RTSH 2: 246–47
****	January 28, 1676/7	Richard Howell	SHTA Liber A2: 113
****	January 23, 1678/9	James Herrick	SHTA Liber A2: 122
Pisachan	June 4, 1685	James Hildreth, Jeremiah Jagger	SHTA Book D2: 187
Pisacomog	January 7, 1679	Edward Howell	SHTA Liber A2: 121
****	June 3, 1682	William Herrick	SHTA Book D2: 86–87
Pisant	March 26, 1677	John Topping, Benjamin Davis, Joseph Fordham	SHTA Liber A2: 114
Piscut	March 26, 1677	John Howell, Benjamin Davis, Joseph Fordham	SHTA Liber A2: 114
Pitiniam	January 9, 1683	Shamgar Hand	SHTA Book D2: 112
Piunquash	December 3, 1681	Henry Pierson	SHTA Book D2: 74
****	January 9, 1683	Shamgar Hand	SHTA Book D2: 112

Plato	March 15, 1679	Richard Shaw, Goodman Garlick	RTEH 1: 430–31
****	April 20, 1681	Philip Leake, John Stratton	RTEH 2: 101
Poaguamo[16]	Nov. 24, 1671	None	SHTA Liber A2: 90
Pobackobaug	December 11, 1670	John Howell, Joseph Raynor	SHTA Liber A2: 85
Pochecun	November 24, c. 1671	None	SHTA Liber A2: 90
Poctoppumsho	February 19, 1679	Thomas Cooper Jr.	SHTA Liber A2: 123
Pockanera	November 24, c. 1671	None	SHTA Liber A2: 90
Poese	April 21, 1682	John Tooker Jr.	RTBH Book B: 110
Poliakees	April 28, 1675	Richard Howell	SHTA Liber A2: 100
Poireo	December 11, 1670	John Howell, Joseph Raynor	SHTA Liber A2: 85
Pokctoppumsho	February 19, 1679	Thomas Cooper Jr.	SHTA Liber A2: 123
Pokatowne	December 28, 1681	Joseph Raynor	SHTA Book D2: 71
Pomamorond	January 20, 1679	Richard Howell	SHTA Liber A2: 122
Pomamson	January 20, 1679	Richard Howell	SHTA Liber A2: 122
Ponguamo (Sachem)	November 24, c. 1671	None	SHTA Liber A2: 90
****	February 25, 1682	Matthew Howell	SHTA Book D2: 74
****	April 19, 1684 (sachem)	John Howell	SHTA Book D2: 168
Portone (Oliver)	January 23, 1679	James Herrick	SHTA Liber A2: 124
Pown	December 20, 1697	William Smith	PSB: 15–16
Poyoasko	January 30, 1678	Josiah Hobert, James Herrick	SHTA Liber A2: 119
Pumhose	January 23, 1678	Daniel Sayre	SHTA Liber A2: 124
Pumpsha	December 17, 1697	William Smith	PSB: 9–10
****	December 27, 1698	William Smith	PSB: 29
****	December 23, 1715	William Smith	PSB: 45
****	December 26, 1716	William Smith	PSB: 45
Quadoqueno	December 27, 1677	Thomas James, John Stratton	RTEH 1: 408–9
Quaesquahege	April 21, 1682	John Tooker Jr.	RTBH Book B: 110

(continued)

Appendix 5 table (*continued*)

Name	Date	English Investor	Source
Quaosharquam	February 19, 1679	Thomas Cooper Jr.	SHTA Liber A2: 123
Quaquaghaug	June 17, 1672	John Cooper	SBD: 36–38
Quaun	March 9, 1675	Thomas James, John Stratton Sr.	RTEH 1: 373–74
Quanuton (Quenaton)	November 24, c. 1671	None	SHTA Liber A2: 87
****	May 29, 1672	Captain Topping, John Topping	SHTA Liber A2: 93
Quequecum (Hector)[17]	December 27, 1677	Thomas James, John Stratton	RTEH 1: 408–9
****	March 18, 1681	John Stratton	RTEH 2: 97
****	March 8, 1683	Robert Keidy	RTEH 2: 120
Quogano	May 29, 1672	Thomas Topping, John Topping	SHTA Liber A2: 93
Quogue (Timothy)	1704/5–1718	William Smith	PSB: 25–26
Quombomo	May 29, 1672	Thomas Topping, John Topping	SHTA Liber A2: 93
Quonshoo	January 23, 1679	James Herrick	SHTA Liber A2: 124
Quoquashas	January 30, 1678	Josiah Horbert, James Herrick	SHTA Liber A2: 119
Quoseque	December 2, 1675	Thomas James, William Edwards	RTEH 1: 381–82
Raepone	April 21, 1682	John Tooker Jr.	RTBH Book B: 110
Reassowunk	December 2, 1675	Thomas James, William Edwards	RTEH 1: 381–82
Red headed Will	January 28, 1677	Richard Howell, Joseph Fordham	SHTA Liber A2: 68
****	March 24, 1681	John Wheeler	RTEH 2: 98–99
Robin Indian	March 26, 1702/3	William Smith	PSB: 41–42
Saamok	February 19, 1679	Thomas Cooper Jr.	SHTA Liber A2: 123
Sacaspan	November 24, c. 1671	None	SHTA Liber A2: 90
****	June 17, 1672	John Cooper	SBD: 36–38
Sacutaca	December 27, 1697	William Smith	PSB: 29–30
Samons	1697	William Smith	PSB: 25

Samson	February 16, 1683	John Kirle	RTEH 2:119
Sasaktakon	March 24, 1681	John Wheeler	RTEH 2: 98–99
Sasaquad	November 24, c. 1671	None	SHTA Liber A2: 90
Sassakaton	March 24, 1681	John Wheeler	RTEH 2: 98–99
Sananegon	January 23, 1679	Daniel Sayre	SHTA Liber A2: 124
Saquirum	April 30, 1683	John Jessup	SHTA Book D2: 117–18
Sauspan	June 17, 1672	John Cooper	SBD: 38
****	January 30, 1678	Josiah Hobert, James Herrick	SHTA Liber A2: 119
Scanderbag	December 2, 1675	Thomas James, William Edwards	RTEH 1: 381–82
****	March 13, 1679	Richard Shaw, Goodman Garlick	RTEH 1: 430–31
****	April 7, 1679[18]	Jacob Schellinger	RTEH 2: 78–79
Scommaug (Scomake, Scummangue)	March 9, 1675	Thomas James, John Stratton	RTEH 1: 373–74
****	December 27, 1677	Thomas James, John Stratton	RTEH 1: 408–9
Scowot	April 7, 1675	Richard Howell, Joseph Raynor	SHTA Liber A2: 99–10
****	April 19, 1679	John Jessup	SHTA Liber A2: 122
****	March 29, 1680	John Jessup	SHTA Liber A2: 136
Sequenanquas (a.k.a. Robin)	April 21, 1682	John Tooker Jr.	RTBH Book B:110
****	August 12, 1685	William Thompson, Abraham Dayton	RTBH Book B: 241–42
Sequana	March 27, 1680	John Hildreth, John Carwithy	SHTA Liber A2: 136
****	February 25, 1682	Mathew Howell	SHTA Book D2: 74
****	May 30, 1682[19]	Obadiah Rogers	SHTA Book D2: 84
****	April 30, 1683	John Jessup	SHTA Book D2: 117–18
Shine	February 16, 1683	John Kirle	RTEH 2: 119
Shotnose	July 4, 1675	Jacob Schellinger	RTEH 1: 378–79
Simon	March 5, 1681	Benjamin Conklin	RETH 2: 95–96
Skowwat	April 19, 1679	John Jessup	SHTA Liber A2: 122

(continued)

Appendix 5 table (*continued*)

Name	Date	English Investor	Source
Soranort	May 15, 1681	Thomas Higbe	RTH 1: 295–96
Soquatash	1705/6	William Smith	PSB: 23–24
Soquirum	April 30, 1683	John Jessup Jr.	SHTA Book D2: 117–18
Sqwoanshene	April 30, 1683	John Jessup	STHA Book D2: 117–18
Squanshuck	December 11, 1670	John Howell, Joseph Raynor	SHTA Liber A2: 85
Sqwonshane	April 30, 1683	John Jessup Jr.	SHTA Book D2: 117–18
Sreewons	February 19, 1679	Thomas Cooper Jr.	SHTA Liber A2: 123
Straphons	December 20, 1697	William Smith	PSB: 7–8
Sugian Indian	May 18, 1681	John Jessup Jr.	SHTA Book D2: 53
Sungatchuse	July 2, 1675	Jacob Schellinger	RTEH 1: 378–79
Suncutturus	June 17, 1672	John Cooper	SBD: 36–38
Sutt	July 10, 1682	Matthew Howell, Thomas Cooper	SHTA Book D2: 93
****	June 18, 1683	Joseph Marshall, Richard Howell	SHTA Book D2: 127
Tachumme	December 2, 1675	Thomas James, William Edwards	RTEH 1: 381–82
Tagian	June 17, 1672	John Cooper	SBD: 36–38
Tantoquin (Will)	December 27, 1677	Thomas James, John Stratton	RTEH 1: 408–9
Tapshana	December 18, 1697	William Smith	PSB: 5–6
Tarumpin	May 15, 1681	Thomas Higbe	RTH 1: 295–96
Taubane	December 2, 1675	Jacob Schellinger	RTEH 1: 379–80
Tauckaumnia (Tackiamials)	December 11, 1670	John Howell, Joseph Raynor	SHTA Liber A2: 85
****	June 17, 1672	John Cooper	SBD: 36–38
Teman	March 29, 1681	John Jessup	SHTA Liber A2: 126
****	April 10, 1683	Joseph Raynor	SHTA Book D2: 119
****	June 18, 1683	Joseph Marshall, Richard Howell	SHTA Book D2: 127

Tenirse (a.k.a. Vergins)	April 19, 1679	John Jessup	SHTA Liber A2: 122
****	December 3, 1681	Henry Pierson	SHTA Book D2: 73
Terh	January 7, 1679	Edward Howell	SHTA Liber A2: 121
Toack (Teech, Teack)	December 11, 1670	John Howell, Joseph Raynor	SHTA Liber A2: 85
****	December 27, 1680	Isaac Raynor	SHTA Book D2: 49
****	January 16, 1682	Thomas Jessup	SHTA Book D2: 73
****	June 18, 1683	John Marshall, Richard Howell	SHTA Book D2: 127
****	June 4, 1685	James Hildreth, Jeremiah Jagger	SHTA Book D2: 168
Toby	March 31, 1679	Thomas James, Thomas Chatfield	RTEH 2: 77
****	January 9, 1680	John Wheeler	RTEH 2: 86–87
****	March 5, 1681	Benjamin Conkling	RTEH 2: 95–96
Toby (Pudding)	1703/4–1717	William Smith	PSB: 33
****	December 26, 1716	William Smith	PSB: 45
Tohomon (Tehemon)	April 17, 1679	John Jessup	SHTA Liber A2: 122
****	January 7, 1682	John Jessup	SHTA Book D2: 72
****	July 10, 1682	Matthew Howell	SHTA Book D2: 93
****	April 10, 1683	Joseph Raynor	SHTA Book D2: 119
****	June 18, 1683	Joseph Marshall, Richard Howell	SHTA Book D2: 127
Tokomomo	April 7, 1675	Richard Howell, Joseph Raynor	SHTA Liber A2: 99–100
Toman	March 29, 1680	John Jessup	SHTA Liber A2: 136
Tomhage (Abel)	December 27, 1677	Thomas James, John Stratton Sr.	RTEH 1: 407–9
****	October 28, 1684	John Miller Jr.	RTEH 2: 152–53
Tom Indian	May 8, 1678	James Herrick	RTSH 2: 55
Tom Indian Jr.	December 8, 1703	William Smith	PSB: 43–44
Toney Indian	1704/5–1721	William Smith	PSB: 37–38
****	December 23, 1715	William Smith	PSB: 45
****	December 26, 1716	William Smith	PSB: 45

(continued)

Appendix 5 table (*continued*)

Name	Date	English Investor	Source
Tooroups	June 13, 1680[20]	Thomas Biggs	RTBH Book B: 44
****	January 18, 1681	John Throp	RTBH Book B: 62–63
Torgeny (Forgeny?)	March 29, 1680	John Jessup	SHTA Liber A2: 126
Toquanuck	May 5, 1681	John Howell, Joseph Raynor	SHTA Book D2: 52
Toutow	June 17, 1672	John Cooper	SBD: 36–38
Towis, Toj (Ben)	March 9, 1675	Thomas James, John Stratton Sr.	RTEH 1: 373–74
*****	December 27, 1677	Thomas James, John Stratton	RTEH 1: 408–9
Towntuck (Sam)	1697–1706	William Smith	PSB: 23–24
Towsacume	November 15, 1670	Josiah Laughton	RTSH 2: 56–57
Towsacum	December 27, 1677	Thomas James, John Stratton	RTEH 1: 408–9
Umbassu (Ambusso)	July 4, 1675	Jacob Schellinger	RTEH 1: 378–79
Uncommouit	December 27, 1677	Thomas James, John Stratton	RTEH 1: 407–9
Unquonimo (Unquonomon)	December 27, 1677	Thomas James, John Stratton	RTEH 1: 407–9
****	March 24, 1681	John Wheeler	RTEH 2: 98–99
Ungomunt	March 9, 1675	Thomas James, John Stratton	RTEH 1: 373–74
*****	April 1, 1681	Samuel Mumford	RTEH 2: 99–100
Wachaquoshut	July 10, 1682	Matthew Howell, Thomas Cooper	SHTA Book D2: 93
Wahumbank, Wahambaho	May 30, 1682	Obadiah Rogers	SHTA Book D2: 84
****	April 10, 1683	Joseph Raynor	SHTA Book D2: 119
Wamabaho, Wamabacho, Wamapaho	May 21, 1672	James Herrick, John Laughton	SHTA Liber A2: 93
****	December 27, 1680	Isaac Raynor	SHTA Book D2: 49
****	January 16, 1682	Isaac Raynor	SHTA Book D2: 72
Wamby	June 17, 1672	John Cooper Jr.	SBD: 36–38
Wammos, Wopomsh (a.k.a. Smith)	January 28, 1677	Richard Howell, Joseph Fordham	SHTA Liber A2: 113

****	January 7, 1679	Edward Howell	SHTA Liber A2: 121
****	February 25, 1682	Mathew Howell	SHTA Book D2: 74
****	July 10, 1682	Mathew Howell	SHTA Book D2: 93
Wamosboha	January 20, 1679	Richard Howell	SHTA Liber A2: 122
Wampanaromps (Sachem)	January 28, 1677	Richard Howell, Joseph Fordham	SHTA Liber A2: 68
Wampaquat (Hames)	July 4, 1675	Jacob Schellinger	RTEH 1: 378–79
****	December 27, 1677	Thomas James, John Stratton	RTEH 1: 408–9
Wamspaho	January 16, 1682	Isaac Raynor	SHTA Book D2: 73
Wanashaquahege	December 3, 1681	Henry Pierson	SHTA Book D2: 73
Wanpetum	December 2, 1675	Thomas James, William Edwards	RTEH 1: 381–82
Wapachukis (Humphrey)[21]	December 20, 1697	William Smith	PSB: 13–14
Warnabaioliow	June 18, 1683	Joseph Marshall	SHTA Book D2: 127
Waseramas (Jeremy)	March 19, 1682	Andrew Gibb	RTBH Book B: 105
Washam (Waishom)	January 30, 1678	James Herrick, James Marshall	SHTA Liber A2: 119
****	September 28, 1681	Joseph Fordham	SHTA Book D2: 72
****	July 10, 1682	Matthew Howell, Thomas Cooper	SHTA Liber A2: 93
Washayonos	April 19, 1684	John Howell	SHTA Book D2: 168
Washouse	January 18, 1681	John Throp	RTBH Book B: 62–63
Wauby	June 17, 1672	John Cooper	SBD: 36–38
Wausi	December 27, 1677	Thomas James, John Stratton	RTEH 1: 408–9
Waukus	December 27, 1697	William Smith	PSB: 29
Waumbuaho	May 20, 1673	James Herrick	RTSH 2: 246–47
Wauphege, alias Porridge	December 9, 1685	Richard Floyd	Strong, May 1957, 20(5): 89–90
Wawmaheo	1697–1706/7	William Smith	PSB: 27–28
Wawashaquahoge (Bumbrest)	December 3, 1681	Henry Pierson	SHTA Book D2: 73
Webonuck (Wiannock)	December 11, 1670	John Howell	SHTA Liber A2: 85

(continued)

Appendix 5 table (*continued*)

Name	Date	English Investor	Source
****	June 17, 1672[22]	John Cooper	SBD: 36–38
Weeis	December 19, 1681	Thomas Cooper, Samuel Barnes	SHTA Book D2: 71
Weehouse	June 18, 1683	Joseph Marshall, Richard Howell	SHTA Book D2: 127
Wemapaug	March 26, 1677	John Topping, Benjamin Davis, Joseph Fordham	SHTA Liber A2: 114
Wenanamy, Wenanimo, Wenanamy	January 7, 1679	Edward Howell	SHTA Liber A2: 121
****	July 10, 1682	Matthew Howell	SHTA Book D2: 93
****	April 19, 1684	John Howell	SHTA Book D2: 168
****	October 15, 1684 Appended to bottom of above contract	John Howell	SHTA Book D2: 168
Wenepag	January 23, 1679	John Rose	SHTA Liber A2: 124
Weramps	1707	William Smith	PB: 2
Weomps	July 4, 1675	Jacob Schellinger	RTEH 1: 378–79
****	December 2, 1675	Thomas James, William Edwards	RTEH 1: 381–83
****	February 19, 1679	Thomas Cooper Jr.	SHTA Book D2: 123
****	April 7, 1679	Jacob Schellinger	RTEH 2: 78–79
****	January 9, 1680	John Wheeler	RTEH 2: 86–87
****	March 5, 1681	Benjamin Conklin	RTEH 2: 95–96
****	April 10, 1683	Name illegible	SHTA Book D2: 119
Weramps	January 18, 1681	John Thorp	RTBH Book B: 62–63
****	September 8, 1683	John Jenners	RTBH Book B: 169–70
Weran Wecan?	January 23, 1679	Daniel Sayre	SHTA Liber A2: 124
Wetanauhhum	December 27, 1677	Thomas James, John Stratton	RTEH 1: 407–9
Weunnahum (sachem)			

Name	Date	Witnesses	Reference
Wewetesowet	July 4, 1675	Jacob Schellinger	RTEH 1: 378–79
Whowhus	December 27, 1677	Thomas James, John Stratton	RTEH 1: 407–9
Will Indian	March 24, 1681	John Wheeler	RTEH 2: 98–99
Witaquiaham	June 18, 1683	Joseph Marshall, Richard Howell	SHTA Book D2: 127
Witness	March 24, 1681	John Wheeler	RTEH 2: 98–99
****	April 1, 1681	Samuel Mulford[23]	RTEH 2: 99–100
Wobetom (Awabeton, Awabetum Awaupetun)	December 2, 1675	Thomas James	RTEH 1: 381–82
****	March 24, 1681	John Wheeler	RTEH 2: 98–99
****	October 28, 1684	John Miller	RTEH 2: 152–53
Womamboha	January 28, 1677	Richard Howell, Joseph Fordham	SHTA Liber A2: 113
Wombanoromm	March 13, 1679	Richard Shaw, Goodman Garlick	RTEH 2: 430–31
Wompanaromps (sachem)	January 28, 1677	Richard Howell, Joseph Fordham	SHTA Liber A2: 113
Wompaquat (a.k.a. Haimes)	March 9, 1675	Thomas James, John Stratton	RTEH 1: 373–74
****	July 4, 1675	Jacob Schellinger	RTEH 1: 378–79
****	December 27, 1677	Thomas James, John Stratton	RTEH 1: 378–79
Wompy	March 29, 1680	John Jessup, Thomas Jessup	RTEH 1: 407–9
****	January 16, 1682	Isaac Raynor	SHTA Liber A2: 136
****	June 14, 1682	Samuel Barnes	SHTA Book D2: 71
****	June 4, 1685	James Hildreth, Jeremiah Jagger	SHTA Book D2: 107–8
Wonanamo	January 7, 1679	Edward Howell	SHTA Book D2: 187
Wonapaug	February 25, 1682	Matthew Howell	SHTA Liber A2: 121
Wonepom	February 25, 1682	Matthew Howell	SHTA Book D2: 72
Wopomsh (Smith)	February 25, 1682	Matthew Howell	SHTA Book D2: 72
Wopsha	September 28, 1681	Joseph Fordham	SHTA Book D2: 72
Woris	December 19, 1681	Thomas Cooper, Samuel Barnes	SHTA Book D2: 72
Wunnakaumtakkum (Cowkeeper)	December 27, 1677	Thomas James, John Stratton	SHTA Book D2: 71
			RTEH 2: 407–9

(continued)

Appendix 5 table (*continued*)

Name	Date	English Investor	Source
****	January 28, 1677	Richard Howell, Joseph Fordham	SHTA Liber A2: 113
****	December 27, 1677	Thomas James, John Stratton	RTEH 2: 407–9
Wunnanaugema[24] (Anthony)	November 14, 1671	None	SHTA Liber A2: 90
****	March 9, 1675	Thomas James, John Stratton Sr.	RTEH 1: 373–74
****	January 28, 1677	Richard Howell, Joseph Fordham	SHTA Liber A2: 113
****	December 27, 1677	Thomas James, John Stratton	RTEH 1: 407–9
****	April 19, 1684	John Howell	SHTA Book D2: 168
Wushagonas	April 30, 1683	John Jessup Jr.	SHTA Book D2: 117–18

[1] It appears that Thomas James recruited Addam away from Schellinger's crew.

[2] Apunsha's name appears on an incomplete entry in the East Hampton records made by Thomas James on March 9, 1674/5. The full contract was entered on December 2, 1675, for the 1675–76 season, but Apunsha was not listed, and neither was an Indian named Joseph.

[3] On November 22, 1677, Sarah Cooper, John Cooper Jr.'s widow, complained to Governor Andros that Artor, Jeffrey, Obadiah, Omagunsies, Papasequin, and Plimmy had jumped from her contract with them. Her husband died in 1677. Source: New York State Historical Archives, British Manuscripts Vol. 26, 153, 157.

[4] The contracts dated February 29, 1682, and June 26, 1682, are both for the 1682–83 season. James Cooper signed up Artor and Cohonood (Cohonded) a second time.

[5] Checkano signed the July 25, 1687, deed for Southampton (RCSS 26–27).

[6] John Cooper is listed as one of the company investors, but he died in 1677. Possibly he put up the money before his death and arranged for the share in his name to be collected by his widow, Sarah. Sarah identified herself as a widow in her November 1677 complaint. His estate inventory was entered on March 8, 1677/8, wherein Sarah was named executor (RCSS 73–76).

[7] December 27, 1686, Cayesen signed a land transaction with Andrew Gibb (RCSS 251–53).

[8] There were at least two Indians who took the English name "Harry." One signed with three Southampton companies (1672, 1677, 1678); a second, identified as Harry (a.k.a. Quaquehide), in 1675 and as Harry (a.k.a. Woossooio) in 1681 (RTEH 1: 373; RTEH 2: 94). The latter two Harrys are listed as Montauketts. They may be two different men or, perhaps, were the same Montaukett who changed his Algonquian name while keeping his English name. A Montaukett named Harry was a party to the Montaukett land transactions in 1703. He is not identified here with an Algonquian alias. It is likely that the Harry who signed with the Southampton companies was likely a Shinnecock and the other (a.k.a. Quaquehide and Woossooio) were (was) Montaukett.

[9] The contracts between Harry and John Stratton are puzzling. On January 6, 1681, Harry agreed to hunt whales for John Stratton Sr. Here he is identified as "Harry alias Quequaheid, Indian of Montaukett." Two months later, on March 18, Harry signs another contract with John Stratton Sr. and his son, John Stratton Jr. In the second agreement he is identified only as "Harry," suggesting that perhaps two Montauketts who took the name Harry both hunted for Stratton during the 1681–82 season.

[10] Sarah Cooper, John Cooper's widow, complained to Governor Andros that Artor, Papasequin, Obadiah, Jeffrey, Plimny, Omagunsies, and two others whose names are not legible, had signed with her for the 1677–78 season and then signed with other investors, one of whom was Richard Howell, who had signed Artor and Jeffrey in violation of her contract (SHTA Liber A2: 113). To further confuse the matter, John Topping signed Jeffrey two months later (SHTA Liber A2: 114). The widow's complaint can be found in the New York State Historical Archives, British Manuscripts (Vol. 26, 153, 157). She appealed again on December 12, 1677, but Andros did not respond to her complaint.

[11] Jeremia (Jeremie) signed with Edward Howell on January 22, 1678/79, and on February 19, 1678/79, with Thomas Cooper. There is no further reference to this. Apparently Howell did not contest the loss of Jeremy to Cooper. Jeremy signed with John Raynor on March 5, 1684, for the 1684–85 season and then signed with Samuel Muncey on August 7 for the same season. It appears that he jumped two contracts.

[12] A variant of the name John (John Man, John Indian, John Passin) appears on eleven contracts. Here we see the problem posed by the adopted English names. It is likely, based on the location of the company owners and the specific descriptions in the contracts, that the names represent four Indians. One was a Shinnecock who signed on with seven companies operating out of Southampton, one was an Unkechaug, so identified in two contracts, and two were Montauketts. One is named on East Hampton contracts in 1675 and 1677, and the other, a younger man identified in 1683 as the son of Wobetom, is the Montaukett whaler whose name is inscribed on the glass bottle in the Pantigo burial (RTEH 2: 132–33).

[13] This contract appears to be related to the January agreement above. It is possible that a rival had approached Judas encouraging him to jump from Herrick's contract. In this same contract Herrick signed Tom Indian and John Indian.

[14] There are two Indians identified as "Will" in addition to their Algonquian names, Manheeg and Tantoquin (RTEH 1: 407–9), one identified only as Will (RTEH 2: 98–99), one listed as "Red Headed Will" (SHTA Liber A2: 113), and one who took the English form, Will Beanes (PSB).

[15] It appears that Obadiah signed with Hildreth on June 14, 1682, and then jumped to Cooper's company two weeks later. There is no record of a complaint by Hildreth.

[16] Poaguamo signed the 1671 whaling contract as a witness, not to be confused with Ponguma (Ponguamo, Pongomo, Pomguamo), who signed the same contract as a member of the whaling company. He had earlier signed the 1666 endorsement of Thomas Topping's purchase of land from Shinnecock sunksquaw Weany (Indian Papers 1640–70, 4). He went whaling for Mathew Howell in 1682 and for John Howell in 1684. The 1684 contract identifies him as a sachem. The last references to him were on documents related to a major land transaction in 1703. He is identified as a sachem in both of those documents (RTSH 2: 176–78, 179–80, 358–59). Assuming that he was around twenty in 1666, he would have been in his mid-thirties when he went whaling. He became a prominent and influential sachem in his mid-fifties. He was married to the sister of Wiangonhut, the Unkechaug sachem.

(continued)

Appendix 5 table (*continued*)

[17] Hector is identified as Quequecum on the December 27, 1677, contract with Thomas James. On March 18, 1681, and March 8, 1683, he is only identified as Hector. They probably are the same man because the contracts are all from East Hampton.

[18] It appears that Scanderbag jumped from his contract with Richard Shaw signed on March 13 to sign up with Jacob Schellinger three weeks later on April 7, 1679. There is no record of a complaint by Shaw.

[19] Sequana appears to have signed with Rogers in violation of his contract with Mathew Howell.

[20] This contract was for cutting out blubber, not for whaling.

[21] There is an Unkechaug Indian named Wawpachukis who took the name Humphrey. He worked for Tangier Smith in 1697 twenty years later.

[22] Webonuck was a witness on Cooper's June 17 contract, not a crew member.

[23] Samuel Mulford (April 1, 1681, RTEH 2: 100) accused John Wheeler of tampering with an earlier agreement he had made with Witness.

[24] Anthony is identified here as a Shinnecock. His name appears again on two more contracts with Southampton companies (January 28, 1677, SHTA Liber A2: 113; April 19, 1684; SHTA Book D2: 168). Wunnananaugema, a Montaukett Indian, took the name Anthony on contracts in 1675 (March 9, 1675, RTEH 1: 373) and in 1677 (December 27, 1677; RTEH 1: 407–9). The tribal identification is supported by the geographic locations of the companies. The Southampton companies were likely to hire Shinnecocks, whereas the Indians hired by East Hampton companies were more likely to have come from the nearby Montaukett villages.

Notes

Chapter 1. The Whale in Aboriginal Long Island Culture

1. The route of right whale mothers passing along the south shore of Long Island was observed in February 1984 when fifteen right whales, including four cows with newborn calves from twelve to fifteen feet long, were sighted off Georgia and Florida. They were sighted again in August and September in the Bay of Fundy. This pattern was observed in other years, suggesting that most cows repeat this pattern (Kraus et al. 1986, 141). More recently three right whale females tagged by a research team with a satellite device were plotted moving along the shore from Florida northward past Long Island (Andrews 2015).

2. John Braginton-Smith and Duncan Oliver (2008, 87–88) are skeptical of this account, noting that there are no other references to Indian whaling in the records. It is possible, they say, that the Indians were simply traveling to Martha's Vineyard and not whaling at all. It seems unlikely that Mayhew, who was knowledgeable about Indian habits and spoke their language, would make such a mistake. Reeves, Smith, and Johnson (2007, 61) are not so quick to dismiss Mayhew's account. They also note the reports about prehistoric Inuit whaling in Labrador by J. G. Taylor (1988). William Palmer in his PhD dissertation on the whaling port of Sag Harbor suggests that the well-documented references to their canoeing skills and seamanship "could, in large part, account for the traditions that would credit the American Indians not only for the whaleboat, but also for teaching the colonists how to catch whales" (Palmer 1959, 42).

3. Eric J. Dolin has raised questions about prehistoric whaling at sea by Indians on the East Coast (Dolin 2007, 36–38, 387–88, 391). He dismisses the assertions by authors such as John Spears who wrote that "in every clan and tribe along the coast were men accustomed to killing whales" (Spears 1908, 20). Dolin does, however, acknowledge that evidence from the northwestern coast proves that prehistoric Indian hunters were capable of killing whales and that the Indians along the eastern coast had the canoe-handling skills and sharp bone-tipped arrows necessary for the hunt. There is no evidence, however, that the toggle point harpoon was used by the Indians in southern New England and Long Island. Dolin concludes that until there is more evidence we cannot say with any confidence that the Indians hunted whales. His skepticism is shared by Elizabeth Little (1992).

Chapter 2. Drift Whales

1. The primary engines driving the English economy were agriculture and textiles, and both were in trouble in the early decades of the seventeenth century. As a result, many fled to the urban areas (Anderson 1991, 27). It is quite likely that members

of the Lynn company were among them and therefore had had some experience in the complexity of town and borough government.

2.   Anthropologists and historians have developed analytical models for the study of relations between Native Americans and whites as the frontier moved westward from New England and Long Island. Anthropologists Edward Spicer (1962, 519–39) and Ralph Linton ([1940] 1963, 463–52) divided the postcontact period into two phases, "non-directed acculturation" and "directed acculturation." The first is characterized by a free exchange of ideas and material goods and a voluntary adaptation of items and practices that do not change lifeways in any fundamental degree. Two decades later Richard White described this phase as a "middle ground" where two cultures meet on fairly even military terms (1983, 1991). The second phase followed military conquest and occupation wherein the Native peoples found themselves under European jurisdiction. This latter phase was characterized by directed acculturation in which their lifeways were often changed under coercion: religious ceremonies restricted, the choice of leaders manipulated, and villages moved and individuals entrapped in various forms of debt peonage (Strong 1995a).

3.   Shortly after the arson incident in Southampton, Gardiner brought Wyandanch to meet with Richard Woodhull, a former Southampton resident who had recently moved to Setauket, a small settlement on the north shore of Long Island, west of Southampton. Woodhull wanted to expand the boundaries of Setauket southward to the Atlantic shore. Wenecoheague, an Unkechaug sachem, signed the deed below Wyandanch's mark, acknowledging his endorsement (Strong 2011, 47–53). Wenecoheague was the first of many Long Island sachems who were forced to join Mandush as he watched his land diminish. Wyandanch with his English allies held the upper hand at the moment.

Chapter 4. Origins of "Ye Whaling Design" on Long Island

1.   Although Jean-Pierre Proulx (1993, 23–24) and Martin Conway (1906, 40) suggest that the Basques may have learned about whaling from the Norse in the eighth century, David Laist strongly disagrees, arguing that this is based on unsubstantiated conjecture (Laist 2017, 102–3). While it is true that a Norwegian named Ochther told King Alfred in the ninth century that whale hunters traveled the Norway coast, there is no evidence that they used the toggle harpoon head developed by the Thule Inuit whalers (Jenkins 1921, 59). The Norse, as noted in chapter 1, used techniques that were suited to their environment, driving whales into the fjords and shallow bays where they could kill the whales with arrows and spears. There is a reference in the colonial documents to the use of similar strategies by the Unkechaug (see chapter 1).

2.   Lord Cornbury, in his 1708 report to the Commissioners for Trade and Plantations, noted that in 1707 New York sent four thousand barrels of oil to London and that in 1708 the colony had "not made above 600" (NYCD 5: 59–60).

3.   Elizabeth Little estimated that the peak years were from 1687 to 1707 based on a report for the 1686–87 year and on the British customs data that began in 1697. She was unaware of the data in the whaling contracts.

4. The only other source of information about a specific company is found in the "Pigskin" ledger book kept by the William Smith family on the Mastic Peninsula in the town of Brookhaven. The ledger includes specific information about the family whaling operations from 1694 to 1721. This material is discussed in a case study in a subsequent chapter.

5. The ten men included Captain Theophilus Howell, Nathaniel Howell, Henry Pierson, James Hildreth, Manassa Kemp, Israel Howell, Jonah Howell, Theodore Pierson, Henry Ludlam, and Amyruhaan Riscoe. The Howell and Pierson families had been engaged in whaling for nearly four decades.

Chapter 5. New Needs, Old Traditions

1. The two account books, RFL 1 (1686–90) and RFL 2 (ca. 1720–32), were located by the author in the collections of the Huntington Library Archive in San Marino, California, in 2011. The first, RFL 1, cited in previous chapters, was the subject of an article by Strong and Lamont. "The Richard Floyd Account Book, 1686–1690: A Search for Authorship and Historical Significance," *Long Island History Journal* 24, no. 1 (2015): 92. Unfortunately, no ledgers have been found for the years from 1690 to 1721, nor for the years following 1732.

Chapter 6. Debt Peonage and Indentured Servitude

1. Some examples of the contracts that signed up less than six men were: Josiah Laughton (SHTR 2: 56–57), John Cooper (SBD 84), John Howell (SHTR 2: 56), Anthony Ludlam (SHTA Liber A2: 87), Arthur Howell (SHTA Liber A2: 88), James Herrick (SHTA Liber A2: 82), Daniel Sayre (SHTA Liber A2: 124), Richard Howell (SHTA Liber A2: 135), James Hildreth (SHTA Book D2: 87–88), Shamgar Hand (SHTA Book D2: 112), Ralf Dayton (RTBH Book B: 156), Joseph Davis (RTBH Book B: 175), John Raynor (SHTA Book D2: 172), Samuel Seward (RTBH Book B: 197), Obadiah Seward (RTBH Book B: 197), Samuel Muncy (RTBH Book B: 197), and Abram Dayton (RTBH Book B: 241–42).

2. In twelve instances contracts were negotiated in January. Five of them were signed in 1679, perhaps because an unusual number of whales appeared along the shore that winter. These contracts appear to be hastily drawn up. Four were only one or two sentences. Some of the January contracts do not clearly state whether they apply to that year or the following season.

3. Martha White, John Howell Jr.'s wife, witnessed one of the earliest contracts. In 1671, she signed (with an X) as a Christian witness for her brother-in-law Arthur Howell. Female relatives of whaling families sometimes witnessed contracts, such as the following: Hannah Clarke (January 28, 1677, and March 26, 1677), Hannah Coe (March 10, 1682/3), Mary Cooper (September 12, 1682, and June 26, 1682), Sarah Edsell (May 8, 1682), Mary Fordham (December 10, 1679), Edith Fyler (January 9, 1679/80), Hannah Hildreth (June 4, 1685), Katherine James (January 6, 1680/81), Hannah Morris (June 18, 1683), Martha Owen (June 3, 1682),

Betty Smith (March 5, 1683/84), Sarah Stanborough (March 31, 1679), Hannah Talmage (January 9, 1682/83), and Mary Williams (June 14, 1682).

4.   The witnesses, Benjamin Smith, Jonathan Morehouse, and Clem Salmon, may have had some financial involvement in the company. Of the three, only Smith appears to have had the financial resources necessary to launch a whaling operation. Curiously, the three men were from different towns: Smith from Brookhaven, Morehouse from Southampton, and Salmon from Southold. Smith's ownership of property in southern Brookhaven may explain his interest in whaling, but little is known about the other two men (RTBH Hutchinson, 10, 50; RTBH 1924, 116). Clem Salmon was probably related to William Salmon, one of the founders of Southold, who brought his family to New England in 1635 and later settled in Southold (Robbins 1918, 1). There is no mention in the Southold records of a family member named Clem, but it is possible this was a nickname. Jonathan Morehouse was one of what might be called "the middling sort." In 1683, his estate was valued at sixty-four pounds, well below the valuations of estates belonging to such Southampton whaling investors as John Howell (442 pounds), Joseph Fordham (459 pounds), John Jessup (360 pounds), Sarah Cooper (337 pounds), Thomas Cooper (209 pounds), and Richard Howell (250 pounds) (Howell 1887, 45).

5.   Smith was also concerned about the hostility of many Brookhaven freeholders who resented his occupation of so much of the township. Many of them had supported Jacob Leisler in his opposition to the manorial grants. During the Leislerian revolt, Smith, an outspoken critic of Leisler, said that he feared his neighbors might burn down his house (Lovejoy 1972, 252).

6.   It was possible to pay off debts by selling the products of their traditional hunting and fishing skills. There was a limited market for venison, hides, dried fish, shellfish, and feathers. English households highly valued feathers for bedding. In 1690, for example, Richard Floyd credited an Unkechaug whaler named Pamatqua with six shillings for six pounds of feathers (RFL 11). The surviving records, however, indicate that most debts were paid off with labor.

7.   This is in a transaction between Tangier Smith and the town of Southampton, June 14, 1693, involving a tract of land "lying and being on the east side of a certain house which Stephen Bayley and company used when they went awhaling near a place called Cupsawege about a mile and a half from a gut near a place called green pines." Three more references in 1790 indicate that the location had become a well-known reference point in land transactions (RTBH Hutchinson, 85, 197, 200, 203).

8.   June 7, 1683 (WFEA FIIS 9965, Box 1, Folder 17); November 13, 1688 (RTBH Hutchinson, 70–71); May 12, 1689 (BTH Shaw File); June 10, 1690 (BTH Shaw File); December 8, 1690 (RTBH B, 470–71); April 8, 1692 (BTH Shaw File); October 8, 1692 (WFEA FIIS 6601, Box 1, Folder 10); April 10, 1694 (BTH Shaw File).

Chapter 7. Papasaquin's World

1.   For an account of the incident, see Strong 1994; and Sellers 2015, 156.

2.   Tracing the genealogy of Native American sachems is a particularly challenging endeavor. Wyandanch's son, Wyancombone, who died shortly after 1662, is

identified in the records as the sachem's son. He undoubtedly had others. In 1669, a man named Poniutute is identified only as the Montaukett sachem, not as a descendent of Wyandanch (NYCD 14: 627). A year later Poniutute took the name Moshup, but again there is no specific reference to his lineage (RCSS 167–69). In March 1675, Moshup is identified on a whaling contract as a sachem (RTEH 1: 373–74). In October of that year, he petitioned Governor Andros to return the Montaukett guns. Here he referred to himself as the grandson of Wyandanch (NYCD 14: 699–700). Two years later, he again signed with James as Sachem Moshup (RTEH 1: 408–9). Moshup may have died between 1675 and 1683 because the Montaukett sachem is identified as "the young sachem" (RCSS 134). The following year, the Montaukett sachem is identified for the first time as Aquaas (Aquosh) (RCSS 170–71). In 1687, it appears that Aquaas took the name of his great-grandfather, Wyandanch (RTEH 2: 213–14). The transactions in 1702 and 1703 identify the Montaukett sachem as Wyandanch (RTEH 2: 213–14; Smith 1926a, 48–56).

3. Unfortunately, little else is known about the East Hampton companies because they did not begin entering their contracts into the town records until 1675. The only two whaling companies on record for that season were the Southampton companies organized by James Herrick and John Cooper, who was in the second season of his five-year contract (RTSH 2: 246; SBD 36–38).

4. The company owners were Thomas Jessup (SHTA Book D2: 72), Isaac Raynor (SHTA Book D2: 73), James Cooper (SHTA Book D2: 103), and Andrew Gibbs (SHTA Book D2: 75; RTBH Book B: 105).

5. Delaval, whose father, Thomas, was an influential member of Governor Lovelace's council, had recently thwarted an attempt to make him pay a customs fee for a shipment of 510 gallons of rum (Ritchie 1977, 156–61). Delaval was likely well known to the whaling company owners, who were in constant need of his product.

6. The six men were Thomas James, Josiah Hobart, John Wheeler, Samuel Mulford, Thomas Chatfield, and Robert Dayton. John Mulford, Jeremiah Conklin, Thomas Osborn, and Stephen Hand were closely related to whaling investors. Only Thomas Baker and Thomas Talmadge had no close relative involved in whaling.

7. The Montauketts also agreed to accept a two-thousand-pound bond payable should the Montauketts attempt to sell to an outside party. This "counter bond" was based on the assumption that the Montauketts had been serious about the sale to Van Dam (Smith 1926a, 53–54).

8. The East Hampton officials engaged in an elaborate dance of political intrigue and chicanery to finally get their title. It is a story for another time and place, but here is a brief overview of the events. Van Dam did not accept the attempt to block his purchase, moving against the East Hampton men the following day. He used his influence to order the arrests of John Mulford, Josiah Hobart, John Wheeler, Richard Shaw, John Gardiner, and several other East Hampton men for interfering with Cardale's survey (NYCCM 9: 180–81). The men, led by Mulford, went to New York and consulted with lawyers to defend themselves. They took their stalwart allies, Ungomunt and Wobetom, with them, apparently to testify in support of the East Hampton deed. All of this activity, including the expenses

for the two Montauketts, was paid for by the town (RTEH 3: 64–66). Mulford, perhaps to strengthen his hand, was elected East Hampton town supervisor. On March 25, 1703, Cardale swore to the validity of his report "about doings in Suffolk County," and, in April 1703, nine of the East Hampton men were jailed in New York City (NYS.MSS 47: 88; NYCCM 9: 182). Wheeler was discharged but the others were detained (NYCCM 9: 183). Back in East Hampton the town residents raised funds to pay for legal fees "on account of the Montauk troubles" (RTEH 3: 62). One lawyer got a barrel of cider, and another entry read "more for the lawyers in New York, 6-8-0." Historian Marion Ales noted that the entries on these pages looked suspiciously like bribes (Ales 1993, 52). Samuel Mulford, Thomas Chatfield, and other town officials made at least three trips to Jamaica and New York City over a period of a month costing a total of thirty pounds. Chatfield alone was paid eleven pounds, eighteen shillings for his expenses. The details of these meetings in New York are, of course, not documented, but there is little doubt that the New York lawyers did very well. A year later the legal battle continued as East Hampton allocated 303 pounds "for the defraying of several extraordinary charges and disbursements arising on Montauk" (RTEH 3: 65–66, 78–79). These were significant sums. When Thomas Cooper, a whaling company owner, died in 1692, his total estate was valued at 420 pounds (RCSS 317–19). In May 1704, a packet of ten documents related to the Montauk land controversy was delivered to John Mulford (RTEH 3: 93). The papers included the 1703 deed and the Indians' protest against the sale to Van Dam and Bridges. The last reference to the issue was an entry on October 1712 wherein Samuel Mumford agreed to pay off Rip Van Dam with the sum of one hundred pounds (RTEH 3: 288). Sachems Wyandanch and Sasakataka had been receiving small amounts from four to twenty shillings (RTEH 3: 220).

Chapter 8. Leaving the Shore

1.   The Sayre letter is reprinted in Adams, *History of Southampton* (1918, 232). The original, located now in the Bridgehampton Museum, Bridgehampton, New York, was brought to the author's attention by Julie Green, collection archivist.

2.   Surroot received corn meal, powder, shot, pork, leather for shoes, molasses, pennystone cloth, an old shirt, old stockings, a Dutch blanket, a Dutch shirt, a pair of shoes, lining cloth, an old coat, a knife, and three quarts of cider (RFL 2: 4v, 5, 5v, 6v, 7, 14, 16).

3.   East Hampton Public Library Pennypacker Collection File 1732 OG 21, Pelletreau to Delancy February 17, 1732.

4.   Kate W. Strong, "Some Early Floyd Papers," *Long Island Forum* 20, no. 5 (1957): 89–90. Ned Laine's indenture is in the Osborn Shaw file in the Brookhaven town historian's collections.

5.   As whale ships went further from shore, flensing was done on board. The blubber was stored in barrels and taken to trying stations on shore. This distance posed problems because the blubber would begin to spoil, producing inferior oil. Try-

ing stations such as the one in Dartmouth (New Bedford) operated in the mid-eighteenth century, but as the whaling expeditions moved into distant waters, often for months at a time, portable trying equipment was carried on board and taken to a convenient place on the nearest shore. It was not always a workable solution. Sanderson attributes this innovation to a Basque captain named Francois Sopite, but he has no footnotes in his book and acknowledges that there is no written record describing this innovation. Eric Dolin and others argue that the procedure was probably developed by different people at different times. By the middle of the nineteenth century, the American whaleships were employing furnaces constructed in the center of the main deck (Dolin 2007, 107–8; Sanderson [1956] 1993, 128–29; Ellis 1991, 46).

Bibliography

Archival Sources

BHSL = Brooklyn Historical Society Library, Pierpont Street, Brooklyn, N.Y.

CELP = Calendar of Endorsed Land Papers, 1643–1803, Vol. 2. Albany, N.Y.: Weed, Parsons, 1864.

CHSC = *Connecticut Historical Society Collections*. Hartford: Connecticut Historical Society.

CNYHS = Collections of the New York Historical Society for the Year 1891, *New York State Historical Society*, 1392.

CTD = Colonial Town Deeds, 1678–1693, Southampton Town Clerk's Office, Southampton, N.Y.

DSBD = Department of State Book of Deeds (N.Y. State Archives series 453, vol. 1–9).

EHTA = East Hampton Public Library Long Island Collection, East Hampton, N.Y.

EHTR = East Hampton Trustees Records, 7 vols., ed. Henry Sleight. East Hampton, N.Y.: Town of East Hampton, 1925–1927.

EHLPC = East Hampton Library, Pennypacker Collection, East Hampton, N.Y.

Indian Papers. 1640–1670. Unpublished original documents, Southampton Town Historian's Office. Southampton Town Clerk's Office, Southampton, N.Y.

IWC = International Whaling Commission. 1982. Reports of the International Whaling Commission Special Issue no. 4, Cambridge, Mass.

JLCC = Journal of the Legislative Council of the Colony of New York, 1691–1743, 2 vols. Albany, N.Y.: Weed, Parsons, 1861.

LCNY = The Colonial Laws of New York, Vol. 1. Albany, N.Y.: James Lyon, State Printer, 1894.

LPSS = Letters Patent, 1664–1912, Secretary of State, New York State Library Archives, Albany, N.Y.

NOAA Fisheries Service. 2012. *North Atlantic Right Whale: Five Year Review Summary and Evaluation*. Gloucester, Mass.: Northeast Regional Office.

NYCCM = New York Calendar of Council Minutes, 1668–1783. Vol. 8 and 9. Published in New York State Library 85th Annual Report, *Bulletin 58*. 1902 [1903]. Albany: University of the State of New York.

NYCD = *Documents Relative to the Colonial History of the State of New York*, ed. Edmund Bailey O'Callaghan and Berthold Fernow, 15 vols. Albany, N.Y.: Weed, Parsons, 1856–87.

NYDH = *Documentary History of the State of New York*, ed. Edmund Bailey O'Callaghan, 4 vols. Albany, N.Y.: Weed, Parsons, 1849–51.

NYSH = New York State Historian, *Second Annual Report of the State Historian, 1897*, 2 vols. Albany: New York State Printers.

NYS.MSS = *New York State Historical Archives, British Manuscripts* (Transcripts and Translations of New York Colonial Manuscripts), New York State Archives, Albany, N.Y.

Osborn Shaw Papers, BTH = Brookhaven Town Historian's Office, Farmingville, N.Y.

PSB = Pigskin Book, Bellport-Brookhaven Historical Society Collections, Bellport, N.Y. The ledger was kept by William Tangier Smith of Saint George Manor from 1696 until his death in 1705. His wife and descendants continued to use the book until 1721. After that occasional entries were made in the eighteenth and early nineteenth centuries. The name refers to the binding of the ledger.

RCC = *Records of the Colony of Connecticut* 1850 [1968], ed. J. Hammond Trumbull, 3 vols. Hartford: Brown and Parsons (AMS Press).

RCNP = *Records of the Colony of New Plymouth: Acts of the Commissioners of the United Colonies of New England*, ed. David Pulsifer, 2 vols. New York: AMS Press, 1968. (Vols. 9 and 10 are the records of the United Colonies.)

RCRI = *Records of the Colony of Rhode Island and Providence Plantation in New England*, ed. John Russell Bartlett, 3 vols. (1857). New York: AMS Press (1968).

RCSS = *Records of the Court of Sessions of Suffolk County in the Province of New York, 1670–1688* (1993), ed. Thomas Cooper. Bowie, Md.: Heritage Books.

RFAC 1 = Richard Floyd account book 1687–1690 and RFAC 2 = Richard Floyd Account Book 1729–1732. Huntington Library Manuscripts Department 1151 Oxford Road, San Marino, Calif., 91108. Filed under mss. HM 59961 (RFAC 1) and mss. HM 59424 (RFAC 2). Digital copies of the account books are located in the Suffolk County Historical Society Collections, Riverhead, N.Y.; Brookhaven Town Historians Archives, Farmingdale, N.Y.; and the William Floyd Estate Archives, Fire Island National Seashore, Mastic, N.Y.

RTBH = Book A (1930) *Records of the Town of Brookhaven Book A, 1657–79; 1790–98*, ed. Osborn Shaw. New York: Derrydale Press.

RTBH = Book B (1932) *Records of the Town of Brookhaven, 1679–1756*, ed. Osborn Shaw. New York: Derrydale Press.

RTBH = Book C (1930) *Records of the Town of Brookhaven, 1687–1789*, ed. Osborne Shaw. New York: Derrydale Press.

RTBH = Hutchinson (1880) *Records of the Town of Brookhaven up to 1880*, Patchogue, N.Y.: Office of the *Patchogue Advance*.

RTBH = 1924 *Records of the Town of Brookhaven, 1662–1679*, ed. Archibald Weeks, New York: Tobias Wright.

RTEH = *Records of the Town of East Hampton*, ed. Joseph Osborne, 1887, 5 vols. Sag Harbor, N.Y.: Hunt.

RTH = *Records of the Town of Huntington*, ed. Charles R. Street, 1887–89, 3 vols. Huntington, N.Y.: Town of Huntington.

RTSH = *Records of the Town of Southampton*, ed. William Pelletreau, 1874–77, 8 vols. Sag Harbor, N.Y.: Hunt.

RTSM = *Records of the Town of Smithtown*, ed. William Pelletreau and Harry D. Sleight, 1898–1931, 4 vols. Huntington, N.Y.: Long Islander Print.

SBD = Small Book of Deeds, unpublished records in the Suffolk County Archives, County Clerk's Office, Historical Documents Room, Suffolk County Office Building, Riverhead, N.Y. Transcribed for the county by Orville Ackerly in 1877.

SGMA = Saint George Manor Archives, Saint George Manor, Mastic, N.Y.

Shaw Notebooks. Transcriptions of deeds in the Saint George Manor Archives (closed to public) made in the 1950s by Osborn Shaw (Brookhaven town historian) located in the Brookhaven Town Historian's Office, Farmingdale, N.Y.

SHSA = Southampton Historical Society Archives, Southampton, N.Y.

SHTA = Southampton Town Archives, unpublished town records are in the Southampton Town Clerk's office under the supervision of the town historian, Southampton, N.Y. Liber A2 is in a bound volume entitled *Town Records, 1659–1754*, and Book D2, also bound, is in *Colonial Town Deeds, 1678–1693*.

WFEA = William Floyd Estate Archive at Fire Island National Seashore. National Park Service, Mastic, N.Y.

WP = *Winthrop Papers*, 1929–47, ed. Allyn B. Forbes, 5 vols. Boston: Massachusetts Historical Society.

Published Sources

Adams, James Truslow. (1916) 1962. *Memorials of Old Bridgehampton*. Port Washington, N.Y.: Ira Friedman reprint.

———. 1918. *History of the Town of Southampton*. Bridgehampton, N.Y.: Hampton Press.

Aguilar, A. 1986. A Review of *Old Basque Whaling and Its Effect on the Right Whales (Eubalaena glacialis) of the North Atlantic. Reports of the International Whaling Commission* 10 (special issue): 191–99.

Akrigg, G. P. V. 1968. *Shakespeare and the Earl of Southampton*. Cambridge: Harvard University Press.

Ales, Marion Fisher. 1993. "A History of the Indians on Montauk, Long Island," 5–67. In Gaynell Stone, ed., *The History and Archaeology of the Montauk*. Stony Brook, N.Y.: SCAA.

Alexander, Michael, ed. 1976. *Discovering the New World: Based on the Works of Theodore De Bry*. New York: Harper and Row.

Anderson, Virginia DeJohn. 1991. *New England's Generation: The Great Migration and the Formation of Society and Culture in the Seventeenth Century*. London: Cambridge University Press.

Andrews, Russel. 2015. "Satellite Tagging of North Atlantic Right Whales: Development and Application of Improved Tag Attachment Methods." Paper presented at the North Atlantic Right Whale Consortium Annual Meeting, New Bedford Whaling Museum, November 4–5, 2015.

Ansel, Willits D., et al. 2014. *The Whaleboat: A Study of Design, Construction, and Use from 1850 to 2014*. Mystic Seaport: The Museum of America and the Sea.

Ashley, Clifford W. 1926. *The Yankee Whaler*. New York: Dover Publications.

Axtell, James. 1981. *The European and the Indian: Essays in the Ethnohistory of Colonial North America*. New York: Oxford University Press.

———. 1985. *The Invasion Within: The Contest of Cultures in Colonial North America*. New York: Oxford University Press.

———. 1988. *After Columbus: Essays in the Ethnohistory of Colonial North America*. New York: Oxford University Press.

———. 1992. *Beyond 1492: Encounters in Colonial North America*. New York: Oxford University Press.

Bailey, Paul. 1953. "Shore Whaling Came First." *Long Island Forum* (May): 83–84, 92.

———. 1957. "Early Long Island Whalers." *Long Island Forum* (August): 147.

———. 1959. *Long Island Whalers*. Amityville, N.Y.: Bailey.

Barkham S. H. 1984. "Basque Whaling Establishments in Labrador, 1536–1632: A Summary." *Arctic* 37: 515–19.

Barstow, Belle. 2004. *Setauket, Alias Brookhaven: The Birth of a Long Island Town*. Bloomington, Ind.: Belle Barstow.

Basset, Benjamin. 1792. "Fabulous Traditions and Customs of the Indians." *Massachusetts Historical Society Collections* 1(1): 139–40.

Baumgartner, Mark F., Charles A. Mayo, and Robert D. Kenney. 2007. "Enormous Carnivores, Microscopic Food, and a Restaurant That's Hard to Find," 138–99. In Scott Kraus and Rosalind M. Rolland, eds., *The Urban Whale: North Atlantic Right Whales at the Crossroads*. Cambridge: Harvard University Press.

Bayles, Richard M. 1983. "The Town of Smithtown." In *History of Suffolk County, New York, 1683–1883*. New York: Munsell.

Beale, Thomas. 1839. *A Few Observations on the Natural History of the Sperm Whale*. London: Jan van Voorst (Google digitalized 2006).

Becker, Marshall Joseph. 2005. "Matchcoats: Cultural Conservatism and Change in One Aspect of Native American Clothing." *Ethnohistory* 52(4): 727–66.

Bragdon, Kathleen J. 1996. *Native Peoples of Southern New England, 1500–1650*. Norman: University of Oklahoma Press.

———. 2009. *Native Peoples of Southern New England, 1650–1775*. Norman: University of Oklahoma Press.

Braginton-Smith, John, and Duncan Oliver. 2008. *Cape Cod Shore Whaling, America's First Whalemen*. Yarmouth, Mass.: Historical Society of Old Yarmouth.

Braunlein, John H. 1976. *Colonial Long Island Folklife*. Stony Brook, N.Y.: Museums at Stony Brook.

Breen, T. H. 1989. *Imagining the Past: East Hampton Histories*. New York: Addison-Wesley Publications.

Brereton John. (1602) 1906. "Briefe and True Relation of the Discoverie of the North Part of Virginia," 327–40. In Harry Burrage, ed., *Early English and French Voyages*. New York: Scribners.

Bridenbaugh, Carl. 1974. *Fat, Mutton, and Liberty of Conscience: Society in Rhode Island, 1630–1690*. Providence: Brown University Press.

Brown, M. L. 1980. *Firearms in Colonial America: The Impact on History and Technology, 1492–1792*. Washington, D.C.: Smithsonian Institution Press.

Brown, Moira W., Scott D. Kraus, Christopher K. Slay, and Lance P. Garrison. "Surveying for Discovery, Science, and Management," 105–37. In Scott Kraus and Rosalind M. Rolland, eds., *The Urban Whale: The North Atlantic Right Whale at the Crossroads*. Cambridge: Harvard University Press.

Byers, Edward. 1987. *The Nation of Nantucket*. Boston: Northeastern University Press.

Cave, Alfred A. 1996. *The Pequot War*. Amherst: University of Massachusetts Press.

Chapin, Howard. 1927. "Indian Graves." *Rhode Island Historical Society Collections* 20: 14–32.

Christoph, Peter, ed. 1980. *New York Historical Manuscripts,* Vol. XXII, *Administrative Papers of Governors Richard Nicolls and Francis Lovelace, 1664–1673.* Baltimore: Genealogical Publishing Company.

Christoph, Peter, and Florence Christoph, eds. 1982. *Book of General Entries of the Colony of New York, 1664–1673.* Baltimore: Genealogical Publishing.

————, eds. 1983. *Records of the Court of Assizes for the Colony of New York, 1665–1682.* Baltimore: Genealogical Publishing.

Clapham, Philip J., Sharon B. Young, and Robert L. Brownell Jr. 1999. "Baleen Whales: Conservation Issues and the Status of Most Endangered Populations." *Mammal Review* (Great Britain) 29: 35–60.

Clarke, P. 2001. "The Significance of Whales to the Aboriginal Peoples of Southern Australia." *Records of the South Australian Museum* 34(1): 19–35.

Conkling, Ira B. 1913. *Conklings in America.* Washington, D.C.: Charles Potter and Company.

Conway, Martin. 1906. *No Man's Land: A History of Spitsbergen from Its Discovery in 1596 to the Beginning of the Scientific Explorations of the Country.* Cambridge: Cambridge University Press.

Cooper, Thomas W. 1990. "Southampton's Founding 1640." *Southampton Historical Society Register* 15: 97–105.

————. 1990. "Southampton's Founding 1640 (con't.)." *Southampton Historical Society Register* 16: 11–24.

Crevecoeur, J. Hector St. John de. (1782) 1957. *Letters from an American Farmer.* New York: E. P. Dutton.

Cronon, William. 1983. *Changes in the Land: Indians, Colonists, and the Ecology of New England.* New York: Hill and Wang.

Crosby, Constance A. 1988. 'From Myth to History, or Why King Philip's Ghost Walks Abroad," 183–209. In Mark P. Leone and Parker B. Potter Jr., eds., *The Recovery of Meaning: Historical Archaeology in the Eastern United States.* Washington, D.C.: Smithsonian Institution.

Cumbaa, S. L. 1986. "Archaeological Evidence of the 16th Century Basque Right Whale Fishery in Labrador." *Reports of the International Whaling Commission* 10 (special issue): 187–90.

Dakin, William John. 1963. *Whalemen Adventurers.* Sydney: Sirus Books.

Dankerts, Jaspar, and Peter Sluyter. 1867. *Journal of a Voyage to New York, 1679–80.* Brooklyn, N.Y.: Brooklyn Historical Society.

Davis, William M. 1874. *Nimrod of the Sea or the American Whaleman.* New York: Harper and Brothers.

De Acosta, Jose. 1590. *The Natural and Moral History of the Indies,* translated by Edward Grimston (1604), revised by Clements R. Markham (1880). London: Hakluyt Society.

De Forest, John W. 1852. *History of the Indians of Connecticut.* Brighton, Mich.: Native American Book Publishers.

Denton, Daniel. (1670) 1968. "A Brief Description of New York," 1–57. In Sidney L. Pomerantz, ed., *Historical Chronicles of New Amsterdam, Colonial New York and Early Long Island*, Series II. Port Washington, N.Y.: Ira Friedman.

De Vries, David P. (1655) 1968. "Short Historical and Journal Notes of Several Voyages," 1–136. In Cornell Jaray, ed., *Historical Chronicles of New Amsterdam, Colonial New York and Early Long Island*, Series I. Port Washington, N.Y.: Ira Freidman.

Dolin, Eric J. 2007. *Leviathan: The History of Whaling in America.* New York: W.W. Norton.

Douglas, William, and Jon Bilbao. 1975. *Amerikanuak: Basque in the New World.* Reno, Nev.: University of Nevada Press.

Dow, George F. 1985. *Whale Ships and Whaling.* New York: Argosy-Antiquarian.

Dudley, Paul. 1753. "An Essay upon the Natural History of Whales." *Philosophical Transactions of the Royal Society of London* 33: 256–69.

Edwards, Everett J., and Jeannette Edwards Rattray. 1932. *"Whale Off!" The Story of American Shore Whaling.* New York: Frederick A. Stokes.

Ellis, Richard. 1991. *Men and Whales.* New York: Alfred A. Knopf.

Fisher, Linford D. "'Why shall wee have peace to be made slaves': Indian Surrenderers During and After King Philip's War." *Ethnohistory* 64(1): 91–114.

Fowler, William. 1972. "Bone Implements: How They Were Used." *Bulletin of the Massachusetts Archaeological Society* 33(1–2): 12–19.

Frasier, Thomas R., Brenna A. McLeod, Roxanne M. Gillett, Moira W. Brown, and Bradley N. White. 2007. "Right Whales Past and Present as Revealed by Their Genes," 200–231. In Scott Kraus and Rosalind M. Rolland, eds., *The Urban Whale: North Atlantic Right Whales at the Crossroads.* Cambridge: Harvard University Press.

Friesen, T. Max, and Charles D. Arnold. 2008. "The Timing of Thule Migrations: New Data from the Western Canadian Arctic." *American Antiquity* 73(3): 527–38.

Galenson, David W. 1981. *White Servitude in Colonial America: An Economic Analysis.* London: Cambridge University Press.

———. 1984. "The Rise and Fall of Indentured Servitude in the Americas: An Economic Analysis." *The Journal of Economic History* 4(1) (March): 1–26.

Gardiner, David L. (1840) 1973. *Chronicles of East Hampton.* Sag Harbor, N.Y.: William Ewers.

Gardiner, Lion. (1660) 1980. "Relation of the Pequot Wars," 111–49. In Charles Orr, ed., *The History of the Pequot War.* New York: AMS Press.

Gary, Jack. 2007. "Material Culture and Multi-Cultural Interaction at Sylvester Manor." *Northeast Historical Archaeology* 36: 100–112.

Giambarba, Paul. 1967. *Whales, Whaling, and Whalecraft.* Centerville, Mass.: Scrimshaw Publications.

Gibson, Susan. 1980. *Burr's Hill: A 17th Century Wampanoag Burial Ground in Warren, Rhode Island.* Providence: Brown University, Haffenreffen Museum of Anthropology.

Goddard, David. 2011. *Colonizing Southampton: The Transformation of a Long Island Community, 1870–1900.* Albany: State University of New York Press.

Goddard, Ives. 1978. "Eastern Algonquian Languages," 70–77. In *Handbook of the North American Indians*, ed. Bruce Trigger. Washington, D.C.: Smithsonian Institution Press.

Gookin, Daniel. (1674) 1972. *Historical Collections of the Indians of New England*. New York: Arno Press.

Graham-Campbell, James. 2013. *The Viking World*. London: Francis Lincoln Limited.

Greven, Philip. 1977. *The Protestant Temperament: Patterns of Child-Rearing, Religious Experience, and the Self in Early America*. Chicago: University of Chicago Press.

Halsey, Hugh. 1980. "Howell and Halsey Family Records." *Suffolk County Historical Register* 4: 5–9.

Hamilton, P. K., and M. H. Marx. 1995. "Weaning in North American Right Whales." *Marine Mammal Science* 11(3): 385–90.

Hamilton, P. K., A. R. Knowlton, and M. H. Marx. 2007. "Right Whales Tell Their Own Story: The Right Whale Identification Catalogue," 75–104. In S. D. Kraus and R. M. Holland, eds., *The Urban Whale: North Atlantic Right Whales at the Crossroads*. Cambridge: Harvard University Press.

Hamlin, Paul M. 1939. *Legal Education in New York*. New York: New York University Press.

Heath, Dwight B. 1989. "American Indians and Alcohol: Epidemiological and Socio-cultural Relevance." In Danielle L. Spiegler et al., eds., *Alcohol Abuse Among U.S. Minorities*, National Institute on Alcohol Abuse and Alcoholism Research Monograph No. 18, Rockville, Md.

Hedges, Henry, ed. 1887. *A History of East Hampton, Vol. 1*. Sag Harbor, N.Y.: Hunt.

Horton, Azariah. 1993. "Journals 1741–44," 195–220. In Gaynell Stone, ed., *The History and Archaeology of the Montauk*. Stony Brook, N.Y.: Suffolk County Archaeological Association.

Hosmer, James Kendall. (1908) 1959. *Winthrop's Journal: The History of New England*. 2 vols. New York: Barnes and Noble.

Howell, George Rogers. 1887. *The Early History of Southampton, Long Island*. Albany: Weed, Parsons and Company.

Howell, N. R. 1941. "Long Island Whaling." *Long Island Forum* (September): 207–16.

Hudson, Charles. 1976. *The Southeastern Indians*. Knoxville: University of Tennessee Press.

Huntington, Mark. 1977. "Ancient Shellheaps Near New York City," 1–15. In Gaynell Stone Levine, ed., *Early Papers in Long Island Archaeology*. Stony Brook, N.Y.: SCAA.

Jacobs, Jaap. 2007. *The Colony of New Netherland: A Dutch Settlement in Seventeenth-Century America*. Ithaca: Cornell University Press.

Jacobs, Wilbur R. 1949. "Wampum: The Protocol of Indian Diplomacy." *William and Mary Quarterly* 6(4): 596–604.

Jameson, J. Franklin. 1883. "Montauk and the Common Lands of Easthampton." *Magazine of American History* 9(4): 225–39.

Jenkins, J. T. 1921. *A History of the Whale Fisheries: From the Basque Fisheries of the Tenth Century to the Hunting of the Finn Whale at the Present Date*. London: H. F. and G. Witherby.

Jennings, Francis. 1975. *The Invasion of America: Indians, Colonialism, and the Cant of Conquest*. New York: W. W. Norton.

Johnson, Adrian, ed. 1974. *America Explored: A Cartographical History of the Exploration of North America*. New York: Viking Press.

Kawashima, Yasuhide. 1988. "Indian Servitude in the Northeast," 404–6. In Wilcomb Washburn, ed., *History of Indian-White Relations*. Vol. 4 in *Handbook of North America Indians*. Washington, D.C.: Smithsonian Institution.

Kraus, Scott D., Richard M. Pace III, and Timothy Frasier. 2007. "High Investment, Low Return: The Strange Case of Reproduction in *Eubalaena glacialis*," 172–200. In Scott Kraus and Rosalind M. Rolland, eds., *The Urban Whale: North Atlantic Right Whales at the Crossroads*. Cambridge: Harvard University Press.

Kraus, S. D., J. H. Prescott, A. R. Knowlton, and G. S. Stone. 1986. "Migration and Calving of Right Whales (*Eubalaena glacialis)* in the Western North Atlantic," 139–44. In Robert L. Brownell Jr. et al., eds., *Proceedings of the Workshop on the Status of Right Whales*. Boston: International Whaling Commission, Special Report Vol. 10.

Kraus, Scott D., and Rosalind M. Rolland, eds. 2007. *The Urban Whale: North Atlantic Right Whales at the Crossroads*. Cambridge: Harvard University Press.

Kupperman, Karen O. 2000. *Indians and English: Facing Off in Early America*. Ithaca, N.Y.: Cornell University Press.

Laist, David W. 2017. *North Atlantic Right Whales: From Hunted Leviathan to Conservation Icon*. Baltimore: John Hopkins University Press.

Latham, Roy. 1978a. "Seventeenth Century Graves at Montauk, Long Island," 6–7. In Gaynell Stone, ed., *The Coastal Archaeology Reader: Selections from the New York State Archaeological Association Bulletin*. Stony Brook, N.Y.: Suffolk County Archaeological Association.

———. 1978b. "Three Mile Harbor Sites, East Hampton," 18–19. In Gaynell Stone, ed., *The Coastal Archaeological Reader: Selections from the New York State Archaeological Association Bulletin*. Stony Brook, N.Y.: Suffolk County Archaeological Association.

Laughlin, William S. 1963. "The Eskimo and Aleut: Their Origins and Evolution." *Science* 142: 633–45.

Leach, Douglas Edward. 1958. *Flintlock and Tomahawk: New England in King Philip's War*. New York: W. W. Norton and Company.

Leland, Charles G. 1884. *Algonquin Legends of New England: Myths and Folklore of the Micmacs, Passamaquoddy, and Penobscot Tribes*. London: Sampson Low, Marston, Searle, and Riverton.

Lenkeit, Roberta Edwards. 2001. *Introducing Cultural Anthropology*. Mountain View, Calif.: Mayfield Publishing Company.

Lincoln, Charles Z. 1894. *The Colonial Laws of New York from 1664 to the Revolution*. Albany: James B. Lyton.

Lindquist, Ole. 1994. "Whales, Dolphins, and Porpoises in the Economy and Culture of Peasant Fishermen in Norway, Orkney, Shetland, Faeroe Islands, and Iceland ca. 900 A.D.–1500 A.D." PhD diss., University of St. Andrews, Scotland.

Linton, Ralph, ed. (1940) 1963. *Acculturation in Seven American Indian Tribes*. New York: Peter Smith.

Lipman, Andrew. 2015. *The Saltwater Frontier: Indians and the Contest for the American Coast*. New Haven: Yale University Press.

Little, Elizabeth A. 1981. "The Indian Contribution to Along Shore Whaling at Nantucket," 111–31. In *Nantucket Algonquian Studies*, no. 8. Nantucket, Mass.: Nantucket Historical Association.

————. 1988. "Nantucket Whaling in the Early Eighteenth Century," 111–31. In William Cowan, ed., *Papers of the Nineteenth Algonquian Conference.* Ottawa: Carleton University.

————. 1992. *Indian Whalemen of Nantucket: The Documentary Evidence.* Nantucket, Mass.: Nantucket Historical Association.

Little, Elizabeth A., and J. Clinton Andrews. 1982. "Drift Whales at Nantucket: The Kindness of Moshup." *Man in the Northeast* 23: 17–38.

Lohse, E. S. 1988. "Trade Goods," 396–403. In Wilcomb Washburn, ed., *History of Indian-White Relations.* Vol. 4 in *Handbook of North American Indians.* Washington, D.C.: Smithsonian Institution.

Lott, Roy. 1964. "Indentured Servants in Huntington." *Long Island Forum* 22(6): 125–26.

Lovejoy, David S. 1972. *The Glorious Revolution in America.* New York: Harper and Row.

Lytle, Thomas G. 1984. *Harpoons and Other Whalecraft.* New Bedford, Mass.: Old Dartmouth Historical Society Whaling Museum.

Mancall, Peter C. 1995. *Deadly Medicine: Indians and Alcohol in Early America.* Ithaca: Cornell University Press.

Marshall, Bernice. 1962. *Colonial Hempstead: Long Island Life Under the Dutch and English.* Port Washington, N.Y.: Ira Friedman.

Martin, John Frederick. 1991. *Profits in the Wilderness: Entrepreneurship and the Founding of New England in the Seventeenth Century.* Chapel Hill: University of North Carolina Press.

Mason, Otis T. 1900. "Aboriginal American Harpoons," 219–36. In *Report of the National Museum.* Washington, D.C.: Smithsonian Institution.

Matthiessen, Peter. 1986. *Men's Lives: The Surfmen and Baymen of the South Fork.* New York: Random House.

Mauss, Marcel. 1967. *The Gift: Forms and Functions of Exchange in Archaic Societies.* New York: W. W. Norton.

Moffet, Ross. 1969. "An Unusual Indian Harpoon from Truro." *Massachusetts Archaeological Society Bulletin* 30(3 and 4): 22–24.

Montgomery, Florence. 1970. *Printed Textiles, English and American Cottons and Linens.* New York: Viking Press.

————. 1984. *Textiles in America, 1650–1870.* New York: W. W. Norton.

Mourt, G. A. (1622) 1993. *A Journal of the Pilgrims at Plymouth, Mourt's Relation*, ed. Dwight B. Heath. New York: Corinthian Books.

Murray, David. 2000. *Indian Giving: Economies of Power in Indian-White Exchanges.* Amherst: University of Massachusetts Press.

Newell, Margaret Ellen. 2015. *Brethren by Nature: New England Indians, Colonists, and the Origins of American Slavery.* Ithaca: Cornell University Press.

O'Callaghan, Edmund Bailey. 1966. *History of New Netherland, 1845–1848.* 2 vols. Spartanburg, N.C.: The Reprint Company.

Occom, Samson. (1761) 1980. "An Account of the Montauk Indians on Long Island," 218–19. In Gaynell Stone, ed., *The Languages and Lore of the Long Island Indians.* Lexington, Mass.: Ginn Custom Publishing.

Onderdonck, Henry. (1822) 1923. *Queens County in Olden Times.* Jamaica, N.Y.: Charles Welling.

Palmer, William R. 1959. "The Whaling Port of Sag Harbor." PhD diss. New York: Columbia University.

Paltsits, Victor H., ed. 1910. *Minutes of the Executive Council of the Province of New York: Administration of Francis Lovelace.* 2 vols. Albany: State of New York.

Papageorge, Toby. 1983. "Records of the Shinnecock Trustees, 1792–1983," 141–83. In Gaynell Stone, ed., *The Shinnecock Indians: A Culture History.* Lexington, Mass.: Ginn Custom Publishing.

Pelletreau, William S. 1903. *A History of Long Island from Earliest Times to the Present.* 2 vols. New York: Lewis Publishing Company.

Pettis, Heather, and P. K. Hamilton. 2014. *Report to the North Atlantic Right Whale Consortium, Annual Report Card.* Boston: New England Aquarium.

Plot, Robert. 1677. *Natural History of Oxfordshire.* London: Litchfield C. Brome. Reprinted 1972 by Paul Chicheley, Buckinghamshire.

Priddy, Katherine Lee. 2007. "From Youghco to Black John: Ethnohistory of Sylvester Manor, ca. 1600–1735." *Northeast Historical Archaeology* 36(1): 16–33.

Pringle, Heather. 2008. "Signs of the First Whale Hunters." *Science* 320(5873): 175.

Proulx, Jean-Pierre. 1993. *Basque Whaling in Labrador in the 16th Century.* Studies in Archaeology, Architecture and History. Canada: National Historic Sites, Park Service, Environment Canada.

Rankin, Hugh. 1962. *Upheaval in Albemarle: The Story of the Culpepper Rebellion: 1675–1689.* Raleigh, N.C.: Carolina Charter Tercentenary Commission.

Rattray, Jeannette Edwards. 1953. *East Hampton History Including Genealogies of Early Families.* East Hampton, N.Y.: Rattray.

Reeves, Randall R., and Edward Mitchell. 1986. "The Long Island, New York, Right Whale Fishery 1650–1924," 201–20. In Robert L. Brownell Jr., Peter B. Best, and John H. Prescott, eds., *Right Whales: Past and Present Status, in the Proceedings of the Workshop on the Status of Right Whales, New England Aquarium, June 15–23, 1986.* Cambridge: International Whaling Commission.

Reeves, Randall R., Jeffrey M. Breiwick, and Edward Mitchell. 1999. "History of Whaling and Estimated Kill of Right Whales, *Balaena glacialis*, in the Northeastern United States, 1620–1924." *Marine Fisheries Review* (June 22): 1–96.

Reeves, Randall R., Tim D. Smith, and Elizabeth Johnson. 2007. "Near Annihilation of a Species: Right Whaling in the North Atlantic," 39–74. In Scott Kraus and Rosalind M. Rolland, eds., *The Urban Whale: North Atlantic Right Whales at the Crossroads.* Cambridge: Harvard University Press.

Rice, James D. 2014. "Bacon's Rebellion in Indian Country." *Journal of American History* 102(3): 726–50.

Ritchie, Robert C. 1977. *The Duke's Province: A Study of New York Politics and Society, 1664–1691.* Chapel Hill: University of North Carolina Press.

Robbins, William S., ed. 1918. *The Salmon Records: A Private Register of Marriages and Deaths of the Residents of Southold, New York.* New York: New York Genealogical and Biographical Society.

Romney, Susanah Shaw. 2014. *New Netherland Connections: Intimate Networks and Atlantic Ties in Seventeenth-Century America.* Chapel Hill: University of North Carolina Press.

Rorabaugh, William. 1979. *The Alcoholic Republic: An American Tradition*. New York: Oxford University Press.

Rosier, James. (1605) 1906. "A True Relation of the Voyage of Captain George Waymouth," 355–94. In Harry Burrage, ed., *Early English and French Voyages, 1534–1608*. New York: Barnes and Noble.

Ross, Emma Howell. 1985. *Descendants of Edward Howell (1584–1655)*. Revised by David Faris. Baltimore: Gateway Press.

Russell, Lynette. 2012. *Roving Mariners: Australian Aboriginal Whalers and Whalers in the Southern Oceans, 1790–1870*. Albany: State University of New York Press.

Sahlins, Marshall. 1972. *Stone Age Economics*. Chicago: Aldine-Atherton Publishers.

Salisbury, Neal. 1982. *Manitou and Providence: Indians, Europeans, and the Making of New England*. New York: Oxford University Press.

Sanderson, Ivan Terrance. (1956) 1993. *A History of Whaling*. New York: Barnes and Noble.

Saville, Foster. 1977. "A Montauk Cemetery at East Hampton, Long Island," 19–29. In Gaynell Stone, ed., *Readings in Long Island Archaeology and Ethnohistory*. Stony Brook, N.Y.: Suffolk County Archaeological Association.

Savitt, Todd Lee. 1970. "Samuel Mulford of East Hampton." Master's thesis, University of Virginia.

Scammon, Charles M. 1968. *The Marine Mammals of the Northwestern Coast of North America, Together with an Account of the American Whale Fishery*. Reprint. New York: Dover Publications.

Seed, Patricia. 1995. *Ceremonies of Possession in Europe's Conquest of the New World, 1492–1640*. Cambridge: Cambridge University Press.

Sellers, Jason. 2015. "'An Indian Called Nangenutch or Will': Identity, Status, and Belonging in a Long Island Rape Trial." Paper presented at the Seventh Annual NAISA Conference, June 4–6, 2015, Washington, D.C.

Seybolt, Robert Francis. 1917. *Apprenticeship Education in Colonial New England and New York*. New York: Columbia University Press.

Shoemaker, Nancy. 2001. "Whale Meat in American History." *Environmental History* 10(2): 269–94.

———. 2015. *Native American Whalemen and the World; Indigenous Encounters and the Contingency of Race*. Chapel Hill: University of North Carolina Press.

Silverman, David J. 2001. "The Impact of Indentured Servitude on the Society and Culture of Southern New England Indians." *New England Quarterly* 74: 622–28.

———. 2005. *Faith and Boundaries: Colonists, Christianity and Community among the Wampanoag Indians of Martha's Vineyard, 1600–1871*. Cambridge: Cambridge University Press.

Simmons, William S. 1970. *Cauntowwit's House: An Indian Burial Ground on the Island of Conanicut in Narragansett Bay*. Providence: Brown University Press.

Skinner, Alison. 1914. "The Algonkin and the Thunderbird." *The American Museum of Natural History Journal* 17: 71–72.

Sleight, Harry. 1931. *Whale Fishing on Long Island*. Bridgehampton, N.Y.: Hampton Press.

Smith, Raymond. 1926a. *In Re Montauk*. East Hampton, N.Y.: East Hampton Town Trustees.

———, ed. 1926b. *In Re Montauk.* East Hampton, N.Y.: East Hampton Trustees.

Smith, Ruth Tangier. 1978. *The Tangier Smith Family.* Smithtown, N.Y.: Ruth Tangier Smith.

Spears, John R. 1908. *The Story of New England Whaling.* New York: Macmillan Company.

Spicer, Edward. 1962. *Perspectives in American Indian Culture Change.* Chicago: University of Chicago Press.

Starbuck, Alexander. (1878) 1964. *History of American Whale Fishing.* 2 vols. New York: Argosy-Antiquarian.

Stone, Gaynell, ed. 1983. *The Shinnecock Indians: A Culture History.* Suffolk County Archaeological Association. Lexington, Mass.: Ginn Custom Publishing.

Strong, John A. 1983. "Sharecropping the Sea: Shinnecock Whalers in the Seventeenth Century," 231–65. In Gaynell Stone, ed., *The Shinnecock Indians: A Culture History.* Lexington, Mass.: Ginn Custom Publishing.

———. 1985. "Late Woodland Dog Ceremonialism on Long Island in Comparative and Temporal Perspective." *The Bulletin: Journal of the State of New York Archaeological Association.*

———. 1986. "Shinnecock Whalers: A Case Study." In William Cowan, ed., *Seventeenth Century Assimilation Patterns.* Ottawa: Carleton University.

———. 1988. "Indian Biography Project," 213–23. In William Cowan, ed., *Papers of the Nineteenth Algonquian Conference.* Ottawa: Carleton University.

———. 1989. "Shinnecock and Montaukett Whalemen." *The Long Island Historical Journal* 2(1): 17–29.

———. 1990. "The Pigskin Book: Records of Native American Whalemen." *The Long Island Historical Journal* 3(2): 253–59.

———. 1993. "The Ancestors: Montauk Prehistory," 601–11. In Gaynell Stone, ed., *The History and Archaeology of the Montauk.* Stony Brook, N.Y.: SCAA.

———. 1994. "The Imposition of Colonial Rule over the Montauk Indians of Long Island." *Ethnohistory* 41(4): 561–87.

———. 1995a. "Indian Labor During the Post-Contact Period on Long Island," 13–39. In Joann P. Krieg and Natalie Naylor, eds., *To Know the Place.* Interlakin, N.Y.: Heart of the Lakes Press Publishing.

———. 1995b. "Native American Whalers: The New Elites in Seventeenth Century Algonquian Society on Long Island." Paper presented at the Mystic Seaport Conference on Race, Ethnicity, and Power in Maritime America, September 14, 1995.

———. 1996. "Wyandanch, Sachem of the Montauks," 48–73. In Robert S. Grumet, ed., *Northeastern Indian Lives, 1632–1816.* Amherst: University of Massachusetts Press.

———. 1997. *The Algonquian Peoples of Long Island from Earliest Times to 1700.* Interlakin, N.Y.: Empire State Books.

———. 1998. *"We Are Still Here!" The Algonquian Peoples of Long Island Today.* Interlakin, N.Y.: Empire State Books.

———. 2001. *The Montaukett Indians of Eastern Long Island.* Syracuse, N.Y.: Syracuse University Press.

———. 2007. "The Autonomous Commonwealth: Southampton, 1640–1644." *Long Island Historical Journal* 19(1–2): 1–19.

———. 2011. *The Unkechaug Indians of Eastern Long Island: A History.* Norman: University of Oklahoma Press.

———. 2012. "A Fatal Friendship: Lion Gardiner and Wyandanch, Sachem of the Montauketts," 147–95. In Tom Twomey, ed., *Origins of the Past: The Story of Montauk and Gardiner's Island.* Bridgehampton, N.Y.: East End Press.

———. 2015. "Data Related to Drift Whales and Shore Whaling in the 17th and 18th Centuries." Paper presented at the 2015 Annual North Atlantic Right Whale Consortium (NARWC), New Bedford Whaling Museum. New Bedford, Mass.

Strong, John A., and Mary Laura Lamont. 2015. "The Richard Floyd Account Book, 1686–1690: A Search for Authorship and Historical Significance." *The Long Island History Journal* 24(1): 1–39.

Strong, Kate W. 1957. "Some Early Floyd Papers." *Long Island Forum* 20(5): 89–90.

Szasz, Margaret Connell, ed. 2001. *Between Indian and White Worlds: The Cultural Broker.* Norman: University of Oklahoma Press.

Taylor, J. Garth. 1984. "Historical Ethnography of the Labrador Coast," 508–21. In David Damas, ed., *The Arctic.* Vol. 5 in *Handbook of the North American Indian.* 15 vols. Washington, D.C.: Smithsonian Institution.

———. 1988. "Labrador Inuit Whale Use During the Early Contact Period." *Arctic Anthropology* 25(2): 120–30.

Thomas, Peter. 1985. "Cultural Change on the Southern New England Frontier, 1630–1665." In William W. Fitzhugh, ed., *Culture in Contact: The Impact of European Contacts on Native American Cultural Institutions, A.D. 1000–1800.* Washington, D.C.: Smithsonian Institution Press.

Tooker, William Wallace. 1911. *Indian Place Names on Long Island.* Port Washington, N.Y.: Ira Friedman.

Tower, Walter S. 1907. *A History of the American Whale Fishery.* Philadelphia: University of Pennsylvania.

Towner, Lawrence W. 1998. *A Good Master Well Served: Masters and Servants in Colonial Massachusetts, 1620–1750.* New York: Garland Publishing.

Tuck, J. A., and J. A. Logan. 1990. "A Sixteenth Century Basque Whaling Post in Southern Labrador." *Association for Preservation Technology Bulletin* 22(3): 65–72.

Ulrich, Laurel Thatcher. 2001. *The Age of Homespun: Objects and Stories in the Creation of an American Myth.* New York: Vintage Press.

Van Der Donck, Adriaen. (1655) 2008. *A Description of New Netherland,* ed. Charles Gehring and William Starna. Lincoln: University of Nebraska Press.

Varga, Nicholas. 1960. "Electoral Procedures and Practices in Colonial New York." *New York History* 41: 249–77.

———. 2010. "The Development and Structure of Local Government in Colonial New York," 186–215. In Brian P. Janiskee, ed., *Local Government in Early America: The Colonial Experience and Lessons from the Founders.* New York: Rowman and Littlefield.

Venables, Robert W. 1993. "A Chronology of Brotherton History to 1850," 515–32. In Gaynell Stone, ed., *The History and Archaeology of the Montauk.* Stony Brook, N.Y.: Suffolk County Archaeological Association.

Wallace, Anthony. 1996. Foreword to Robert Grumet, ed., *Northeastern Indian Lives*. Amherst: University of Massachusetts Press.

Ward, Harry. 1972. *The United Colonies of New England, 1643–1690*. New York: Vantage Press.

Warren, Wendy. *New England Bound: Slavery and Colonization in Early America*. New York: Liveright Publishing Company.

Welters, Linda. 1993. "From Moccasins to Frock Coats and Back Again: Ethnic Identity and Native American Dress in Southern New England," 6–41. In Patricia A. Cunningham and Susan Voso Lab, eds., *Dress in American Culture*. Bowling Green, Ohio: Bowling Green State University Press.

Whitbourne, Richard. 1620. *A Discourse and Discovery of Newfoundland*. St. Johns: Center for Newfoundland Studies, University of Newfoundland.

White, Richard. 1983. *The Roots of Dependency: Subsistence, Environment, and Social Change Among the Choctaws, Pawnees, and Navajos*. Lincoln: University of Nebraska Press.

———. 1991. *The Middle Ground: Indians, Empires, and Republics in the Great Lakes Region, 1650–1815*. New York: Cambridge University Press.

Willey, Nancy Boyd. 1949. "The Whaling Era on Long Island," 533–56. In Paul Bailey, ed., *Long Island: A History of Two Great Counties, Nassau and Suffolk*. New York: Lewis Historical Publishing.

Williams, Roger. (1643) 1973. *A Key into the Language of America*, ed. John J. Teunissen and Evelyn J. Hinz. Detroit: Wayne State University Press.

Willmont, Cory. 2005. "From Stroud to Strouds: The Hidden History of the British Fur Trade." *Textile History* 36(2): 196–239.

Wood, William. (1634) 1968. *New Englands Prospect*. New York: Da Capo Press.

Wooley, Charles. (1701) 1968. "A Two Year Journal in New York, 1678–1680," 1–97. In Cornell Jaray, ed., *Historic Chronicles of New Amsterdam, Colonial New York and Early Long Island*, Series I. Port Washington, N.Y.: Ira J. Friedman.

Index

References to illustrations appear in italic type. Tables are indicated by (t) after the page number.

aboriginal Long Island culture, 3–20; calling the whales, 18–19; images of precontact Indian whalings, 8–11; and whaling ceremonies, 15–18. *See also* accounts of precontact Indian whaling; North Atlantic right whale

absenteeism: fines imposed for, 100; and Indian stereotypes, 151

accounts of precontact Indian whaling: and antler harpoon points (Saville), *14*–15; and ceremonies and artifacts, 15–*16*, *17*–18, 19; and expedition led by Arundell (1605), 11; and mica tablet (1840s), 16–*17*, 19; and spirit forces, 17–18, 20; and whale-hunting scene by Bailey, 13–14; and whaling descriptions, 12–13

acculturation, directed and nondirected, 127, 204ch3n2

"Act for the Encouragement of Whaling" (1708), 151–53

Akuctattrias, 105

alcohol (deadly medicine): and "Act for the Encouragement of Whaling," 151–53; consumption by Indians and whites, 85–86, 94; and debt peonage, 100, 109, 123, 163; and Indian stereotypes, 88, 92, 148, 151–53; and manipulation of Indian labor, 86–87, 88, 94, 95; and Meneges, 94, 95; monopoly by owners, 113; prohibition of, 88–90, 98, 157

alliance sachems, 143, 155

Andros, Edmund (governor): and English governance restored, 133; and failure to support Sarah Cooper, 138; Lovelace's successor, 135; ordinance of, 88; Schellinger appeal approved by, 137

Anglo-Dutch War, 132–33

Ansel, Willits, *58*, 61–62

antler harpoon points (Saville), *14*

Apocock Creek, western boundary of Shinnecock lands, 45

Aquaas (later Wyandanch the 2nd), 144, 145, 146, 147–48

Artor: and coats as payment, 81; and Cooper, 105–6, 108, 120; testimony of, 138

Arundell, Thomas, 11

Axtell, James, *Beyond 1492*, 10

Bailey, Paul, 13

Baker, Thomas, 41, 47, 136–37

baleen: and baleen plates, *4*–*5*, *23*; groupings of whales, 3–4; and imports, 76; profits from, 77; and uses, 21–*22*. *See also* drift whales; shore whaling

barter system, 79, 104, 105

Basques, as whalemen, 10–11, *57*–*58*, 204n1

Basset, Benjamin, 19

beached whale at Smith Point, Long Island, *22*

Beale, Thomas, 13–14

Biggs, Thomas, 89–90, 91

blubber being minced, *74*

Bolton, Reginald Pelham, 15

Bond, Robert, 53, 72

Bragdon, Kathleen, *Native Peoples of Southern New England* (Bragdon), 17, 19, 98, 121

Breen, T. H. (historian), 70, 99, 123

Brereton, John: on Basque "catcher boats," 57–*58*; *Relation*, 57

Bridges, John, 147–48

Brockholes, Anthony, 90

Bunbrest, 112, 122, 197

burial rituals, 97

burials, excavations of, *84*, 95–98, *96*

Cabot, John, 25

calling the whales, 18–19

canoes, 9–13, 58

Cawbutt, 120

Cawhlutoowit (good deity), 16

ceremonies. *See under* accounts of precontact Indian whaling

Charles, King (1644), 47, 133
Christian witnesses, for deeds and labor contracts, 101–2, 105, 164, 205n3
Clark, George, 152
Clove, Anthony, 133
coats, demand for, 80–83
Cobish, 42, 47, 50
Comes, John, 134, 136, 207n3
Commission on Indian Affairs: formed by Nicolls, 49–50; Howell appointed to, 106–7; Lovelace's referral to, 103; and Nangenutch rape case, 129–130
commodity prices: and Cooper's list, 111; and start-up costs, 70–73. *See also* economics of whaling
conflicting sovereignties, 41–56; and contested beaches, 54–56; and land claim turmoil, 41–45; and rulings by Nicolls and Lovelace, 55–56. *See also Cooper v. Ogden*; Duke's colony; Wyandanch
Conkling, Benjamin, 64, 140, 149
Conkling, Jeremiah, 130
Conkling, Joseph, 160
contract system (1670–1672): and adoption of English names, 106, 159; and Andros ruling on, 104; and barter system as basis, 79, 104, 105; and challenge to (1671), 105–6, 206n4; and contract contents, 100; and contract "jumping," 101–2; and fines imposed on whalers, 100; and Indian dependency pattern, 118–20; and Lovelace's ruling (1670), 103; and recruiting competition, 100–102, 205ch6nn1–2; and sachems' authority declining, 119–120; and shore whaling, 104–5; and Southampton Town ordinance (1672), 108–9; and Topping's complaint to Andros, 103–4; and witnesses to contracts, 101–2, 205ch6n3
Cooper, John Jr.: and 1668–69 season, 68; and commodity price list, 111; company formed with Stevens by, 69; and Connecticut purchase, 47–48; and contract of June 17, 1672, 100, 109–13; and contract with Artor, 81, 105, 120; death of, 137; and gun powder ordinances, 85; and leases from Gardiner, 37–39; rights to drift whales reaffirmed, 51–52; and taking of whales illegally, 55. See also *Cooper v. Ogden*

Cooper, John Sr.: death of, 109; large landowner in Lynn, Mass., 22–23; witness to Topping lease (1658), 35
Cooper, Sarah, 137–38
Cooper, Thomas, 28, 43, 63–64
Cooper v. Ogden (October 1667), claims made in, 52–54
Cornbury, Lord (Governor): Indians blamed for oil production decline by, 151; inner circle of, 147; New York and New Jersey governor, 76; on price of a barrel of oil, 111; wampum received by, 147
Courageous, James, 162
Court of Assizes, 48–53
Cronon, William, *Changes in the Land*, 99
Crosby, Constance, on burial rituals, 97
cultural impact of "ye whale design," 79–98; coat men and clothmakers, 80–85; grave goods, 95–98; trade and labor, 79–80. *See also* alcohol; Meneges
Curious Method of Catching Whales (de Bry), 9
customs records of imports: beginning in 1696, 76, 204ch4n2; estimates for 1708, 152; records from 1697–1734, 159; report for 1703, 116

Davis, William, *Nimrod of the Sea*, 60–61
de Acosta, Jose: *Curious Method of Catching Whales*, 9; *Natural and Moral History of the Indies*, 9
deadly medicine. *See* alcohol
de Bry, Theodor: *Curious Method of Catching Whales* (de Bry), 9; *Harpooning Whales* (engraving), *10*
debt peonage and indentured servitude, 99–126; challenging the system, 105; dependency, dispossession, and survival, 106n6, 118–120; and global marketplace, 99; and overlapping systems of control, 120–23; Southampton town ordinance (1672), 109–13. *See also* contract system; debt peonage on Saint George Manor; Floyd, Richard
debt peonage on Saint George Manor, 113–18; debt records in "Pigskin book," 114; and debts recorded, 115 (t); and debts to Smith family by Unkechaugs, 115–16; reservation granted to Unkechaugs, 114–15; and

stereotypes held by Martha Smith, 117–18; Unkechaugs as labor supply, 113–14; and value shares (1706–07), 118 (t); and whalers' shares, 116–17

De Forest, John, 80

de Hooges, Antoine, earliest account of flensing a drift whale, 25–26

Delancy, Stephen, account of 1731–32 whaling season, 156

Delavel, John, 145, 207n5

De Vries, David (Dutch entrepreneur), 65

Dimon, Thomas, 102, 133–34, 137

Dongan, Thomas (governor), Andros's successor, 143–44, 145

drift whales, 21–40; commercial potential of, 21–23; Dutch account of first encounter, 25–26; and exportation to Europe, 32; and flensing procedures, 28–29; profits from, 28, 31–32; town ordinance on, 26–27; and trying furnaces, 29–30, *30–31*; and violence on middle ground, 32–34. *See also* Cooper, John Jr.; Gardiner, Lion; Wyandanch

Duke's colony (1664), 48–52; and *Cooper v. Ogden*, 52–54; and disputes, 50–51; and Indian Affairs commission, 49–50; and Nicolls as governor, 48–49; and Town of Brookhaven, 47, 51

Duke's Laws, 48, 92, 98

Dutch, the: and confrontation by Cooper, 133; and defeat of English, 132; expansion of whaling in 1632, 65; on first whale encounter, 25–26

East Hampton: and Colonial Council actions, 146–48; company formed with Moshup, 134–35, 207n3; founding of, 27, 35; and Montauketts, 148–150, 207n7; and patent process (1684), 143–45, 207n5; and patent terms, 146; and 1703 compromise, 148–150, 149 (t), 207n8

economics of whaling, 70–75; and contracts, 76, 204ch4n3, 205n4; and family networks (1670–185), 70; licenses issued in 1711, 77, 205n5; profits from, 75–76; and property comparison, 73, 75; 1686–87 whaling season, 77; and start–up costs, 70–73. *See also* customs records of imports

Edwards, Everett Joshua. See *Whale–off*

Edwards, William, 134

end of an era, 151–163; decline of, 151–53; last days (1732–1750), 156–59; leaving the shore, 159–162; shore whaling (mid–eighteenth century), 153–54; Unkechaug whalers (1720–1732), 154–56; whaling agents for new era (1803–1805), 162–63

English whaling in early seventeenth century, 57–78; overview, 57–58; canoes to whaleboats, 58–64; profits and risks, 65–68, 75–78. *See also* Cooper, John Jr.; economics of whaling; whale hunting

European goods, demand for, 80–83, 95, 98

flensing a whale, *73*

Floyd, Richard: account books of, 82, 205ch5n1; and dispossession of Indian land, 123–25, 206n7; and goods Meneges received from, 93–94; and last indentures (1730), 157, 208n4; and Meneges, 93–94; and Unkechaugs, 154–55, 159

Fordham, Joseph, 27

Fordham, Rev. Robert, 27, 34

Gardiner, David Lion, *Chronicles of East Hampton*, 15–16, 38

Gardiner, Lion: death of, 46; and "Enaughquamuck" negotiations, 39–40; and expansion of holdings, 32; leases secured by, 35–37, 38; and Pequot War, 128; settler in 1639, 15, 25; and Wyandanch alliance, 33

Gary, Jack, 18

Gibb, Andrew, 102, 140, 207n4

Gie (Unkechaug sachem): as crop tender, 90; as whaling crew member, 93, 183

Glooscap (creator spirit), 18

Goddard, David, 99

Goddard, Ives, 11

Gosmer, John, 33, 34, 37

Gosnold, Bartholomew, 10

Griffin, Owen, 11

guns: seizing of, 89–90, *131*, 135; as status symbol, 85

Halsey, Joseph, 153

Halsey, Thomas Jr., 50

Halsey, Thomas Sr.: and case against Topping, 50; and guns seized from Indians, 89; and Ogden purchase, 37; Southampton founder, 23; and wife's murder, 33
Harpooning Whales (engraving) (de Bry), *10*
harpoon points, bone: found in East Hampton by Saville, *14*–15; Rosier's reference to, 12
Harrington, Mark, 18
Hellyer, Simon (whaling crew member), 64
Henry, William, 156
Herrick, James, 160
Herrick, John, 47
Herrick, William, 160, 161, 162
"hiving out," defined, 23
How, Daniel, 23
Howell, Arthur, 69, 80, 105, 137
Howell, Deborah, 108
Howell, Edward, 23, 34, 140
Howell, John: and contract with Shinnecocks, 101; as governor's appointee, 50; as justice of the peace (East Riding), 106–7; and Quashawam, 47, 49; as squadron leader, 28; as Suffolk County clerk, 145
Howell, Matthew, 106, 140, 141
Howell, Richard: as company owner, 68; and Connecticut purchase, 47–48; and contract jumping incidents, 103; Cooper's suit against, 45; and family squabbles, 138; and testimony, 53; and Waters, 55
Howell, Stephen, 160, 162
Howell, Thomas, 158
Hudson, Henry, 25
Humphrey (a.k.a. Matomapait), 102
Hunter, Robert (governor), 77, 153
hunting and catching whales, images of, 8–*10, 9*
hvalrekst (whale drive), 19

indentured servitude: examples of, 121–22; and indebtedness as labor control, 122–23, 125–26; and Jambush, 153–54; origins of, 121, 123; and overlapping systems, 120

Jacob, David, 161–62
Jacob, Hugh, 162–63
Jacob Indian, 154
Jambush, indenture of, 153–54
James, Philip, 154, 155, 156

James, Rev. Thomas: arrival in East Hampton (1651), 32; and East Hampton company formed, 133–34, 145; and family networks, 102; and guns demanded from Montauketts, 131; Montaukett debt purchased by, 130; and Montaukett land purchase blocked, 41; and rights to beached whales, 36; and Toby, 139; and Tom Indian indentured to, 149; witness to indenture, 122
Jefferson, Thomas, 3
Jennings, Francis, 40
Jennings, John, 93
Jessup, John, 53–54
Jessup, John Jr., 141, 144
Jessup, Thomas, 113, 141
Jessup, Zebulon, 162

kettles: and burial goods, 97; high value of iron and copper, 84; as trying furnaces, 29–*30*, 72–73; Warwakmy receives six, 81
Kieft, Willhem, 27
King Philip's War: and Indians under suspicion, 135; and Meneges, 89–90, 92; and Philip's death, 137

labor system. *See* indentured servitude
Laist, David, *North Atlantic Right Whales*, 8, 12
Lane, Daniel, 51, 54
Laughton, Josiah, 81, 101
lay share agreement, 109, 134, 157
Lenape legend, a, 18
Lindquist, Ole, 19
Linneaus, Carl, 7
Lipman, Andrew, *Saltwater Frontier*, 78
Little, Elizabeth, 12, 14
Long Island in seventeenth century (map), *24*
Longworth, Thomas, and trickery, 147–48
Loper, James: competing with James for whalers, 134, 136–37; and family connections, 137; as shore whaling legend, 138–39; and suit against Comes, 134; and suit against Quasique, 139. *See also* Schellinger, Jacob
Lourandos, Henry, 15
Lovelace, Francis (governor): and alcohol prohibition, 88–90, 98, 157; appeals by Winecroscum and Tobacus, 55–56; imprisonment of, 132–33; and Nangenutch

rape case, 129–130; Nicolls's successor, 55, 88; and Ninigret agreement, 131–32; and Quaquashawge, 119–120; and ruling on contract violations, 103

Ludlam, Anthony, 105

Lynn, Mass., 21–23, 32, 72, 80, 203ch2n1

Mahaine (Meheane) (Unkechaug), fines imposed on, 123–24

Mahue, John, 90, 91, 94

Mandush (Shinnecock sachem): and Weany, 42, 45, 47, 50–51; and Wyandanch settlement, 33–34

Manecopungun, 144, 146

Manitou, 97–98

Mason, John, 34, 72, 128

Mastic Peninsula (map), *107*

Mayhew, Thomas, Jr., 13

Mecox whaleboat launch area: location of, 81, 101; whales killed at, 116

Meneges (Tom Indian): and alcohol, 94, 95; background of, 89; and Biggs, John, 89–90; as bilingual translator, 80, 95; and Brookhaven planting rights, 93; and case study of weapon ban, 89–90; and goods from Floyd's company, 93–94; lessons from story of, 94–95; and Mahaine, 123; and whaling crews, 92–93; and Woodhull, 91. *See also* Robinson, John

metal items, demand for, *84–85*

middle ground, violence on, 32–34, 204ch2n2

Miller, John, 21

miogarosormr (water serpent being), 17–18

Montaukett burial site (iron pot), *84*

Montauketts: and Long Island (map), *24*; and Nangenutch rape case, 129–130; and Niantic alliance, 128–29; and Ninigret agreement, 128–130; and pending state recognition, 163; villages of, 23–25; whale ceremony of, 19. *See also* East Hampton; Ninigret

Moshup (Montaukett sachem), 19, 130, 135–36

Mulford, John: and arrest (1703 compromise settlement), 150, 207n8; and Commission on Indian Affairs, 103, 129; as justice of the peace, 51, 53; and land purchase attempt, 41; and land purchase from Montauketts,

145, 207n6; and seizure of Montaukett guns, 129; and Wobetom, 95

Mulford, Samuel, 148–49, 153

Mutcheshesumetooh (evil deity), 16

names of whalers and investors on contracts (1670–1685) (appendix 5), 179–202

Nangenutch (Montaukett), and attempted–rape conviction, 129–130

Niantic alliance, 128–132. *See also* Ninigret

Nicolls, Matthias, 48

Nicolls, Richard, 48

Nimrod (Unkechaug), 154, 157, 158, 159

Ninigret (Niantic sachem): and Great Dance, 130, 135; and Montauketts, 25, 36, 41, 128–130, *131*

Norse whalers: and fin and tail sacrifice, 15, 16; and mythology, 17–18; and spear whaling, 19; and whaleboats, 71

North Atlantic right whale: decline in population of, 153; description of, 3; images of, *4–5*; migratory corridor for (map), 6; naming of, 7; near extinction of, 159–160; number of, 7–8; reproduction of, 3, 7, 203ch1n1

North Atlantic Right Whales (Laist), 8, 12

Occom, Samson, 16, 159

Ogden, John, 27–28, 32, 34, 37; and land purchases, 41–43; and move to New Jersey, 46–47; whaling design proposed by, 65–69

oil being bailed into cooling vat, *74*

Oldfield, John, 66–67, 70

Osborn, Daniel, Papasaquin's daughter indentured to, 142, 149

Osborn, John, 142–43, 144

Oyster Bay conflict, 56

Papasaquin: background of, 127–28; and dispossession of Montaukett lands, 142; and distrust of English, 146, 150; and indenture of children, 142; and retirement from whaling, 141; and Shinnecock connections, 132, 140; as whaler with Benjamin Conkling, 140; as whaler with Howell, 140–41; as whaler with James, 133; as whaler with Schellinger, 138–39; and Wyandanch's gun to Ninigret, 130–*31*

Papasaquin's world, 127–150; overview, 127–28; and dispossession of Montaukett lands, 142–150; and Niantic alliance, 128–132; and whaling years, 132–141. *See also* Papasaquin

Passamaquoddy mythology, 18

Pauwas, 93

Pelletreau, Francis, 156, 208n3

Pelletreau, William, 99–100

Pequot War, 34, 80, 128, 129

Pierson, Henry, 93

Pierson, Rev. Abraham, 27

Poole, Jonas, 57

Powwowing, prohibition of, 98

Pumpsha (whaler), hired by Tangier Smith, 114–18

Quaquashawge, 119–120

Quashawam (daughter of Wyandanch), 41, 46–47, 97

Rattray, Jeanette. See *Whale-off*

Raynor, Isaac, 92–93

Raynor, Joseph: as constable, 138; and contract with Shinnecocks, 101; Cooper's suit against, 45; and Quasawam, 47; Southampton freeholder, 39, 52; whales taken illegally by, 55

Raynor, Thruston, 34

Reeves, Randall, 8–9, 159

reservation granted to Unkechaugs, reservation granted to Unkechaugs, 206n5

Reuben, 156, 157

Richbell, John, 37, 39

Rider, John, 48, 52–53

right whale. *See* North Atlantic right whale

rituals: and fin and tail sacrifice, 15; and fins and tails reserved, 35, 43; and grave goods, 97. *See also* accounts of precontact Indian whaling

Robinson, Jane, 92

Robinson, John, and Unkechaug incident, 91–92

Rogers, Obadiah, 141

Rogers, Uriah, 160, 161, 162

Romney, Susan Shaw, 47

Rosier, James, 11–12

Ryder, Robert, *43–44*

Sasakataka, 144

Saville, Foster, 14, 95

Sayer, Thomas, 33

Sayre, Daniel, and letter to Clark, 152, 208n1

Schellinger, Jacob: background of, 68–69; and bonds for whalers, 100; and East Hampton company, 68; and indenture contract with Papasaquin, 142; Manhansetts hired illegally by, 136; and whale design delay, 134. *See also* Loper, James

Scott, John, 32

Scudder, David, 92

Seelye, Robert, 46

Sharpe, John, 48, 52–54

Shaw, Edmund, 53

Shinnecock Reservation, 18

Shinnecocks, 140; company formed by, 105; contracts with Howell and Raynor, 101; location of, 23–25; and Papasaquin, 132, 140; recognition of federally, 163

shore whale catch estimates (1697–1734) (appendix 4), 177–78 (t)

shore whaling: ending of, 57; increase in, 104–5; in Labrador and Greenland, 13; in mid–eighteenth century, 153–54; and two cultures, 78

Smith, Martha, 117–18

Smith, Richard, 28, 32

Smith, William Henry (Tangier's son), 114, 154, 156

Smith, William Tangier: death of, 156; and ledger (1706–1707), 108–9; property of, 206n7; reservation granted to Unkechaugs, 114, 154; of St. George Manor, 94, *107*

Southampton: and arson incident, 34, 204ch2n3; contentious climate in, 34–35; founding of, 21, 23; murder by a Shinnecock, 33

spear whaling strategy, 19

Sporri, Felix Christian, 67–68

Starbuck, Alexander, *History of American Whale Fishing*, 68–69

Stevens, Nicholas, 69

Stevens, Thomas, 77

St. George Manor (appendix 3): ledger book (1706–1707), 176 (t); whale catches (1694–1721), 175 (t)

Stratton, John, 102

Stratton, Richard: and Thomas James's company, 133, 145, 149, 186; Wobeton's son indentured by, 120–21
Surroot (Unkechaug), 157, 159. and Floyd, 154, 155, 208n2
Sylvester Manor house (Shelter Island), 18

Tackapousha (Massapequa sachem), 37
Talmadge, Thomas, 43
Talmadge, Widow, 31
Tarrant, Mataukus (Shinnecock Nation), *31, 63, 64*
Thomas, Peter, 35
Thompson, John, 93
thunderbird spirit, images found on Long Island, *17*, 18
Tobacus (Unkechaug sachem): confronts whaling company, 132; land purchased from, 47; Mahaine's fine arranged by, 123; and Meneges, 89, 90, 135; and reserving fins and tails, 43; supports Brookhaven Town, 51, 52; and town meeting on drift whales (1668), 54–55; waning status of, 119; and Winecroscum, 35, 39
Toby (Unkechaug), 122, 139
Toech, 93
Tooker, John Jr., 122
Tooker, Joseph, 91, 93, 102
Tooker, William Wallace, 18
Topping, Elnathan, 103
Topping, John, 107–8
Topping, Thomas: arrival in Southampton, 27; and complaint on "damned pagans," 90; Cooper Jr sued by, 45–46; in court session, 45–46; death of, 75; and family tension, 47; and Indian Affairs commission, 49; and land purchased overlapping with Ogden, 42–43; leases secured by, 35–36; objections to ruling by Lovelace, 103; and political positions, 107–8; and property dispute, 50–51; as squadron leader, 28; and Wyandanch, 38
Towsacom, contract with Laughton, 101
trying furnaces, 29–30, *30–31*
trying station on shore, *75*

Uktena (Cherokee deity), 17
Ulrich, Laurel, *Age of Homespun, The*, 81, 82–83
Underhill, John, and Pequot War, 28

Ungomunt, 148
Unkechaug Nation, recognition of, 163
Unkechaugs: as labor supply, 113–14; whalers (1720–1732), 154–56. See also *specific names* (e.g., Tobacus)

Van Dam, Rip, 147–48
Van Der Donck, Adriaen, *Description of New Netherland*, 20
Vickers, Daniel, 121

Wacus (sachem), 156
Wahumbaho, 141
Wamabaho, 93
Wamahow, 118
Warawakmy, 81
warps for whaleboats: and English demands with Dutch, 133; use and costs, 64, 72
Warren, Joe, 26
Washam, Thom, 154–55
Waters, Anthony, 39, 43, 55
Wauphague (Unkechaug "chief man"), and dispossession of Indian land, 123, 125
Weany (sunksquaw), 42, 45, 47, 50–51
Weramps, 156
whaleboats, 57–59, *58*, 71, 101. See also whale hunting
whale hunting: companies in 1668–69, 68; and crew responsibilities, 60–62, 64; descriptions of, 59–61; Englishmen absent from, 63; and harpooning, 62–63, 64; Sporri's account in 1662, 67–68
Whale-off (Edwards and Rattray): on boat-handling maneuver, 62; on hunting methods, 60–61; on trying operations early twentieth century, 28–30; on whale boat size, 57–58, 71
whale oil: boiling of, *74*; and European market, 99; profits from, 56; uses of, 21–22. See also drift whales; economics of whaling
whales, drift. See drift whales
whales in New York Harbor, *66*
whaling, prehistoric, disagreements on, 20, 203n3
whaling companies, 134–35; competition and, 136; with Cooper and Stevens, 69; in East Hampton with Moshup, 107n3, 134–35; and Floyd's company, 93–94;

whaling companies (*continued*)
and Southampton company, 23. *See also* economics of whaling
whaling contract examples (appendix 1), 164–170; first on record (1670), 164–65; John Cooper Jr.'s contract (1672), 166–68; between Papasaquin and B. Conkling (1681), 169–170; Papasaquin's contract with Schellinger (1679), 168–69; Shinnecock contract (c. 1671), 165–66
whaling contracts by season (appendix 2): season 1686–1687, 174 (t); seasons 1670–1685, 171–73 (t)
whaling seasons: 1710–1711, 152 (t); 1721–1726 (decline in catches), 155–56; 1731–1732, 156–57; 1732–1733, 157. *See also* whaling contracts by season (appendix 2)
whaling stations (eastern Long Island) (map), *44*
Whatnews, 92
Wheeler, John, 139–140
Whitbourne, Richard, 10–11
White, Richard, 32, 118–19, 204ch2n2
Will (Umpatrina), 154, 156

Williams, Roger: on boat handling skills, 19; *Key into the Languages of America*, 3; on whale meat distribution, 12, 16
Winecroscum (Unkechaug sachem), 43, 51–52, 54
Winthrop, John Sr., 25
Wobetom, 95–98, *96*
Wood, William, 12–13, 203n2
Woodhull, Richard, 32, 55, 67, 89; and Unkechaug weapons, 89
Wooley, Rev. Charles, *Two Years Journal in New York*, 59, 71, 75–76
Wuch–i– kit– taw– but (widow of Wyandanch), 41, 42, 43, 46, 97
Wyancombone (son of Wyandanch): death of, 43; and Gardiner, 38; and gift of land, 42; Grand Sachem heir, 41, 46
Wyandanch (Montaukett sachem), 33–34; death of, 39–40, 41, 42, 119, 128, 129; family of, 131; and Gardiner, 25, 36, 39; last transaction of, 39; named "the Grand Sachem," 34; and settlement with Mandush, 33–34; and shift in policy, 38
Wyandanch family, 142

About the Author

John A. Strong is a professor emeritus of history and American studies at Long Island University. He is the author of numerous books, including *The Montaukett Indians of Eastern Long Island* and *The Unkechaug Indians of Eastern Long Island*.